CoursePrep
ExamGuide/StudyGuide
MCSA Exam 70-218

Managing a Microsoft Windows 2000 Network Environment

THOMSON

COURSE TECHNOLOGY

Australia • Canada • Mexico • Singapore • Spain • United Kingdom • United States

THOMSON

™

COURSE TECHNOLOGY

MCSA 70-218 CoursePrep StudyGuide and *MCSA 70-218 CoursePrep ExamGuide* by Joseph P. Sellers is published by Course Technology

Product Manager
Charles Blum

Managing Editor
Will Pitkin

Production Editor
Danielle Power

Manufacturing Manager
Laura Burns

Marketing Manager
Jason Sakos

Editorial Assistant
Nick Lombardi

Cover Design
Betsy Young and
Abby Scholtz

Compositor
GEX Publishing Services

Disclaimer
Course Technology
reserves the right to revise
this publication and
make changes from time
to time in its content
without notice.

ISBN 0-619-13015-6
ISBN 0-619-13016-4

TABLE OF CONTENTS

SECTION 4 CONFIGURING, MANAGING, SECURING, AND TROUBLESHOOTING ACTIVE DIRECTORY ORGANIZATIONAL UNITS AND GROUP POLICY 153

SECTION 5 CONFIGURING, SECURING, AND TROUBLESHOOTING REMOTE ACCESS 203

PREFACE

The CousePrep ExamGuide and CoursePrep StudyGuide are the very best tools to use to prepare for exam day. Both products provide thorough preparation for the MCSA 70-218: Managing a Microsoft Windows 2000 Network Environment exam. These products are intended to be utilized with the core "Guide to" textbook, *MCSA Guide to Managing a Microsoft Windows 2000 Network* (0-619-13012-1), by Conan Kezema. CoursePrep ExamGuide and CoursePrep StudyGuide provide you ample opportunities to practice, drill, and rehearse for the exam!

COURSEPREP EXAMGUIDE

The *CoursePrep ExamGuide for MCSA Exam 70-218: Managing a Microsoft Windows 2000 Network Environment*, ISBN 0-619-13016-4, provides the essential information you need to master each exam objective. The ExamGuide devotes an entire two-page spread to each certification objective for this exam, helping you to understand the objective, and giving you the bottom line information—what you *really* need to know. Memorize these facts and bulleted points before heading into the exam. In addition, there are four to seven practice test questions for each objective on the right-hand page—over 250 questions total! CoursePrep ExamGuide provides the exam fundamentals and gets you up to speed quickly. If you are seeking even more opportunity to practice and prepare, we recommend that you consider our most complete solution, CoursePrep StudyGuide, which is described below.

COURSEPREP STUDYGUIDE

For those really serious about certification, we offer an even more robust solution—the *CoursePrep StudyGuide for MCSA Exam 70-218: Managing a Microsoft Windows 2000 Network Environment*, ISBN 0-619-13015-6. This offering includes all of the same great features you get with the CoursePrep ExamGuide, including the unique two page spread, the bulleted memorization points, and the practice questions. In addition, you receive a password valid for six months of practice on CoursePrep, a dynamic test preparation tool. The password is found in an envelope in the back cover of the CoursePrep StudyGuide. CoursePrep is a Web-based pool of hundreds of sample test questions. CoursePrep exam simulation software mimics the exact exam environment. The CoursePrep software is flexible and allows you to practice in several ways as you master the material. Choose from Certification Mode to experience actual exam-day conditions or Study Mode to request answers and explanations to practice questions. Custom Mode lets you set the options for the practice test, including number of questions, content coverage, and ability to request answers and explanation. Follow the instructions on the inside back cover to access the exam simulation software. To see a demo of this dynamic test preparation tool, go to *www.courseprep.com*.

FEATURES

The *CoursePrep ExamGuide* and *CoursePrep StudyGuide for MCSA Exam 70-218: Managing a Microsoft Windows 2000 Network Environment* books include the following features:

Detailed coverage of the certification objectives in a unique two-page spread: Study strategically by really focusing in on the MCSA certification objectives. To enable you to do this, a two-page spread is devoted to each certification objective. The left page provides the critical facts you need, while the right page features practice questions relating to that objective. You'll find that the certification objective(s) and sub-objectives(s) are clearly listed in the upper left-hand corner of each spread.

An overview of the objective is provided in the ***Understanding the Objective*** section. Next, ***What You Really Need to Know*** lists bulleted, succinct facts, skills, and concepts about the objective. Memorizing these facts will be important for your success when taking the exam. ***Objectives on the Job*** places the objective in an industry perspective and tells you how you can expect to utilize the objective on the job. This section also provides troubleshooting information.

Practice Test Questions: Each right page contains four to seven practice test questions designed to help you prepare for the exam by testing your skills, identifying your strengths and weaknesses, and demonstrating the subject matter you will face on the exams and how it will be tested. These questions are written in a fashion similar to real MCSA exam questions. The questions test your knowledge of the objectives described on the left page and also the information in the *MCSA Guide to Managing a Microsoft Windows 2000 Network* (ISBN 0-619-13012-1). You can find answers to the practice test questions in the answer key at the back of the book, and on the CoursePrep Web site, **www.courseprep.com**, where you can also find additional Web-based exam preparation questions.

Glossary: The glossary lists and defines key terms and acronyms that you need to know for the exams, and it is included in the back of the book as a reference.

How to use this book

The *CoursePrep ExamGuide* and *CoursePrep StudyGuide for MCSA Exam 70-218: Managing a Microsoft Windows 2000 Network Environment* are all you need to successfully prepare for the MCSA certification exam if you have some experience and working knowledge of managing Microsoft Windows 2000 networks. This book is intended to be utilized with a core text, such as *MCSA Guide to Managing a Microsoft Windows 2000 Network (0-619-13012-1)*, also published by Course Technology. If you are new to this field, use this book as a roadmap for where you need to go to prepare for certification, and use the *MCSA Guide to Managing a Microsoft Windows 2000 Network* to give you the knowledge and understanding that you need to reach your goal. Course Technology publishes a full series of MCSE/MCSA products that provide thorough preparation for the all of the MCSE/MCSA exams. For more information, visit our Web site at **www.course.com/networking**, or contact your sales representative.

Section 1

Creating, Configuring, Managing, Securing, and Troubleshooting File, Print, and Web Resources

1.1 Publish resources in Active Directory. Types of resources include printers and shared folders.

PUBLISH RESOURCES, SUCH AS PRINTERS AND SHARED FOLDERS.

UNDERSTANDING THE OBJECTIVE

Windows 2000 Active Directory allows the network administrator to publish shared resources in the Active Directory database. This simplifies and secures Active Directory users' access to these resources. Shared folders, shared print devices installed on Windows 2000 computers, and print devices installed on other operating systems can be published.

WHAT YOU REALLY NEED TO KNOW

- ◆ The resource to be published must be a network share or print device that follows the **UNC** naming convention. The most consistent results are obtained by using shared resources (folders and printers) hosted on Microsoft Windows 2000 Server computers. However, published resources are not restricted to Microsoft Windows 2000 Server computers. To publish a resource, it is required that the object to be published use **IP** as a network protocol.

- ◆ The person who creates the published resource must have appropriate permissions in **AD** to create that resource. Also, AD security permissions, **NTFS** permissions (if applicable), and shared folder permissions must be configured for the object. The object to be published in AD must be accessible across the network from a Windows 2000 domain controller, and the UNC path to the resource must be known.

- ◆ A design implementation plan that maps the AD location where the published objects will exist should be created before the resources are published. **OU**s should already exist or be created to serve as a parent object for the shared resources.

- ◆ If down-level clients are used in the domain, they should be tested to verify their connectivity with the published resources. All clients should be able to map network drives to the published objects in AD.

- ◆ Appropriate **GPOs** must be configured to secure the resources in AD. The AD design team must determine which AD users will have access to the published resources.

OBJECTIVES ON THE JOB

Publishing shared network resources into the AD allows the network administrator to effectively control both access and security for the resources. The publishing technique is simple and easily implemented.

PRACTICE TEST QUESTIONS

1. **Publishing resources in Active Directory is an easily implemented enhancement for shared resources in your network environment. What network protocol is required to publish shared resources?**
   a. AppleTalk
   b. NWLink
   c. NetBEUI
   d. IP
   e. L2TP with IPSec

2. **Which of the following is a requirement for the administrator creating published resources in AD? (Choose all that apply.)**
   a. membership in the Schema Admins group
   b. SmartCard access to a Windows 2000 Professional computer with Service Pack 1a installed
   c. the permission to create objects in AD
   d. access to the Windows 2000 Professional Resource Kit and tools
   e. access to the Windows 2000 Server installation media
   f. the name of the OU that will host the published object

3. **What levels of security can be applied to objects published in AD? (Choose all that apply.)**
   a. NetBIOS Scope IDs
   b. shared folder permissions
   c. NTFS permissions
   d. NTLM security permissions
   e. AD security permissions

4. **AD users can map network drives from _____.**
   a. My Network Places
   b. File Manager
   c. AD Users and Computers
   d. AD Domain and Trusts

5. **An administrator is trying to configure security settings for a published folder in AD. She is unable to view the Security tab even though she has seen the tab displayed on other administrative stations. How can she change Active Directory Users and Computers to view the Security tab for the published folder? (Choose all that apply.)**
   a. Log off and log on as a member of the AD Published Folders Admin group.
   b. Delete the published object, and then reinstall the published object.
   c. Enable the Ordinary users can view published objects policy in the Windows 2000 GPO for the domain.
   d. Use the View option in Active Directory Users and Computers to turn on the Advanced Features option.

1.1.1 Perform a search in Active Directory Users and Computers.

SEARCHING AD FOR PUBLISHED OBJECTS

UNDERSTANDING THE OBJECTIVE

One of the many benefits of publishing objects in AD is that administrators and users gain the ability to search AD for published objects. Administrators can search in Active Directory Users and Computers directly, and AD users may search AD using several tools.

WHAT YOU REALLY NEED TO KNOW

- ◆ The AD is a large, searchable database. AD can store information about published resources such as shared folders.

- ◆ Administrators can search AD by using the Active Directory Users and Computers tool. Domain users can conduct searches using either this tool or a customized version called a task pad. Administrators can use the **ADSI** tool to search for specific information.

- ◆ When searching AD for shared folders using Active Directory Users and Computers, the search may be conducted using either the Shared Folders tab or the Advanced tab. In both tabs, the user conducting the search must select what to search for in the Find list and where to look using the In list. There also is a Browse button available.

- ◆ The Shared Folders tab allows search strings by name or keywords. On the Advanced tab, you can search one of the following fields: Description, Keywords, Managed by, Name, and Network path. After you choose a field, you must set a condition. The conditions are Starts with, Ends with, Is (exactly), Is not, Present, and Not present. When you have selected a field and a condition, you must enter a value to search on, and then you must click the Add button to enter the search criteria into the search window. A Remove button is also present to clear old searches. After the search criterion is populated, you click the Find Now button to begin the search.

- ◆ If the search is successful, you may now perform several different tasks with the search result. These tasks include Rename, Delete, Move, Open, Explore, Find, Map Network Drive, Create Shortcut, and View Properties.

OBJECTIVES ON THE JOB

If you publish resources in AD for your users and for yourself, you must know how to search AD to find these resources. Searching AD using Active Directory Users and Computers allows you, the administrator, to easily search for and manipulate these resources. Publishing resources in AD allows your users to easily search for and use these resources.

PRACTICE TEST QUESTIONS

1. **The Active Directory Users and Computers Find Shared Folders tool lists the search fields on the Advanced tab.**
   a. File managed by, Network path, Name, Description, and Keywords
   b. Description, Keywords, Managed by, Folder name, and Windows network path
   c. Description, Keywords, Managed by, Name, and Network path
   d. Keyword description, Managed by, Folder name, Network path, and Author
   e. Stream description, Keyword, Network location, Managed by, and Version

2. **By default, users can use which AD tool?**
   a. AD Users and Computers
   b. AD Domains and Trusts
   c. AD Sites and Services
   d. none of the above

3. **The Shared Folders tab in Active Directory Users and Computers Find Shared Folders allows a search in AD for folder name and _____.**
   a. embedded data streams
   b. creation date
   c. keywords
   d. owner

4. **Using the Active Directory Users and Computers _____ tab, users can search the entire AD structure or only parts of it, such as a specific domain.**
   a. AD Search
   b. Find\Shared Folders
   c. Shared Folder Search
   d. Net Share Find

5. **Administrator_A wants to give her users the ability to search AD directly for published folders. What is the best technique and tool for this purpose?**
   a. Administrator_A should give her users access to Active Directory Users and Computers, but assign delegated permissions to control access.
   b. Administrator_A should give her users access to Active Directory Users and Computers without delegated permissions.
   c. Administrator_A should create a task pad view for her users.
   d. Administrator_A doesn't need to do anything because her users can use the Windows Search tool.

6. **After a successful search has been completed and the desired folder is listed in the search results view, the user will need to use _____ to map a drive to the published folder.**
   a. My Network
   b. My AD Places
   c. My Network Places
   d. My Places

1.1.2 Configure a printer object.

PUBLISH PRINTER OBJECTS

UNDERSTANDING THE OBJECTIVE

Besides publishing shared folders in AD, you can publish print devices. This technique allows you to centralize your print devices to provide your AD users easy access to them.

WHAT YOU REALLY NEED TO KNOW

- ◆ Any print device hosted on a print server or user's personal workstation can be published in AD if the device meets two conditions. First, it must be shared as a network resource. Second, it must use IP as a protocol and have a UNC.

- ◆ When a print device is installed on a Windows 2000 Server computer that belongs to an AD domain, that print device is automatically published in the AD. This is the default behavior of AD. The exceptions to this rule are **USB** print devices that must be manually shared and published into AD.

- ◆ Print devices hosted on non-Windows 2000 Server computers must be manually added to the AD. Print devices hosted on Windows NT 4.0 Server computers can be added through the use of a VB script named pubprn.vbs.

- ◆ After a print device is added to AD, the administrator can use the features of AD to enhance the device's functionality. The administrator can use AD to map the physical location of the print device (street address, floor, and so on) into AD against a logical subnet. Another feature of AD support for published print devices is the orphan pruner, which is a program that checks the status of print devices published in AD. Because objects listed in AD must exist and be online, the orphan pruner periodically checks published print devices in AD and removes those devices from AD that do not respond to the orphan pruner query.

- ◆ The orphan pruner by default runs every eight hours. If a print device does not respond to three consecutive orphan pruner queries, the orphan pruner removes that print device from AD.

- ◆ To add print devices manually to the AD, you must first configure the orphan pruner pruning interval to "never." Failure to make this configuration setting will cause any print devices that you publish manually in AD to be removed automatically by the orphan pruner the next time the service runs.

- ◆ While data is being printed, it is sent asynchronously from the print server to AD for processing after a one-second delay. If the print server is unable to contact AD with this initial attempt, it continues to attempt a connection to the AD until two hours have elapsed. When the two-hour mark has been reached, the print server continues to make connection attempts using this new, two-hour interval.

OBJECTIVES ON THE JOB

AD allows administrators to publish print devices into AD so that these resources are available to AD users. Your ability to map print devices allows your users to search for these devices.

PRACTICE TEST QUESTIONS

1. Print devices that are hosted on _____ print servers can be published in AD.
   - a. UNIX
   - b. NetWare 3.12
   - c. DLC-based
   - d. Banyan Vines

2. You have published several print devices. Now clients are complaining that one particular device named ACCT_PRN1, while visible in Active Directory, is not responding. How can you troubleshoot through AD?
   - a. Access the print device through Active Directory Users and Computers.
   - b. Access the print device by clicking Start, pointing to Settings, and then clicking Printers.
   - c. Use the PERL script in the Server Resource Kit to troubleshoot the device.
   - d. Call the local user at the site who was delegated as the point of contact.

3. The orphan pruner is a configurable service that runs by default every _____.
   - a. 24 hours
   - b. 8 hours
   - c. 30 minutes
   - d. 6 days
   - e. 2 days

4. An administrator is trying to locate published print devices in Active Directory Users and Computers. The administrator has located a computer known to have shared print devices. The shared print devices are seen in My Network Places and they respond when the ping command is used against them. What must the administrator do to view these resources in Active Directory Users and Computers?
   - a. Log off and log on as a user with administrative privileges.
   - b. Delete the print devices, reboot the server, and reinstall the print devices.
   - c. Enable the Ordinary users can view published print devices GPO in AD.
   - d. Use the View option in the Active Directory Users and Computers to turn on the Users, Groups, and Computers as containers option.
   - e. The administrator must install QOS on his or her computer.

5. As part of your daily network maintenance routine, you must install new print drivers on the print server located in Boston. However, you are located in Plano. You know that the folder containing the print drivers is shared and that the name of the print server is BostonPrint. What is the correct path to access this folder?
   - a. \\BostonPrint\print
   - b. \\BostonPrint\printers
   - c. \\bostonprint\print$
   - d. \\BOSTONPRINT\PRINTDRIVERS

1.2 Manage data storage. Considerations include file systems, permissions, and quotas.

MANAGE DATA STORAGE

UNDERSTANDING THE OBJECTIVE

Windows 2000 allows administrators to configure different methods of data management. Data management consists of several different technologies that allow an administrator to control data.

WHAT YOU REALLY NEED TO KNOW

- ◆ Windows 2000 allows system administrators to control data on Windows 2000 Server and Professional computers.

- ◆ Windows 2000 supports six different file systems; each has specific uses and parameters. The file systems **FAT12**, **FAT16**, **FAT32**, **CDFS**, **UDF**, and **NTFS**. FAT12 is used only on 3.5" and 5.25" floppy disks and will be used on partitions that are less than 16 MB in size and formatted with FAT. FAT16 can be used for partitions larger than 16 MB but smaller than 4 GB, and individual files may not be larger than 2 GB. FAT32 can be used for partitions up to 8 TB (theoretically); however, if created under Windows 2000, a FAT32 partition cannot be larger than 32 GB. Also, individual files may not be larger than 4 GB. NTFS supports a theoretical size limit of 16 EB (16 million GB); however, Windows 2000 limits the size of a single partition to 128 TB. The only limit of file size is the amount of space available on a partition up to the limits stated.

- ◆ CDFS is the original format for recorded data CDs. It has limitations: the combined directory and filename cannot be longer than 32 characters, and directory trees cannot be more than eight layers deep. CDFS has been replaced by a newer format called UDF, which allows filenames up to 255 characters in length, maximum combined directory and filename paths of 1023 characters, and the use of mixed uppercase and lowercase for names. Windows 2000, however, supports read-only access for UDF-formatted CDs.

- ◆ Windows 2000 allows administrators to use different tools to format disks. The Disk Management snap-in can be used to format disks if a **GUI** interface is desired. Command line tools are also supported for use at the command prompt.

- ◆ Disk Management allows an administrator to use snap-in remote systems to delete, create, format, and share partitions across the network.

OBJECTIVES ON THE JOB

Data storage management is one of the most important daily tasks for a Windows 2000 administrator. The correct configuration of NTFS permissions, shared folder permissions, and AD permissions is extremely important for securing a Windows 2000 installation.

PRACTICE TEST QUESTIONS

1. **NTFS supports a maximum file size of _____.**
   - a. 4 GB
   - b. 128 TB
   - c. 16 EB
   - d. unlimited

2. **The _____ snap-in allows the administrator to connect remotely to other computers and manage those partitions.**
   - a. Disk Management
   - b. UDF Format
   - c. Print object
   - d. Connectivity

3. **CDFS supports directory trees _____ layers deep.**
   - a. 23
   - b. 12
   - c. 8
   - d. 32

4. **The UDF file system supports a combined directory and filename path of up to _____ characters.**
   - a. 128
   - b. 50
   - c. 1023
   - d. 1056

5. **Windows 2000 can be installed on which of the following file systems? (Choose all that apply.)**
   - a. FAT12
   - b. HPFS
   - c. FAT32
   - d. NTFS

6. **Windows 2000 limits the size of a single partition to _____.**
   - a. 16 EB
   - b. 128 TB
   - c. 8 picabytes
   - d. 500 GB

1.2.1 Implement NTFS and FAT file systems.

FILE SYSTEM IMPLEMENTATION DETAILS

UNDERSTANDING THE OBJECTIVE

Windows 2000 supports two main file systems for installation: NTFS and various versions of FAT. The administrator must understand the file systems and know which one to use in the installation and configuration of Windows 2000.

WHAT YOU REALLY NEED TO KNOW

- ◆ Windows 2000 supports FAT12, FAT16, FAT32, NTFS v1, and NTFS v2.

- ◆ Of all the FAT versions supported by Windows 2000, only FAT12 will never be used to host the operating system because it is used only on partitions sized 16 MB or smaller. Because Windows 2000 Professional requires at least 500 MB for a minimal installation of the operating system, FAT12 is excluded. Windows 2000 (any version) could be installed on a FAT16 partition (up to the 4 GB size limitation); however, this is discouraged because of security issues. The one exception to this rule would be a Windows 2000 computer used as a development platform. Here, the ability to access the boot partition from FAT would be a distinct advantage, provided that the development tools support installation on a non-NTFS partition and that the administrator has implemented other security measures. Another limitation of FAT16 is the small size (comparatively) of the usable partition; it is only 4 GB. Realistically, this size is not usable for the Windows 2000 OS in a production environment.

- ◆ FAT32 can be used to host a Windows 2000 system. Microsoft recommends FAT32 as the partition format of choice if the machine being built is intended to dual boot Windows 2000 and another operating system, such as Windows 98. Windows 98 cannot access an NTFS partition, but Windows 2000 can access a FAT32 partition.

- ◆ The preferred partition format for Windows 2000 is NTFS for many reasons. One of the most important reasons to use NTFS on a Windows 2000 installation is that no version of FAT provides the local security that NTFS does. Versions of FAT support only network-based security, which is security implemented through shared network folders, not the NTFS local security. NTFS supports native compression and **EFS** and is more efficient at larger partition sizes. NTFS also uses data streams to embed additional data into NTFS files (which is useful for application programs).

OBJECTIVES ON THE JOB

Selecting the correct file system for a Windows 2000 installation is one of an administrator's most important decisions. It is strongly recommended that the Windows 2000 administrator choose the NTFS file system for any Windows 2000 installation.

PRACTICE TEST QUESTIONS

1. **User_A has configured a laptop computer to dual boot Windows 98 and Windows 2000 Professional. The Windows 98 partition is formatted with FAT32. The Windows 2000 Professional partition is formatted with NTFS. User_A has files on the Windows 98 partition that have been compressed by Windows 98. User_A wants these files to be available in Windows 2000. What should User_A do to accomplish this goal?**
   a. Boot the laptop to Windows 2000 Professional and access the desired files from the Windows 98 compressed folder using Windows 2000 Professional.
   b. Boot the laptop to Windows 98 and copy the files from the Windows 98 FAT32 partition to the Windows 2000 NTFS partition.
   c. Boot the laptop to Windows 98, and copy the files from the Windows 98 FAT32 partition to an uncompressed folder on the Windows 98 partition. Then reboot the laptop to the Windows 2000 NTFS partition and copy the files from the uncompressed Windows 98 FAT32 folder to a folder on the Windows 2000 Professional NTFS partition.
   d. Use a third-party utility to convert the Windows 2000 NTFS partition to a FAT32 partition.

2. **If you have a business reason to install Windows 2000 on a FAT partition, you can format the partition with _____.**
   a. HPFS
   b. CDFS
   c. FAT12
   d. FAT32

3. **You have a business requirement to implement a file system that supports data streams and EFS. Which file system or systems could you implement? (Choose all that apply.)**
   a. NTFS v1
   b. HPFS
   c. FAT32
   d. NTFS v2

4. **Based on your current understanding of available Windows 2000 file systems, if you need to write a single 16 GB file to a partition, which file system should you implement? (Choose all that apply.)**
   a. FAT32
   b. USMDOS
   c. NTFS v1
   d. NTFS v2

1.2.2 Enable and configure quotas.

MANAGEMENT OF USER ACCOUNTS WITH QUOTAS

UNDERSTANDING THE OBJECTIVE

Windows 2000 supports the application of disk quotas on the platforms of both Windows 2000 Professional and Windows 2000 Server to assist the administrator in controlling hard drive space.

WHAT YOU REALLY NEED TO KNOW

◆ Windows 2000 supports quotas for volumes, not quotas for directories. If your environment requires a product that supports directory quotas, you should consider a third-party solution.

◆ Quotas are supported only on partitions formatted with NTFS v2, the version of NTFS found in Windows 2000. When a system is upgraded to Windows 2000, the version of NTFS also is upgraded and so it supports quotas without additional action on the part of the system administrator. Also, quotas can be enabled only on local volumes, not mapped connections. However, quotas can be configured without difficulty through the Windows 2000 Terminal Server client on Windows 2000 Terminal servers.

◆ Windows 2000 quotas are implemented based on the user's file ownership rights on the volume configured with quotas. If the user moves a file from one folder to another folder on the quota-enabled volume, the quota usage does not change. If the user copies a file from one location on the quota-enabled volume to another location on the same volume, the user's file usage on that volume is increased by the size of the file. Duplicated files increase the quota measured against the user.

◆ An administrator can configure a default quota for the entire volume or differing quotas for specific users on the volume. If default quotas have been configured, new clients receive this quota limit for their resources. After this is configured, an administrator can view the following quota information: default quota limits, per-user quota information, and quota tracking levels.

◆ Quotas can be implemented on computers locally (for example, on a shared workstation or a user's personal computer), or they may be implemented on a Windows 2000 file server configured with NTFS on the volume being used for storage.

◆ After quotas have been enabled, the administrator needs a method to track quota usage. The tool for this function is Event Viewer. Use the Event Viewer to export your quota reports to a tool such as Excel for data analysis and archival storage.

OBJECTIVES ON THE JOB

Quotas allow the network administrator to limit the amount of space a user may occupy with his or her associated folders and files. Quotas function on Windows 2000 Server and Windows 2000 Professional computers.

PRACTICE TEST QUESTIONS

1. **Which of the following systems can support volume quotas? (Choose all that apply.)**
   a. Windows 2000 Professional with the FAT32 file system
   b. Windows 95 with the FAT32 file system
   c. Windows 2000 Professional with the NTFS v2 file system
   d. Windows NT 4.0 Server with the NTFS v1 file system

2. **If an administrator wishes to, he or she can enable only _____, and not quota enforcement.**
   a. EFS
   b. quota tracking
   c. EFS quota tracking
   d. quota tracking with EFS

3. **A client is trying to copy additional files from Folder_A to Folder_B and is consistently unsuccessful. He receives a message that says he has exceeded the quota limits and must delete files before being allowed to proceed. The user insists that sufficient space exists under the assigned quota, and because compressed files are being used, they should not receive this message. Both folders are hosted on a Windows 2000 Server computer that has enforced quota limits enabled on the volume. Why is the user unable to copy the files? (Choose all that apply.)**
   a. EFS permissions have been configured to block the copy.
   b. Compression attributes are ignored when calculating quota usage values.
   c. The Windows 2000 file server is not using NTFS as its file format.
   d. Copied files on a quota-protected volume are counted twice against the user's quota.
   e. The user is not using Windows 2000 as a client.

4. **Clients using Windows _____ can use disk quotas.**
   a. 95
   b. 98
   c. Me
   d. 2000

5. **_____, once enabled, can never be disabled.**
   a. Compression quotas
   b. NTFS quotas
   c. EFS quotas
   d. Volume quotas

1.2.3 Implement and configure Encrypting File System (EFS).

EFS UTILIZATION

UNDERSTANDING THE OBJECTIVE

Windows 2000 now supports EFS, which is a form of **PKI**. EFS allows either users or administrators to encrypt files or folders with a PKI technology to protect these resources from unauthorized access.

WHAT YOU REALLY NEED TO KNOW

- ◆ Windows 2000 EFS is supported only on NTFS v2. No other file system supports EFS. After it is enabled, EFS is transparent to applications and can be made transparent to the user if implemented correctly. Before rolling out EFS in your network environment, make certain to create secure recovery agents.

- ◆ If not carefully planned and implemented in a domain environment, EFS is unbreakable by the administrator and can make resources unrecoverable. It is best to create a new, empty folder, apply EFS to it, and either move existing resources into it or create new resources in it.

- ◆ Files or folders configured with EFS are protected only while hosted on NTFS v2 volumes. If the files or folders are moved or copied to partitions formatted with other file systems, the encryption is removed.

- ◆ EFS encryption can be enabled through a GUI interface in My Computer or through Windows Explorer. A command line tool, CIPHER, may also be used to apply encryption.

- ◆ Encryption can be beneficial for users of portable computers such as laptops. The ability to encrypt local resources allows the user to have security on his or her machine no matter where he or she is. The security does not apply to off-line folders and files, however. The recommended technique for enabling encryption on a portable computer is to apply encryption on the empty My Documents folder first. New files or folders created in the My Documents folder will be encrypted automatically.

- ◆ Encryption can be disabled by unchecking the EFS check box in the Advanced Properties for an individual file or folder. Turning on the System attribute for a file or folder can prevent EFS because the OS will not allow system resources to be encrypted.

OBJECTIVES ON THE JOB

EFS allows you to apply security either locally on an individual computer or in a domain environment to enforce security on files and folders. EFS is a security tool that benefits users and can be easily implemented by administrators of Windows 2000.

PRACTICE TEST QUESTIONS

1. **Windows 2000 EFS can protect what kinds of objects? (Choose all that apply.)**
   a. folders hosted on an NTFS v2 partition
   b. files contained in a folder hosted on an NTFS v2 partition
   c. files contained in a folder hosted on an NTFS v2 partition that was converted from NTFS v1
   d. print devices shared on a Windows 2000 print server

2. **If a computer dual boots between Windows 98 and Windows 2000 Professional, and EFS has been enabled on a Windows 2000 folder named Test that resides on an NTFS partition, this folder is not accessible from the Windows 98 installation.**
   a. True
   b. False

3. **EFS can be applied to removeable media by using the _____ command.**
   a. cipher /a /media
   b. encrypt /-a:
   c. cipher /a: now
   d. none of the above

4. **A client computer running Windows 2000 Professional uses Offline folders. The folder that hosts these files is located on a Windows 2000 file server with NTFS v2. EFS is enabled on the file server-based files. Because the user has full control access to her file share on the file server, the user can access the file server and verify that the files and folders stored there are EFS protected. However, the user noticed that the Offline versions of these files are not protected by EFS. The user wants the Offline copies on the laptop computer to also be EFS protected. How can you implement this protection on the laptop?**
   a. Log on as the local system administrator and enable EFS on the Offline folder store.
   b. Implement the local Support EFS on Offline store security policy.
   c. Tell the user that because the Offline folder store is a system object, EFS is not supported. Give the user the option of disabling Offline file storage and implementing their storage for these drives locally, and then applying EFS.
   d. Move the CSC folder to a FAT32 partition and implement EFS that way.

5. **EFS can be enabled through what interface? (Choose all that apply.)**
   a. Windows 2000 Explorer
   b. Windows 2000 My Computer
   c. Windows 2000 My Network Places
   d. Command prompt and the CIPHER tool

1.2.4 Configure volumes and basic and dynamic disks.

DISK MANAGEMENT TECHNIQUES

UNDERSTANDING THE OBJECTIVE

Windows 2000 offers greater functionality and flexibility in the configuration of hard drives than that which was previously available in operating systems. These enhanced capabilities are provided through the use of dynamic disks.

WHAT YOU REALLY NEED TO KNOW

- ◆ Windows 2000 supports dynamic disks natively and is the only operating system to do so. Because of the disk overhead created by implementing dynamic disks, after a Windows 2000 computer implements dynamic disks, the computer cannot boot any other operating system except Windows 2000, and then only the installation of Windows 2000 that created the dynamic disks. In addition, after dynamic disks have been implemented, you cannot switch back to basic disks without destroying the operating system data.

- ◆ A benefit of the Windows 2000 hard drive implementation, which is not dependent on dynamic disks, is the ability to create new partitions that do not need to be mapped as drive letters, but that can instead be mounted as folders. This removes the limitation of previous Microsoft operating systems, which could support only 26 drive mappings, including network drives.

- ◆ A spanned volume consists of no more than 32 areas of free space (either 32 physical drives or 32 areas of unused space on one volume) that have been logically combined into a single drive. One benefit of a spanned volume is the ability to add space to the original volume by extending the volume. However, only NTFS partitions can be extended. Striped volumes, also called RAID 0 volumes, are implemented with a minimum of two physical drives to a maximum of 32 physical drives. A striped volume simultaneously writes data in 64 KB stripes across all elements of the set. Because they are writing and reading simultaneously to the set, striped volumes exhibit good-to-excellent read and write performance. They do not, however, provide any kind of fault tolerance—nor do spanned volumes.

- ◆ Only Windows 2000 Server products support all four advanced implementations of disk management; Windows 2000 Professional supports spanned volumes and striped volumes.

OBJECTIVES ON THE JOB

The ability to create dynamic disks in Windows 2000 is an important management tool for system administrators who must manage hard drive resources under Windows 2000. The use of dynamic disks provides better support and reliability for network users and clients.

PRACTICE TEST QUESTIONS

1. **You have implemented a RAID 5 array on a Windows 2000 server. There are eleven 512 MB drives in the array. What is the total size of the array, and how much space in the array is dedicated to parity information?**
   a. Total size is 5.6 TB and there are 512 MB of parity information.
   b. Total size is 5.6 PB and there are 5.1 GB of parity information.
   c. Total size is 5.6 GB and there are 512 MB of parity information.
   d. Total size is 5.6 GB and there is one array element for parity information.

2. **Which version of Windows 2000 supports spanned volumes? (Choose all that apply.)**
   a. Windows 2000 Professional
   b. Windows 2000 Server
   c. Windows 2000 Advanced Server
   d. Windows 20000 Datacenter Server

3. **Windows 2000 striped volumes can be extended if _____ to NTFS v2 first.**
   a. formatted
   b. converted
   c. copied
   d. moved

4. **A Windows 2000 _____ volume can support an operating system. (Choose all that apply.)**
   a. spanned
   b. mirrored
   c. Raid 5
   d. disk duplex

5. **A Windows 2000 dynamic disk will support _____ 26 partitions.**
   a. only
   b. more than
   c. less than
   d. none of the above

6. **If you are not satisfied with your _____ implementation, you cannot revert to the basic disk scheme without formatting the drive and destroying the operating system data on the drive.**
   a. mirrored drive
   b. spanned volume
   c. dynamic disk
   d. volume set

1.2.5 Configure file and folder permissions.

CONFIGURING NTFS PERMISSIONS

UNDERSTANDING THE OBJECTIVE

The NTFS permissions are powerful tools. Their use allows an administrator to apply basic security to Windows 2000.

WHAT YOU REALLY NEED TO KNOW

◆ NTFS permissions are available only on NTFS-formatted partitions. The NTFS format can be applied using an additional command-line switch: format *drive_letter /fs:ntfs* : The Disk Manager snap-in tool also can be used to apply the NTFS format. A third option is to use the convert command at the command prompt to convert a previously formatted volume that contains data to NTFS. The syntax for this command is convert *drive_letter* :

◆ NTFS permissions are effective against all users, including the administrator, if so configured. It is possible for a user to deny access by the administrator to an object.

◆ Windows 2000 NTFS v2 has very specific permissions. The administrator has a wide range of control over the level of access he or she can grant to users. A separate NTFS permission is the Change Permission permission. If granted to a user, the user is allowed to personally configure NTFS permissions. This setting can be allowed or denied. The NTFS settings are configured using the Security tab on the Properties sheet for Windows 2000 file and folder objects.

◆ One NTFS access permission available to the administrator and users is the No Access permission. The No Access permission overrides all other permissions and is absolute. No Access controls even the administrator. The default NTFS permission is Everyone – Full Control.

◆ NTFS permissions can be applied to files and folders and can also be configured separately for files and folders. NTFS file permissions always supersede NTFS folder permissions. The NTFS file and folder permissions also combine to provide the most restrictive combination of permissions on NTFS resources.

◆ When using NTFS permissions, only those users or groups published on the permissions list will be checked for access to the resource.

OBJECTIVES ON THE JOB

NTFS permissions are the primary tool you will use as an administrator to control access to your Windows 2000 file and folder resources. They provide safe, secure, and controllable access to resources, based on your administrative model for the environment that you support.

PRACTICE TEST QUESTIONS

1. **Windows 2000 NTFS permission can be applied to _____.**
   a. print devices
   b. removable drives such as CD-ROMs
   c. files only
   d. files and folders

2. **A partition can receive the NTFS file system _____. (Choose all that apply.)**
   a. by being formatted with NTFS on creation using the Disk Management snap-in tool
   b. from Windows Explorer
   c. from Windows File Manager
   d. from the FORMAT utility at the command prompt

3. **The NTFS No Access permission is_____.**
   a. absolute for users, optional for administrators
   b. effective only for users from foreign domains
   c. absolute for any user or group who is mapped to the permission
   d. an implicit permission that can be removed

4. **Who can administer NTFS permissions?**
   a. only members of the Domain NTFS Admins group
   b. any user who belongs to the Domain Users group
   c. any user who belongs to the Domain Users group and has received the Administer NTFS permission
   d. anyone who is mapped against a user account or group that has the Change Permission permission

5. **Windows 2000 NTFS permissions are identical to _____ permissions.**
   a. Windows Me
   b. Windows NT 3.5.1
   c. Windows NT 4.0
   d. Windows NT 3.1

6. **When Windows 2000 NTFS file and folder permissions combine, the most _____ permissions are the resulting permissions.**
   a. flexible
   b. restrictive
   c. user-friendly
   d. comprehensive

7. **Windows 2000 NTFS _____ are configured on the NTFS tab in the Object Properties dialog box.**
   a. shares
   b. quotas
   c. permissions
   d. encryption settings

1.2.6 Manage a domain-based distributed file system (DFS).

THE DISTRIBUTED FILE SYSTEM IN WINDOWS 2000

UNDERSTANDING THE OBJECTIVE

Windows 2000 DFS is a unique solution to the problem of providing and maintaining redundancy in your network environment. DFS can be implemented in two different versions in Windows 2000. The first version is known as stand-alone DFS. The second version is known as domain-based DFS and will be discussed here.

WHAT YOU REALLY NEED TO KNOW

- ◆ DFS is a tool that allows administrators to distribute file resources throughout a network environment by hosting the files on more than one file server. The administrator then uses the DFS tool to tie those resources into what appears to the users as a single, logical network share. As a result, users are no longer required to know the path to multiple network file server computers to gain access to resources. Users instead are presented with a single share point that contains the resources they need.

- ◆ Domain-based DFS has the additional benefit of integrating with AD and using AD for management and synchronization. Using the domain-based form, when a file or folder is updated or modified on one DFS share, that change is replicated to all other DFS shares at the next domain controller replication event.

- ◆ To configure DFS, you must first create a DFS root. This root is a shared resource that exists in your network environment and is accessible using a UNC path. The DFS console is located in the Administrative Tools folder under Programs on the Windows 2000 Start button.

- ◆ Domain-based DFS, because it integrates with AD, provides the most secure and robust DFS implementation. It removes the single point of failure from shared network resources and is ideal for use in Web servers, FTP server computers, or other server implementations where the shared resources must be constantly available to the network users.

- ◆ DFS also provides network administrators with a nonconfigurable form of load balancing because clients requesting network resources will be randomly directed to different file servers when they connect. This load balancing also extends to incidents of file servers crashing. With DFS implemented in your environment, as long as a DFS host is online, network users will be able to access shared resources in your environment.

OBJECTIVES ON THE JOB

You should know how to properly configure DFS in your network environment. It is a robust tool that can provide stability and redundancy for your network users. It is included in the standard installation of Windows 2000 Server and Windows 2000 Advanced Server.

PRACTICE TEST QUESTIONS

1. **What features of DFS make it a valuable tool for the network administrator to implement? (Choose all that apply.)**
   a. integration with UNIX file Server computers
   b. configuration-free network load balancing
   c. integration with MS-DOS computers with network shares hosted using TCP/IP as a protocol
   d. the ability to hide the details of different server deployments and file share locations from your users by presenting a single logical view of the network

2. **How many different versions of DFS are implemented in Windows 2000?**
   a. one—a domain-based DFS
   b. two—a domain-based DFS and a stand-alone DFS
   c. three—a domain-based DFS, a stand-alone DFS, and a workgroup DFS
   d. four—a domain-based DFS, a stand-alone DFS, a workgroup DFS, and an IIS DFS

3. **Which of the following network services would benefit from integration with domain-based DFS? (Choose all that apply.)**
   a. IIS 5.0 Web sites
   b. IIS 5.0 FTP sites
   c. software distribution points
   d. common shared workgroup files

4. **Windows 2000 domain-based DFS can be hosted on any computer that uses _____ as a protocol and that can create and host shares that follow the UNC naming convention.**
   a. UDP
   b. ICMP
   c. IP
   d. SNMP

5. **Windows 2000 domain-based DFS requires which of the following to function?**
   a. Active Directory
   b. WINS
   c. Windows 2000 Server computers that are either domain controllers or member server computers
   d. a valid DFS license

6. **If two users are sharing a DFS share and both are saving files into the share, then one user deleting files _____ affect the other user.**
   a. cannot
   b. will
   c. might
   d. More-specific information is needed to answer the question.

1.2.7 Manage file and folder compression.

USING AND MANAGING NTFS COMPRESSION

UNDERSTANDING THE OBJECTIVE

One of the many advantages of the NTFS file system is NTFS compression, which is useful for administrators who need to configure storage on NTFS volumes.

WHAT YOU REALLY NEED TO KNOW

◆ NTFS compression is available only on NTFS volumes and is built into the file. It is not a third-party, add-on product. Individual files may be compressed without affecting the folder that contains them. An entire folder could be compressed but compression could be removed from a few specific files within the folder. Compression is inherited by child objects from parent objects. Files and folders with NTFS compression enabled are not accessible by other operating systems, such as Windows 95 or Windows 98. They are accessible from other installations of Windows 2000, however.

◆ Certain key files needed for system start-up should not be compressed. These files are ntldr, boot.ini, and NTDETECT.COM. If these files are compressed, they become unusable and the computer cannot start. In addition, although a pagefile may be compressed, such a compression is useless because the operating system must uncompress the pagefile to use it. In addition to the files mentioned, specific folders on the volume should not be compressed. Most notably among them is the WINNT folder, which contains the operating system itself.

◆ Compression can be enabled in different ways. The simplest method is through the Explorer tool. Select the file or folder that you want to compress, and then select the Properties page for that object. At the bottom of the Properties page is the Advanced button. Click the Advanced button, and at the bottom of the next page, you will find the settings for compression. The method using My Computer is almost identical. A third method uses the command line tool, Compact, which can force compression to be applied, remove compression after it has been applied, and report compression statistics.

◆ NTFS compression is transparent to the user and to applications. It is possible for an administrator to enable compression on a user's volumes and folders without the user's knowledge. The compressed sizes of files will not be used by Windows 2000 disk quotas for tracking space usage, however.

OBJECTIVES ON THE JOB

When implementing Windows 2000, consider the benefits of applying NTFS compression on your volumes. You will find that NTFS saves significant space, is easy to use, and is transparent to applications and users.

PRACTICE TEST QUESTIONS

1. **NTFS compression can be applied using which tool? (Choose all that apply.)**
   a. COMPACT
   b. File Manager
   c. My Computer
   d. Windows Explorer
   e. the Disk Management snap-in

2. **Which of the following lists key files that are needed by the operating system and that must not be compressed?**
   a. ntoskrnl.exe, ftdisk.sys, boot.ini, and IO.SYS
   b. IO.SYS, MSDOS.SYS, regedit.exe, and win.ini
   c. ntldr, boot.ini, and NTDETECT.COM
   d. AEvent.Evt, SYSTEM.SAV, BOOT.INI, and cache.dns

3. **NTFS compression can be configured by _____.**
   a. the Everyone group
   b. the Domain Admins group
   c. anyone with appropriate permissions
   d. the creator/owner of the resource only

4. **Windows 2000 NTFS compression cannot be applied on what type of volume?**
   a. Windows NT 4.0 partitions on computers that dual boot
   b. Windows 2000 NTFS formatted volumes that host shares for Apple Macintosh clients
   c. volumes containing Windows 98 installations on computers that dual boot
   d. Windows 2000 spanned volumes formatted with NTFS

5. **A user calls your help desk to complain about being denied file storage space on a network file server with disk quotas in place. Supposedly, the user has exceeded the assigned quota limit. You discover that NTFS compression has been placed on the user's file server storage point. The user insists that the quota limit has not been exceeded. You know that the client is not using NTFS locally. What could be the cause of the problem?**
   a. The client doesn't have permission to access the resources.
   b. NTFS compression reports only the actual object sizes to the Windows 2000 disk quota management tool, not the compressed sizes.
   c. The user's quota limits have been set too low and need to be adjusted.
   d. The client needs to move the data stored on the network from the network to the local drive.

6. **The command-line utility _____ can be used to apply compression to resources on Windows 2000 FAT16 partitions.**
   a. Compress
   b. Stac
   c. Compact
   d. none of the above

1.3 Create shared resources and configure access rights. Shared resources include printers, shared folders, and Web folders.

USING SHARED RESOURCES IN WINDOWS 2000

UNDERSTANDING THE OBJECTIVE

Windows 2000 supports the ability to create shares and to make resources available to users on your network. Different kinds of shares can be created.

WHAT YOU REALLY NEED TO KNOW

- ◆ As a network administrator, one of the more valuable tools available to you is the network share. Network shares allow you to make commonly used resources available to many users in your network environment, instead of just to those users who have the resources connected to their local computers.

- ◆ Objects that can be shared in Windows 2000 include folders on any supported file system, volume and partition roots, CD-ROM and floppy disks, and print devices.

- ◆ Windows 2000 allows an administrator to create multiple shares on the same resource. This is beneficial if you need to create a share with two different naming conventions or differing shared folder permissions.

- ◆ The only security settings that can be enabled on a FAT partition under Windows 2000 are shared folder permissions. Also, any protocol supported under the Windows 2000 OS allows the creation of network shares, provided that networking support (which is optional) has been installed and configured.

- ◆ There is a key difference between sharing a resource on a Windows 2000 Server computer and sharing a resource on a Windows 2000 Professional computer. Windows 2000 Server by default permits more than 4.29 billion simultaneous connections to a shared resource. Windows 2000 Professional permits only 10 simultaneous connections to a shared resource.

- ◆ Shares in Windows 2000 can be created in several different ways. Probably the most common method is through the Explorer tool. However, resources can also be shared through My Computer, Computer Management, or Server Manager. The Computer Management snap-in also allows the administrator to create shares on a remote machine (without having physical access to the machine) by using only a network connection. Several tools also exist in the Windows 2000 Server Resource Kit that can assist with managing and manipulating shared resources in Windows 2000.

OBJECTIVES ON THE JOB

Creating and using shares is one of the most common daily tasks of the network administrator. Windows 2000 provides the administrator and the user a simple, secure way to make local resources installed on any supported file system available to users of the network.

PRACTICE TEST QUESTIONS

1. **Sharing resources in Windows 2000 is easily implemented and optimizes your resources in a network environment. What protocol is required to create shared resources? (Choose all that apply.)**
   a. AppleTalk
   b. NWLink
   c. NetBEUI
   d. IP

2. **Windows 2000 does not support file shares on the _____ file system.**
   a. NTFS v1
   b. HPFS v2
   c. NTFS v2
   d. FAT12

3. **A client has requested that you publish some resources on the company intranet site. What should be your first step?**
   a. Copy the files needed by the intranet site to a folder on the IIS server.
   b. Tell your client that the request cannot be implemented, and suggest that the files needed by these Web sites should be copied to the machines locally.
   c. Change the protocol used on both the client and the file server from NetBEUI to IP so that IPSec Transport mode can be enabled.
   d. Use the Properties tab for the folder and enable Web Sharing on the folders, as needed by the resources, with the appropriate names and security settings.
   e. Transfer the files needed by the resources to a file server that uses the LANManager protocol.

4. **Active Directory guests map network drives to shared folders using the _____ tool.**
   a. AD Sites and Services
   b. AD Shares and Trusts
   c. AD Users and Computers
   d. Control Panel Map Remote

5. **To configure a print device as a shared device on a Windows 2000 Server computer, you must:**
   a. install the device; the default settings will share the device to the network.
   b. install the device and create manual shares.
   c. use the Pubprn.vbs script.
   d. install only to a stand-alone computer, and then restart the computer.

1.3.1 Share folders and enable Web sharing.

BASIC SHARED FOLDER TECHNIQUES

UNDERSTANDING THE OBJECTIVE

The Windows 2000 administrator must know how to create shared folders on a Windows 2000 computer. Administrators also must understand Web Sharing, an additional tool that simplifies the creation of secure intranet and extranet Web sites. The Web Sharing feature is an implementation of shared folders that will become more important as the Windows 2000 OS continues to grow and evolve into an enterprise-grade OS for the corporate environment.

WHAT YOU REALLY NEED TO KNOW

◆ For Windows 2000 Professional, only members of the Administrators group or members of the Power Users group can create shared objects. For Windows 2000 Server or Advanced Server, the same restriction applies. However, a Windows 2000 Server or Advanced Server configured as a **DC** does not support the Power Users group; therefore, only the Administrators group and the Server Operators group have the necessary rights to create shared objects.

◆ The combination of shared folder permission and NTFS permissions represents the toolset that the Windows 2000 administrator will implement to make local resources available to the network environment. When configuring objects for sharing, the administrator must implement the most rigorous security settings possible, yet balance them with user access needs.

◆ Shared folders can be created using different tools, including, but not limited to, Explorer, My Computer, and Computer Management\Shared Folders.

◆ When configuring shared folders, the administrator may select how many connections will be allowed to simultaneously access this share. The default is Maximum Allowed. For a Windows 2000 Professional computer, this means only 10 connections per resource. For a Windows 2000 Server computer, this same setting means 4.29 billion connections. You might want to reduce this value.

◆ A final technique for creating shares is the Administrative or so-called Secret shares. They are configured so that they do not appear in My Network Place in Windows 2000 or any other Microsoft Network view. This configuration is achieved by placing a $ character, without spaces, at the end of the share name.

OBJECTIVES ON THE JOB

Shared folder techniques in Windows 2000 are an important part of daily management that administrators need to understand and utilize. The Web Sharing that is now supported also allows administrators to implement advanced tools, such as the Microsoft Portal Server product, into their network users' environment.

PRACTICE TEST QUESTIONS

1. What special character must be appended to a share name to create an Administrative share? (Choose all that apply.)
   - a. #
   - b. &
   - c. $
   - d. Æ
   - e. @

2. Windows 2000 Professional allows only _____ to simultaneously connect to a single shared resource.
   - a. 100 users
   - b. 5 users for a FAT partition and 10 users for an NTFS volume
   - c. 10 users
   - d. 21×10^1 users

3. Which tool cannot be used to create shared folders? (Choose all that apply.)
   - a. Server Manager
   - b. Explorer
   - c. Program Manager
   - d. My Computer

4. Members of the Power Users group on a Windows 2000 Domain Controller can create shared folders.
   - a. True
   - b. False

5. UserA has a laptop that uses Windows 2000 Professional. UserA has created an extensive Web-presentation and wants to publish it on the company Web site. UserA has asked you to place this presentation on the company Web site for viewing. Choose the simplest implementation.
   - a. Copy the files to a file server running Windows 2000 and IIS 5.0, and then create a virtual Web server. Configure the Web server appropriately and restart IIS for the changes to take effect.
   - b. Copy the files to a file server running Windows 2000, and then create a virtual Web directory pointing back to the server hosting the presentation. Configure the Web server appropriately and restart IIS for the changes to take effect.
   - c. Copy the files to a file server running Windows 2000 and IIS 5.0, and then create a Web Share on the folder. Configure the Web server appropriately and restart IIS for the changes to take effect.
   - d. Copy the files to a file server running Windows 2000 and IIS 5.0, and then create a virtual Web server. Implement domain-based DFS for availability, and then configure the Web server appropriately. Restart IIS for the changes to take effect.

1.3.2 Configure shared folder permissions.

SHARED NETWORK RESOURCES

UNDERSTANDING THE OBJECTIVE

Shared network resources allow the Windows 2000 administrator to make resources, including file and application folders and Web folders, available to authorized users in their environment.

WHAT YOU REALLY NEED TO KNOW

◆ Shared network resources are supported on any file system used by Windows 2000, including any version of FAT. Shared folder permissions are the only security protection available for resources residing on partitions formatted with any version of FAT. Shared folder permission can be applied to folders or drives (for example, the folder that holds the latest downloaded anti-virus signature files) or to a CD-ROM drive that is on a computer.

◆ Shared folder permissions are much simpler to use and configure than NTFS permissions. Shared folders can be created using a scripted process. The three shared folder permissions are Full Control, Change, and Read. These permissions can be allowed or denied. The deny permission overrides all other permissions. Unlike NTFS permissions that can be applied at the file and folder level, shared folder permissions apply only at the folder level. Like NTFS permissions, shared folder permissions are cumulative if multiple shared folders are in the same path; however, this practice is strongly discouraged.

◆ When shared folder permissions and NFTS permissions are in place on an object, the resultant permissions are the most restrictive combination of permissions.

◆ The number of connections available to each shared resource depends on the version of Windows 2000 hosting the share. Windows 2000 Professional shares are restricted to only 10 simultaneous connections. Windows 2000 Server defaults to 4.29×10^9 simultaneous connections.

◆ Users who have appropriate permissions may map drives to folders on Web server computers and use those mapped drives as a local drive resource. Several specific conditions must be met before Web folders can be implemented: the Web server must support **WEC**, FrontPage extensions, and **DAV** protocols. Microsoft **IIS** and other Microsoft tools satisfy all these conditions.

OBJECTIVES ON THE JOB

Shared resources in a Windows 2000 network environment allow the administrator to optimize and control the utilization of corporate resources. When combined with NTFS permissions, the network administrator can implement a secure and efficient environment for the users.

PRACTICE TEST QUESTIONS

1. Shared folders can be created on _____ partitions. (Choose all that apply.)
   a. FAT12
   b. FAT32
   c. NTFS v2
   d. HPFS

2. Web folders are supported on Web server computers that meet specific constraints. What are the constraints? (Choose all that apply.)
   a. The network protocol is NetBIOS.
   b. The FrontPage extensions are available.
   c. The Web server supports WEC.
   d. The DAV protocols are supported.
   e. The network protocol is TCP/IP.

3. Administrator_A wants to hide a folder containing installation files from view on the network, but not continually share and unshare the folder. What steps should Administrator_A take to achieve this goal? (Choose all that apply.)
   a. Configure appropriate shared folder permissions.
   b. Create the hidden share by appending "&" after the share name.
   c. Configure the appropriate NTFS permissions for the resource.
   d. Place an A record for the resource into DNS.

4. A network user is trying to create a shared folder on a laptop for 17 members of the workgroup to simultaneously access the resource. However, the user has complained that not all of the team members can simultaneously access the shared folder. What might cause this? (Choose all that apply.)
   a. Some of the users have incorrect permissions.
   b. Some of the users have incorrect subnet settings.
   c. Some of the users have incorrect IP information.
   d. Some of the shared folder permissions may be incorrect.
   e. Some of the users have incorrect gateway settings.

5. You have files on a Windows NT 4.0 file server and would like to make them available to your AD clients who use Windows 2000 Professional. The Windows NT 4.0 file server belongs to a Windows NT 4.0 domain, and it is the PDC for the domain. How can you add this resource from a foreign domain into your Windows 2000 AD as a published source?
   a. Install the Hi-encryption version of Service Pack 5 on the Windows NT 4.0 server and then reboot.
   b. Open AD Users and Computers and create the published object.
   c. Create a manual mapping in the WINS database and configure WINS lookup for DNS.
   d. Install the Hi-encryption version of Service Pack 6a on the Windows NT 4.0 server and then reboot.

1.3.3 Create and manage shared printers.

SHARING PRINT DEVICES IN WINDOWS 2000

UNDERSTANDING THE OBJECTIVE

Beyond sharing folders and partitions in Windows 2000, the administrator can also create shares for print devices. This makes it possible to reduce the number of individually assigned print devices and redirect users to print devices that exist in your network environment.

WHAT YOU REALLY NEED TO KNOW

- ◆ Any kind of print device that can be installed on a Windows 2000 computer, whether Professional or Server, can be shared on the network.

- ◆ When a Windows 2000 Server computer is configured as a print server, a directory is created on the server to hold print drivers for the device. This folder is shared administratively as Printer$. This sharing allows the administrator to connect to this share and install new print drivers across the network without having physical access to the print server. There are no configurable share permissions for print devices.

- ◆ When a client connects to a shared print device, his or her operating system determines how the client will obtain print drivers. If the client is using a DOS-based or non-Microsoft OS, the client must obtain the print drivers from a source designated by the administrator and install the drivers manually. Clients who use Windows 95, Windows 98, Windows NT 4.0, or Windows 2000 will automatically download the correct print driver when they connect to the printer. The Windows 2000 Server installation media does not provide print drivers for any other OS except for Windows 2000. If additional clients are to be supported, the administrator must obtain them elsewhere.

- ◆ If you are installing your print device shares on a Windows 2000 Server computer that belongs to an AD domain, the administrator has an additional configuration setting available. The additional setting allows the print device to be published in AD.

- ◆ If the print devices are installed on a Windows 2000 Server computer that is running IIS 5.0, the administrator can also implement Web-based printing, which allows users to access and manage their documents and their printers using a Web browser interface.

OBJECTIVES ON THE JOB

Windows 2000 offers the administrator useful and powerful techniques for managing and maintaining network print devices. All these advanced techniques begin with the creation of shared network print devices and their correct implementation in your environment.

PRACTICE TEST QUESTIONS

1. All _____ clients who connect to a Windows 2000 print server will automatically download the correct drivers.
   a. UNIX
   b. Microsoft
   c. Apple
   d. OS/2

2. The shared permissions for Windows 2000 print devices are:
   a. Full Control, Print, Manage, and No Access
   b. Full Control, Manage Documents, and Print
   c. AD User Print, No Access, Full Control, Print, and Manage
   d. There are no configurable share permissions.

3. UserA is trying to connect to a Windows 2000 print server with a workstation which is running OS/2 2.1. The user can see the print server on the network, can connect to the print server, and connect to the printer itself. However, the output from the device is unintelligible. What is the resolution for this user?
   a. Disconnect the mapped printer and reset the user's security settings. Have the user restart the computer and then reconnect to the printer.
   b. Go to the IBM OS/2 2.1 user's page and search for the FAQ documentation.
   c. Uninstall the user's network adapter card and protocols. Restart the computer, and then reinstall the adapter and the protocols.
   d. Obtain the correct OS/2 2.1 printer drivers and install them manually.

4. UserB is trying to print a document and has sent the document several times, but it has not printed. Windows 2000 Professional is UserB's OS. UserB can access the printer properties and see five different copies of the document, but can delete only the extra copies of the document. Determine a resolution for this user.
   a. The user has an incorrect printer driver and needs a replacement driver installed. Reinstall the correct driver to solve the problem and test for the user.
   b. Check the priority and scheduled print times for this user's printer.
   c. The user has installed a print driver for the MIPS versions of Windows 2000 Professional. Delete this driver and install the correct driver for the Intel platform.
   d. Check the spooler settings for the user's printer.

5. Web-based printing means: (Choose all that apply.)
   a. the ability to print Web site pages
   b. the ability to administer print devices using the Internet and a browser
   c. the ability to connect to print devices using the Internet and a browser
   d. sending documents to the print device through Internet Explorer

1.3.4 Configure shared printer permissions.

WINDOWS 2000 SHARED PRINTER PERMISSIONS

UNDERSTANDING THE OBJECTIVE

After you have established shared print devices in Windows 2000, you must configure the permissions for these resources. Windows 2000 shared printer permissions can provide you a great deal of administrative control over your users.

WHAT YOU REALLY NEED TO KNOW

- ◆ One of the settings that can be enabled is the location of the print device—the actual physical location of the device. Supplying this information allows the administrator to map this location against the subnet of the device, if it is a network print device. This can be useful for users who can now search AD for print devices closest to them. Another one of the AD options available to the administrator is the default setting for List in the Directory.

- ◆ The properties sheet for print devices allows for configuration of the port properties for the device. You can also add a port, delete a port, configure a port, and enable printer pooling. The printer pooling technique allows the administrator to map multiple print devices against a single printer. With printer pooling enabled, when a client sends a document to the printer, it is spooled and then delivered to the first print device in the pool that is free to accept the document. There are two issues associated with printer pooling. The print devices in the printer pool must be the same type of device. This is required because the physical devices will be using the same logical software component. The second issue is that the clients do not know which print device will service their print request, so you should place the print devices close together.

- ◆ The administrator will also find a Security tab that allows for the configuration of printer permissions for the device. There are three of these top-level security settings: Print, Manage Printers, and Manage Documents. By default, all users receive the Print permission; however, if a user is delegated the Manage Documents right, he or she still needs the Print permission.

- ◆ The administrator can also enable auditing for the print devices to track usage and access times. In addition, the Advanced tab allows you to enable the "Keep printed documents" setting and retain documents in the spooler to be printed later.

OBJECTIVES ON THE JOB

Print devices in Windows 2000 have advanced configuration settings that are available to the network administrator. These settings can provide enhanced functionality for users and more manageability for the administrator.

PRACTICE TEST QUESTIONS

1. **What security permissions are available for Windows 2000 print devices? (Choose all that apply.)**
   a. Print Documents
   b. Print
   c. Manage Documents
   d. Manage Printers

2. **IIS is required for what service to function? (Choose all that apply.)**
   a. Standalone Certificate Authority
   b. Web-based printing
   c. Trivial File Transfer Protocol
   d. Quality of Service

3. **You support approximately 250 users who frequently use the company's 10 print devices. However, only some of these devices are available on the network; the others are installed locally on individual machines. Users frequently complain about the length of time it takes to print a document. How could you optimize the printing experience for your users? (Choose all that apply.)**
   a. Enable a separator page.
   b. Configure the Use Printer Pooling GPO in AD.
   c. Enable printer pooling for your network.
   d. Disconnect local printers from users' workstations and attach them to the network instead.

4. **Users have the right, by default, to manage documents for _____.**
   a. other users
   b. themselves
   c. team members
   d. Guests

5. **Windows 2000 print devices can be shared and made available to clients running _____. (Choose all that apply.)**
   a. UNIX
   b. DOS
   c. Apple Macintosh
   d. Red Star Linux

6. **What setting can be enabled to keep documents on the print spooler until the administrator has a chance to print them out to view their contents?**
   a. Reprint documents
   b. Hold mismatched documents
   c. Keep printed documents
   d. Print directly to the printer

1.4 Configure and troubleshoot Internet Information Services (IIS).

TROUBLESHOOTING WEB SERVICES

UNDERSTANDING THE OBJECTIVE

One of the key services of Windows 2000 Server is IIS. This tool provides a service that, while not required for operation of Windows 2000 Server computers in stand-alone or member server roles, is very important for Windows 2000 DCs. It is mandated for machines such as **CAs** and is an implementation enhancement for other domain controller roles, such as print server and DFS.

WHAT YOU REALLY NEED TO KNOW

- ◆ IIS installs by default on Windows 2000 Server computers. Windows 2000 Professional can also accept an installation of IIS. However, on the Professional platform, IIS installs as a service called **PWS**. PWS is functionally similar to IIS; the differences are the number of connections supported by PWS. IIS defaults to 100,000 connections to a Web site. PWS supports no more than 10 connections at a time.

- ◆ Unlike other Web servers such as Apache Web, IIS is not just a Web server. It is a component of the operating system that interacts and interoperates with the operating system. Microsoft technologies such as Office XP and Share Point Portal Server are just two Microsoft products that integrate with IIS to provide users with an enhanced computing environment.

- ◆ Besides supporting Web sites, IIS also supports FTP services. The FTP server can be configured for upload or download and can also support several different levels of security ranging from anonymous logon to Windows Authenticated logon.

- ◆ The Internet Information Services management snap-in supports the administration of IIS 5.0 in Windows 2000. Besides allowing the administrator to manage the local IIS server, the IIS management console also allows an administrator to connect to and administer other IIS computers.

- ◆ IIS also supports **SMTP** and **NNTP** for Windows 2000. Each of these services also has its own management interface in the IIS console tool.

- ◆ When working with IIS, the administrator must remember to stop and restart IIS after making any changes.

OBJECTIVES ON THE JOB

IIS is an important technology for Windows 2000 Server and will become more important as the product matures. Properly implemented and secured, IIS can be a valuable tool for the administrator. IIS can enhance the network experience for network users and assist the administrator in day-to-day maintenance of the network.

PRACTICE TEST QUESTIONS

1. **Which of the following will install on a Windows 2000 Professional computer? (Choose all that apply.)**
   a. Simple Mail Transfer Protocol
   b. Network News Transfer Protocol
   c. Peer Web Services
   d. File Transfer Protocol

2. **What function does PWS serve in a networked environment?**
   a. It allows users to receive SMTP mail services.
   b. It allows users to manage IIS 5.0 Web server computers.
   c. It allows users to create small Web sites for teams for workgroups.
   d. It allows users to utilize TFTP.

3. **Apache Web Server is usually found on the _____ OS.**
   a. Windows 2000 Server
   b. Windows 2000 Web Server
   c. Apple Web Server
   d. UNIX

4. **After an administrator makes configuration changes to IIS, the administrator must:**
   a. reboot the IIS server.
   b. update the IIS metabase.
   c. stop and restart the IIS server.
   d. use the automated cleanup utility.

5. **Peer Web Server can support no more than 10 client connections per Web page. How many users can the IIS 5.0 Default Web Site support, by default?**
   a. unlimited connections
   b. 1,000 connections
   c. 100,000 connections
   d. 50,000 connections at 15% network bandwidth utilization

6. **How can the administrator enable Web-based printing?**
   a. Enable the Web-based printing tool in IIS 5.0.
   b. Reconfigure the Default Web Site to support Web-based printing.
   c. Apply the Web-based printing GPO in AD.
   d. Install the print device on a computer with IIS 5.0 enabled.

1.4.1 Configure virtual directories and virtual servers.

WEB SITE IMPLEMENTATION DETAILS

UNDERSTANDING THE OBJECTIVE

Virtual directories allow the administrator to map Web sites against content directories on other computers.

WHAT YOU REALLY NEED TO KNOW

◆ IIS 5.0 allows the creation of virtual directories for hosted Web sites. A virtual directory is a directory hosted on another computer—not the computer hosting the Web server that belongs to the same Windows 2000 domain as the Web server running IIS 5.0.

◆ To use IIS virtual directories, you must meet several conditions. You must know the UNC path to the computer hosting the directory to be added to the IIS Web site, and you must supply a user name and password to access the other computer.

◆ Using virtual directories allows the IIS administrator to isolate application folders from each other, thereby preventing one Web application from accessing the files for another application. Virtual directories are also useful for enhancing security in your Windows 2000 environment because you create an alias for the virtual directory location. This allows browser users to access your Web site and make use of the Web resources, and it allows the IIS administrator to hide the network identity of the computer hosting the actual directories and files used for the Web site. Users entering the Web site will know only the name of the server hosting IIS, not the name of the server hosting the actual resources.

◆ Virtual servers can also be created on IIS 5.0 servers. A virtual server is another name for a Web site. IIS 5.0 allows the IIS administrator to create additional Web sites in addition to the single default Web site provided by IIS.

◆ Just as the default Web site has a unique IP address and domain name, each virtual server can also have its own IP address and domain name.

◆ Virtual servers can also be configured through the use of port numbers appended to the default IP address for the Web server.

◆ You also can assign multiple IP addresses and domain names to one network adapter card and then control connectivity by using host header files.

OBJECTIVES ON THE JOB

Virtual directories and virtual servers are a useful tool for IIS administrators who want to enhance the functionality and performance of IIS services.

PRACTICE TEST QUESTIONS

1. _____ directories can be used to enhance security for your IIS Web servers.
   a. Local
   b. Remote
   c. DFS
   d. Virtual

2. As the IIS administrator, you need to configure Web resources for your IIS server. However, the servers that contain the resources are UNIX servers. For various reasons, you cannot move the material from these UNIX servers to a Windows 2000 Server computer. IIS _____ directories will solve this problem and allow you to host the resources located on the UNIX servers on your IIS Web site.
   a. UNIX realm
   b. Kerberos authenticated
   c. virtual
   d. local

3. How can virtual servers be created on IIS servers? (Choose all that apply.)
   a. by appending a port number to the IP address of the IIS server
   b. by creating a static entry in the WINS server database
   c. by installing multiple NIC cards in the IIS server and assigning a specific NIC card to a specific virtual server
   d. by assigning multiple IP addresses and domain names to one NIC card, and then controlling access through the use of host header files

4. A user in your domain is trying to configure a virtual directory on the team Web server; however, this user cannot make a connection to the server. What might be the problem? (Choose all that apply.)
   a. The computer hosting the resources is not in the same Windows 2000 domain as the IIS server.
   b. The UNC path is incorrect.
   c. The user account and password are incorrect.
   d. The computer browser service is nonfunctional.

5. Virtual servers are useful for providing _____ Web sites using only one Web server.
   a. departmental
   b. team
   c. individual
   d. group

1.4.2 Troubleshoot Internet browsing from client computers.

INTERNET CONNECTIVITY ISSUES

UNDERSTANDING THE OBJECTIVE

In today's Internet-enabled world, a nonfunctional Web browser is not just an annoyance, it is a business issue. Without a functional Web browser, your clients may not be able to retrieve Internet mail or obtain the latest antivirus updates. As a network administrator, you may be called upon to troubleshoot Internet browsing for your clients.

WHAT YOU REALLY NEED TO KNOW

◆ As your first step in troubleshooting Internet connectivity, you should examine the client IP configuration settings. If they are using static IP, check whether the configuration is correct and the IP address matches the subnet mask. If there is a client gateway, check whether the IP address matches it. If not, reset the static IP information.

◆ If the client is a **DHCP** client, check the DHCP settings. Check whether the lease for the client is active and whether the client has a DHCP mapping to a DHCP server.

◆ Check the client's address. If this is a Windows 2000 client, check the IP address. If it falls in the range 169.254.*x.y,* the computer was unable to contact a DHCP server and has used **APIPA** to self-configure its IP address. When using APIPA, the client will have no network connectivity beyond other APIPA-enabled machines. You must determine why it was unable to contact a DHCP server and then correct the problem. The easiest way to switch from APIPA back to standard DHCP is to ensure that the DHCP server is active and reachable on the subnet of the client being worked on. After this has been verified, access the Properties tab for My Network Places, and then disable the network interface. After the interface has stopped, re-enable it. The adapter should now receive DHCP information.

◆ If the IP address information is correct, you may need to check **DNS** name resolution next. Determine whether other clients can reach out to the Internet. If they can, you have isolated the problem to this computer only.

◆ If the client is a dial-up user, check whether the modem is working. If not, you may need to check the status of the modem. Sometimes the simplest troubleshooting procedure is to uninstall/remove the modem, reboot the computer, and then reinstall the modem.

OBJECTIVES ON THE JOB

Internet Explorer is a tool that you must maintain. It no longer simply provides entertainment on lunch breaks. Companies depend on Internet-enabled e-mail, Internet-hosted corporate portals, and other Internet-enabled tools.

PRACTICE TEST QUESTIONS

1. **Internet Explorer depends on which network protocol for correct operation? (Choose all that apply.)**
   a. IP with IPSec Transport mode enabled
   b. IP with DHCP only
   c. IP with static IP configured
   d. NBT enabled with WINS servers for resolution

2. **Microsoft _____ is an Enterprise-class Web browser that can support clients in a corporate environment, and it is available in versions to match most foreign languages.**
   a. Internet Explorer
   b. intranet explorer
   c. Share Point Team Services
   d. Exchange Messaging Server

3. **Internet Explorer is available for which platforms? (Choose all that apply.)**
   a. Apple Macintosh
   b. Windows 98 SE
   c. Windows 2000 Server
   d. Windows 3.1
   e. Windows NT 4.0 Workstation

4. **Internet Explorer _____ with the operating system in Windows 2000.**
   a. works
   b. integrates
   c. interoperates
   d. merges

5. **An IP address in the range of 169.254.*x.y* means that your computer has successfully obtained a(n) _____ address mapping.**
   a. DHCP
   b. APIPA
   c. DNS
   d. WINS

6. **Internet Explorer can be enabled for automatic updates. In a corporate environment, this may _____.**
   a. cause inconsistent configurations
   b. cause no problems at all
   c. decrease available bandwidth
   d. represent a security breech

1.4.3 Troubleshoot intranet browsing from client computers.

INTRANET BROWSING

UNDERSTANDING THE OBJECTIVE

Many companies are moving more of their internal documentation and administrative functions to the corporate intranet. You may find yourself dealing with a corporate Web site that is used as the employee time sheet recording tool or as a centralized location for team information. Many issues that apply to Internet browsing apply equally for intranet browsing.

WHAT YOU REALLY NEED TO KNOW

◆ There are three types of Web environments recognized today: the Internet, corporate intranets, and extranets. The Internet is the World Wide Web. The intranet is a Web environment contained within your organization or business. An extranet is a Web environment that exists between two or more businesses only

◆ FrontPage with Extensions is a useful and valuable tool for administrators in a corporate environment. It allows you to create Web sites quickly and easily.

◆ Ensure that your network configuration settings for accessing your corporate intranet are correct. If you are using a proxy server, be sure that it has been configured correctly so that clients trying to access the intranet are not redirected to the proxy server, but can bypass it and proceed directly to the intranet.

◆ Be sure that your internal Web sites are configured correctly to deny access to unauthorized employees and public Internet browsers. Your intranet resources should reside on Windows 2000 file servers with virtual directories and NTFS permissions configured. If not, they should have security enabled.

◆ AD GPOs can also be used to control the users and the Web sites they access. You may need to examine these settings to determine whether a new GPO is affecting the client.

◆ If **IEAK** was used to configure the clients for intranet connectivity, you should check the settings used. If IEAK was not used, you should check the Web servers themselves to ensure that they are up and running.

◆ Confirm the status of virus protection agents on the Web servers and the clients. Make sure that all required service packs and hot fixes have been applied to the Web servers.

OBJECTIVES ON THE JOB

If you are implementing a corporate intranet for your company or organization, you should approach troubleshooting from the same perspective as you would for Internet connectivity.

PRACTICE TEST QUESTIONS

1. **A client is trying to access the internal corporate intranet site but cannot connect. The client can connect to the public Intranet site, however. What should you suspect as a possible source of the problem?**
   a. incorrectly configured client-side proxy server settings
   b. incorrectly configured server-side proxy server settings
   c. incorrectly configured DHCP settings
   d. blocked gateway

2. **It is impossible to configure Internet Explorer so that a user cannot change their Internet connection settings by using:**
   a. DPO
   b. ZAK
   c. system policies
   d. local security policies

3. **An administrator wants to configure Internet Explorer to control all aspects of the browser interface presented to the users, including the sites to which they have access. The corporate directive is to deny all Internet sites and allow only intranet and extranet sites. What tools could the administrator use to meet this goal? (Choose all that apply.)**
   a. IEAK
   b. GPO
   c. RIS
   d. ISA

4. **You need to design a new corporate Web page for the intranet site. What tool or tools could you use for this task? (Choose all that apply.)**
   a. Microsoft Word
   b. Microsoft Notepad
   c. Microsoft FrontPage with Extensions
   d. Microsoft Access

5. **A corporate extranet is a Web site that was intended to _____. (Choose all that apply.)**
   a. allow public Internet users to view special offers from your company
   b. allow public Internet users to connect to your research division and order documention and reports
   c. allow public Internet users to connect through a secure link and shop in your E-store without exposing their payment information
   d. all of the above

1.4.4 Configure authentication and SSL for Web sites.

SECURING YOUR WEB SERVICES

UNDERSTANDING THE OBJECTIVE

If you have placed your sites on Windows 2000 Server computers, you can fully integrate Windows 2000 security tools, such as NTFS and shared folder permissions, into your Web sites.

WHAT YOU REALLY NEED TO KNOW

◆ Several different security implementations are available to the network administrator for securing a Web site. The first step is to host the resources on a Windows 2000 server that uses NTFS volumes instead of FAT partitions.

◆ The IIS server will be able to see resources on a local volume and use them for the Web site. If the server hosting the resources is not an IIS server, you will need to create network shares and configure those shares for secure connections.

◆ You can integrate your Web site authentication with AD for a more robust implementation. This allows you to host all Internet resources on the same machine while securing different resources through the use of differing robust NTFS permissions. As a result, all resources will be grouped locally.

◆ As the next step in configuring authentication for your Web sites, decide whether you want to implement **IPSec** or **SSL**. IPSec's advantage is that it doesn't require SSL-aware applications or software. It is transparent to applications running in your environment. It is not a simple protocol to configure, and may present some challenges. SSL, on the other hand, is easy to configure but requires the use of applications that "speak" SSL. This may cause difficulties.

◆ Additional authentication features in IIS consist of how the client will connect. There are five different methods for authenticating Web browser clients in IIS: Anonymous, Basic, Integrated Windows, Digest, and Certificate Mapping. They are listed from the simplest to the most secure.

◆ You may also decide to enable auditing for your IIS resources to more completely track users trying to connect to these files. If you enable auditing, remember that auditing will affect the performance of your Web server.

OBJECTIVES ON THE JOB

IIS 5.0 has the flexibility to configure multiple Web sites on the same Web server, each with a different level of authentication. You may use IPSec and Digest authentication for a secure implementation on one site, while configuring only Anonymous authentication on another site.

PRACTICE TEST QUESTIONS

1. **Your company employs approximately 100 employees. You need to create three different Web sites for your company. One site will be the Internet site with public information available. The second site will be your intranet site, which will house resources for your employees. The third site will be your extranet site, which holds information for your B2B partners. Based on this information, what would be the most secure implementation for your Web sites?**
   a. three separate Windows 2000 Web servers that are configured separately for each Web site with NTFS, IPSec where appropriate, and SSL
   b. one Windows 2000 server running IIS with default authentication configured for all three sites
   c. a hosted service through your company's ISP
   d. none of the above

2. **Which of the following is *not* an authentication method for Windows 2000 IIS 5.0?**
   a. Certificate Mapping
   b. Digest Authentication configured with Pre-Windows 2000 Authentication
   c. Basic Integrated
   d. Enterprise Root CA Mapping

3. **You can access Web sites using SSL by using _____.**
   a. HTTP
   b. HTTPS
   c. IPsec
   d. EFS

4. **Integrated Windows authentication will work through _____.**
   a. IAS
   b. ISA
   c. RRAS
   d. TFTP

5. **If you need to enable auditing on your Web sites, enable auditing and audit logging for all Web sites because this will have the _____ impact on IIS performance.**
   a. smallest
   b. largest
   c. longest lasting
   d. securest

1.4.5 Configure FTP services.

THE FTP SERVICE

UNDERSTANDING THE OBJECTIVE

The **FTP** service in Windows 2000 IIS is a service that allows users to either download or upload files to a network-based repository. It also has some configurable settings, but not as many as the IIS Web sites.

WHAT YOU REALLY NEED TO KNOW

◆ By default, FTP is not started and must be manually started by the administrator before it can be used. Once started, the service continues to run until manually stopped by the administrator.

◆ Unlike Web sites, the FTP site only has five configuration tabs in the Default FTP Site Properties box: FTP Site, Security Accounts, Messages, Home Directory, and Directory Security. On the FTP Site tab, you may configure settings such as the descriptive name of your FTP site, the IP address to use for the site, and the TCP port for the service. You may also configure the number of connections the site will host and the logging options and properties, and you can view current FTP sessions.

◆ The Security Accounts tab contains settings for the accounts that will use the FTP service. The default username is created when IIS is installed and should be in the form *IUSR_Servername*. The default FTP operator is the local administrator.

◆ The Message tab is where you can configure the Welcome, Exit, and Maximum Connections messages that will be shown to visitors of your FTP site.

◆ The Home Directory tab allows you to control where the directories for your FTP sites will be found. Your location options are either on the computer that hosts the FTP server or on a remote server share.

◆ The Directory Security configuration tab allows you to configure access settings for computers only, not users.

◆ FTP does not encrypt either user names or passwords when the service is used.

◆ The FTP service can also be configured to use either all IP addresses on the FTP server, or a specific address.

OBJECTIVES ON THE JOB

FTP can be a valuable service in a Windows 2000 environment, particularly for non-Windows 2000 clients that cannot take advantage of GPO-based software deployment. If properly configured, FTP can provide functionality to other clients, such as Offline Folders or SharePoint Portal Server, that cannot take advantage of the advanced features of Windows 2000.

PRACTICE TEST QUESTIONS

1. Windows 2000 IIS 5.0 FTP Server is a simpler service than Default Web Site.
   Default FTP Site has _____ separate configuration tabs.
   - a. seven
   - b. four
   - c. five
   - d. eight

2. What method does FTP support for user authentication? (Choose all that apply.)
   - a. FTP Basic
   - b. Digest
   - c. Anonymous
   - d. Basic

3. Windows 2000 Server FTP Server can use windows sockets if the FTP service has
   been configured to support it. Assuming an IP address of 169.254.254, what is the
   default windows socket?
   - a. 169.254.2.54.21
   - b. 169.254.254:21
   - c. 169.254.2.54:22
   - d. 169.254.2.54.22

4. Which default user account for FTP site access is correct?
   - a. *TsInternetUser*
   - b. *IUSR_servername*
   - c. *IWAM_servername*
   - d. *IUSR_FTPGuest*

5. The _____ configuration allows the administrator to configure three
   different directory listing styles.
   - a. TFTP
   - b. Share Point
   - c. FTP
   - d. UNIX

6. Automatic Updates for FTP _____ be configured to automatically
   download and install all updates released by Microsoft for the FTP server.
   - a. can
   - b. cannot
   - c. must always
   - d. will

1.4.6 Configure access permissions for intranet Web servers.

CONFIGURING YOUR CORPORATE INTRANET

UNDERSTANDING THE OBJECTIVE

If you are going to use IIS to provide an intranet site for your corporation, you must first configure the resources for your intranet. Are you designing solely to provide a high-speed corporate Web portal or is your goal a secure and robust corporate Web site? Remember that the vast majority of hacking in a corporate environment is not done by outsiders, but by your own employees.

WHAT YOU REALLY NEED TO KNOW

◆ When configuring your corporate intranet site, you should consider several security-related issues. It is very important to ensure that your files and folders are protected, not only from accidental damage caused by your users, but also from intentional damage caused by users who have a destructive agenda.

◆ Will you host your intranet resources on a Windows 2000 file server or on a third-party server such as a NetWare Server or a UNIX server? If you use a Windows 2000 server, you will configure NTFS and shared folder permissions as appropriate. If your resources will be hosted on a third-party implementation, you must configure the appropriate security settings for those products.

◆ When you configure permissions for the Windows 2000 Server computers, remember that the most effective permissions will be achieved by combining NTFS and shared folder permissions.

◆ You may want to consider implementing virtual directories for your intranet. This has the advantage of allowing you to hide the name and locations of the actual host servers for these file resources.

◆ You also need to investigate what kind of authentication services you will provide for your corporate users. Will you integrate with AD, or is a simple anonymous logon sufficient? Remember that integrating with AD gives you the highest level of control in terms of resource access, but AD is also more difficult to configure.

◆ As an additional feature for your corporate intranet, you may choose to implement domain-based DFS to provide some network load balancing and redundancy for your users.

OBJECTIVES ON THE JOB

Windows 2000 has advanced IIS configuration settings that are available to the network administrator. They can provide the users enhanced functionality and the administrator increased manageability.

PRACTICE TEST QUESTIONS

1. When configuring your corporate intranet Web Server computers, you should balance _____ against security.
   a. accessibility
   b. security
   c. performance
   d. manageability

2. The majority of attacks against your intranet sites will come from _____. (Choose all that apply.)
   a. social engineering activists
   b. amateur hackers
   c. disgruntled employees
   d. unqualified administrators

3. You want to build a corporate intranet site to assist users in their daily work. However, some departments deal with confidential medical information that cannot, by law, be exposed to unauthorized parties, even other employees. What can you do? (Choose all that apply.)
   a. Build a separate intranet server for each department. Reconfigure your corporate network by implementing a new subnet design that assigns each department to a separate subnet. Use DHCP in each subnet to assign leases to the clients, and place an intranet server on each subnet for servicing client information requests.
   b. Enable NetBIOS scope IDs for each division. Build a multihomed intranet Web server and assign one scope ID from each division against each network card in the multihomed Web server.
   c. Build your single intranet Web server on a Windows 2000 Server computer. Configure virtual directories to hold the information for each department. Create departmental security groups with the membership lists comprising the employees from each department. Then assign the correct NTFS and shared folder permissions on each folder that contains department-specific information. Configure security permissions on the Web server to secure each virtual directory, and then test for connectivity and correct access rights.
   d. Build a single Web server and depend on each department manager to enforce secure access to the confidential information.

4. _____ directories can exist only on the Windows 2000 server that supports the corporate intranet site.
   a. Logical
   b. Virtual
   c. Local
   d. Remote

5. Virtual servers can exist only on the _____ server that supports the corporate intranet site.
   a. UNIX
   b. Linux
   c. Windows 2000
   d. Sun

1.5 Monitor and manage network security. Actions include auditing and detecting security breaches.

INTRODUCTION TO NETWORK SECURITY

UNDERSTANDING THE OBJECTIVE

One of the most crucial daily tasks of the network administrator is to implement and monitor the security of the network that he or she supports. Windows 2000 allows a great deal of flexibility and control for the network administrator.

WHAT YOU REALLY NEED TO KNOW

- ◆ Windows 2000 security, whether deployed to individual computers or domain controllers or any machine between them, is a proactive technology, not a reactive technology. There is no magic button that you can press and suddenly have your security settings enabled, tested, and working. You are the magic button.

- ◆ As with most other components in Windows 2000, good security implementations begin with good security plans. Decide what you will monitor, whom you will monitor, and how you will monitor. Remember the 5 Ws and the H: Who, What, When, Where, Why, and How. All of these apply to your network environment.

- ◆ For ease of planning, divide your supported computers into groups, such as domain-connected workstations, member server computers, stand-alone server computers, and domain controllers. Be sure to examine other operating systems as well. Are you supporting any Windows NT 4.0 computers, any Windows 98 and Windows 95 computers, or a few Apple Macintoshes? Also, what do you consider to be your outstanding security vulnerability—virus infections, industrial espionage, or hackers?

- ◆ Remember also to extend your security planning to basic network design issues. If you can eliminate 50 percent of your security vulnerabilities by designing a new subnetting scheme and implementing the scheme over a weekend, that is worthwhile, particularly if your salary increases and paycheck depend on a secure network implementation.

- ◆ Ensure that your anti-virus software actually works. If possible, configure it for an automatic download of virus updates. Purchase an anti-virus product that was designed for a network environment.

- ◆ Many different tools and functions also exist in the AD for implementing security in your network environment. Investigate the possibilities afforded by rigorous GPOs. Be sure to consider how the GPOs will affect your clients.

OBJECTIVES ON THE JOB

Securing your Windows 2000 network is one of your primary jobs as an administrator. Consider all aspects of a secure implementation, from securing your e-mail servers and DNS servers to providing security to the clients' local machines and dial-up connections.

PRACTICE TEST QUESTIONS

1. When configuring your corporate security environment, balance
   _____ against manageability.
   - a. accessibility
   - b. security
   - c. performance
   - d. manageability

2. The majority of attacks against your external network interface will come from:
   (Choose all that apply.)
   - a. social engineering activists
   - b. amateur hackers
   - c. disgruntled employees
   - d. professional hackers

3. You support approximately 250 users. Most computers have Windows 2000
   Professional; however, a small group in the graphic arts department uses Apple
   Macintosh computers, and you have one NetWare 4.1 server and one UNIX server.
   One employee's workstation runs on IBM PC DOS 2000. All clients use two
   Windows 2000 file servers for storing their work. No work-related files are stored
   on the local machines. Management has informed you that you must implement an
   antivirus solution for all the company's machines. After researching the directive,
   you conclude that you will be able to implement this solution _____
   (Choose all that apply.)
   - a. because antivirus software exists for the listed platforms
   - b. for the Windows 2000 computers and Apple workstations only
   - c. for the Windows 2000 computers and NetWare servers only
   - d. for the Windows 2000 computers and IBM PC DOS 2000 workstation only

4. _____ authentication technologies include retina scanning and
   voice print.
   - a. Biometric
   - b. Polymetric
   - c. Netmetric
   - d. Human metric

5. Why is a dial-up connection for a remote user not as secure as a cable modem
   connection for the same user?
   - a. Dial-up connections can never be made as secure as a cable modem connection.
   - b. Cable modem connections can never be made as secure as a dial-up connection.
   - c. It depends on the IAS server configuration.
   - d. It cannot be implemented under Windows 2000 RRAS.

1.5.1 Configure user-account lockout settings.

LOCKING USER ACCOUNTS

UNDERSTANDING THE OBJECTIVE

One security detail you should implement in your network is the Account Lockout Policy for user accounts in the domain. Windows 2000 supports the ability to configure lockout options on the user accounts as a security measure.

WHAT YOU REALLY NEED TO KNOW

◆ Windows 2000 supports two different levels of account lockout settings. One level is the local configuration for the local machine only. The second level is the AD configuration for AD users. The first setting affects only the users of the local machine that is running the policy. The second level affects AD users as a GPO, and like all GPOs, it can be assigned at any level in AD, from the domain to a separate OU.

◆ The three settings are Account lockout duration, Account lockout threshold, and Reset account lockout counter after. These settings occur in both the domain GPO and in the local policy. The local policies are configured with default settings. The GPOs in AD are not preconfigured. As the administrator, you must configure them.

◆ Account lockout duration is used to control how long the user's account remains locked out. The default duration is 30 minutes. What you configure with this setting is the amount of time that the user stays locked out when he or she violates the number of allowed logon attempts. The range of values is from 0 minutes to 99,999 minutes (69.4 days).

◆ Account lockout threshold is used to control how many invalid attempts the user can make before the account locks the user out. The default local setting is five attempts. The domain setting is not configured and must be enabled by the administrator. The range of possible values is from 0 attempts, which will not allow the account to lock out, to 999 attempts, which would allow the user 999 invalid logon attempts before locking the account.

◆ Reset account lockout counter means that the user's account will reset its lockout status after five minutes. The range of possible values is from 0 minutes to 99,999 minutes (69.4 days), which is the default setting.

◆ In the AD GPO configuration screen for the account lockout settings, choosing any option brings up the Suggested Value Changes dialog box, which lists suggested changes for the other two settings. Clicking the OK button automatically applies the suggested changes to the other two settings.

OBJECTIVES ON THE JOB

By correctly configuring lockout options, the administrator can control how the accounts for the users respond to user account lockout events.

PRACTICE TEST QUESTIONS

1. **If you need to configure an account lockout for your domain users that will keep their accounts disabled for 45 minutes, allow the users to try to log on six times, and unlock locked accounts after one hour, how should you configure the settings?**
   - a. Account lockout duration = 60, Reset account lockout counter after = 45, and Account lockout threshold = 6
   - b. Reset account lockout counter after = 60, Account lockout threshold = 45, and Account lockout duration = 6
   - c. Account lockout threshold = 60, Reset account lockout counter after = 45, and Account lockout duration = 6
   - d. Reset account lockout counter after = 60, Account lockout threshold = 6, and Account lockout duration = 45

2. **What are the default settings for the local account lockout policy? (Choose all that apply.)**
   - a. Account lockout duration = 60 minutes, Account lockout threshold = 3, and Reset account lockout counter after = 15 minutes
   - b. Account lockout duration = 30 minutes, Account lockout threshold = 5, and Reset account lockout counter after = 30 minutes
   - c. Account lockout duration = 15 minutes, Account lockout threshold = 5, and Reset account lockout counter after = 30 minutes
   - d. Account lockout duration = 30 minutes, Account lockout threshold = 3, and Reset account lockout counter after = 30 minutes

3. **What should you set to make sure that users accounts will never be locked out?**
   - a. Reset account lockout counter after = 0
   - b. Account lockout duration = 0
   - c. Account lockout threshold = 0
   - d. Account lockout duration = 15 minutes

4. **The Account Lockout Policy exists only at the _____ level.**
   - a. local
   - b. remote
   - c. network
   - d. workgroup

5. **The AD Account Lockout Policy will never lock out the _____ account in AD.**
   - a. Guest
   - b. Domain Guest
   - c. Administrator
   - d. DNS Administrator

1.5.2 Configure user-account password length, history, age, and complexity.

USER ACCOUNT PASSWORD CONFIGURATION

UNDERSTANDING THE OBJECTIVE

Different networks have particular methods to implement the password feature. Varying levels of security and differing layers of options for security are available.

WHAT YOU REALLY NEED TO KNOW

◆ Windows 2000 supports six configuration settings for passwords. Each machine and each domain support only one policy. Thus, the settings that you configure for one part of the domain affect all domain users. The settings are Enforce password history, Maximum password age, Minimum password age, Minimum password length, Passwords must meet complexity requirements, and Store password using reversible encryption for all users in the domain. The settings are turned off by default.

◆ The Enforce password history setting allows the administrator to control how many user passwords will be remembered. The default setting in AD is 18.

◆ The Maximum password age setting controls how frequently users must change passwords. The default value for AD is 70 days. The range of values is from 0 days, which means that the password will not expire, to 999 days (2.7 years).

◆ The Minimum password age setting allows the administrator to control how long the user must keep the password before being allowed to change it. In AD, the default setting is 0 days, which means that the password can be changed immediately.

◆ The Minimum password length setting controls how long the password must be for it to be accepted as a password. The default setting in AD is a password at least seven characters in length, but not more than 128 characters in length. The range of values is from 0 characters. The default local setting is to require eight characters.

◆ The Passwords must meet complexity requirements setting defines a complexity policy for passwords. If the policy is defined and enabled, the user's password, beyond meeting restrictions for length and age, must also contain characters from three of the four monitored character sets. The character sets are uppercase characters, lowercase characters, and numerals and nonalphabetic characters (such as !, @, and #).

OBJECTIVES ON THE JOB

As an administrator of a Windows 2000 domain environment, one of your most important daily tasks will be policing and enforcing your password policies.

PRACTICE TEST QUESTIONS

1. **You must configure a password policy that forces users to change their passwords once every three work weeks, where a work week is defined as 40 hours, and that forces them to keep the passwords they select for at least three working days. What settings should you configure?**
   a. Enforce password history = 2, Minimum password length = 7, and Minimum password age = 1
   b. Maximum password age = 5, Minimum password age = 1, and Passwords must meet complexity requirements = Enforced
   c. Minimum password age = 5 and Maximum password age = 1
   d. Store password using reversible encryption for all users in the domain = Enforced, Maximum password age = 21, and Minimum password age = 3

2. **What does the Store password using reversible encryption for all users in the domain setting control? (Choose all that apply.)**
   a. Kerberos authentication for down-level clients who are not using Windows 95
   b. password encryption for users who are Windows 2000 clients and Windows NT 4.0 clients
   c. password encryption for users who are Windows 2000 clients
   d. recoverability of password encryption for users who are Windows 2000 clients

3. **Many of your current users are used to simple passwords—lowercase only, no numerals, and no more than six characters. The previous administrator allowed this situation in the domain. You have decided to change the password policy. To address the two issues given, what settings should you enable at a domain level for your users? (Choose all that apply.)**
   a. Store password using reversible encryption for all users in the domain
   b. Passwords must meet complexity requirements
   c. Minimum password length
   d. Minimum password age
   e. Maximum password age
   f. Enforce password history

4. **You have several workstations in your office that are shared by several different users but that do not belong to the domain. How can you enforce complex passwords?**
   a. Join them to a domain.
   b. Configure local password policies.
   c. Implement SmartCards.
   d. Complex passwords cannot be configured on these machines.

5. **How many password policies are supported in each Windows 2000 AD Domain?**
   a. one
   b. two
   c. three
   d. four

1.5.3 Configure Group Policy to run logon scripts.

SCRIPTS AND GROUP POLICY

UNDERSTANDING THE OBJECTIVE

One of the most powerful components of AD is the GPO. Computers and clients that use Windows 2000 and that belong to a Windows 2000 AD domain can use GPOs to manage and control their computers and user accounts. Administrators configure GPOs for the users and for their computers to enforce their domain security settings, to facilitate software maintenance, and to control the users. GPOs, however, are not useable or enforceable for down-level clients, which are clients that do not use the Windows 2000 operating system. For these clients, the administrator can employ scripts to perform their administrative tasks.

WHAT YOU REALLY NEED TO KNOW

◆ Windows 2000 AD supports five different kinds of scripts. The administrator may apply Startup and Shutdown computer-based scripts. For the user, the administrator may apply Logon and Logoff scripts. The correct processing order at this level is Startup, Logon, Logoff, and Shutdown. If multiple scripts are configured at each level, the administrator may rank them in order; that is, the administrator may set Script #2 to run first, followed by Script #1, then Script #3, and so on. The administrator may also decide to support logon scripts that run against a specific user. All types of scripts, by default, run asynchronously in a hidden window.

◆ There are nine different settings that control the processing of scripts in GPOs. Five are used to control the behavior of the computer. The remaining four are used to control the behavior of the users at the computer. The options for the computer are Run logon scripts synchronously, Run startup scripts asynchronously, Run startup scripts visible, Run shutdown scripts visible, and Maximum wait time for Group Policy scripts. The options for the user are Run logon scripts synchronously, Run legacy logon scripts hidden, Run logon scripts visible, and Run logoff scripts visible.

◆ If you are using scripts in your network and are supporting a mixed environment of Windows 95, Windows 98, Windows NT 4.0, and Windows 2000 computers, you may encounter problems running the scripts on the Windows 95 and Windows NT 4.0 clients. These problems are caused by how these two OSs support .vbs and .js scripts. For these two script families to run on either OS, you must place the scripts into batch files and run them from this environment or install **WSH** on these machines and then run the scripts.

OBJECTIVES ON THE JOB

The use of scripts has been a common administrative technique in a networked environment to automate many repetitive tasks for the administrator. The Windows 2000 administrator can assign scripts through the Group Policy interface in AD.

PRACTICE TEST QUESTIONS

1. You want to automate the cleaning of temporary files from the hard drives of the Windows NT 4.0 computers in your domain. These computers all belong to your Windows 2000 AD domain. You have written a VB script to accomplish this task. How should you implement this script? (Choose all that apply.)
   a. Assign the script to OU where the user account is located.
   b. Create a GPO for the OU where the user accounts reside. Assign the script to this GPO and wait for the scheduled refresh of the GPOs.
   c. Create a computer configuration GPO for the domain. Assign the script to this GPO. Create a group in AD and place the computers running Windows NT 4.0 into this group. Then assign this group to the GPO holding the script. As a last step, deploy WSH using a software-based GPO installation for the Windows NT 4.0 machines only.
   d. Place the script into a shared folder on a Windows NT 4.0 server.

2. If scripts in an AD environment are not being applied correctly, what should you check? (Choose all that apply.)
   a. the Inherit GPO scripts setting in the Advanced section of the GPO
   b. the inheritance flowchart Visio document
   c. the script processing order in the GPO
   d. the assignment of scripts

3. Windows 2000 AD supports what kinds of scripts for computers and users? (Choose all that apply.)
   a. Legacy Logon
   b. Logoff
   c. Startup
   d. Legacy Logoff
   e. Shutdown
   f. Logon

4. The preferred method to apply scripts in Windows 2000 is by using:
   a. System Policies.
   b. Group Policies.
   c. Batch files.
   d. Local Policies.

5. Scripts in Windows 2000 can be applied either as logon scripts or as
   _____.
   a. system on files
   b. logoff scripts
   c. OS scripts
   d. system change

1.5.4 Link Group Policy objects.

OPTIMIZING GROUP POLICY OBJECTS

UNDERSTANDING THE OBJECTIVE

AD GPOs allow administrators to control over 450 separate configuration settings for the objects that reside in AD. These objects include computers, users, shared folders, and print devices. AD supports the ability to link GPOs across OUs and domains.

WHAT YOU REALLY NEED TO KNOW

◆ Linked GPOs provide a tool for administrators to use in their day-to-day administration of a Windows 2000 AD environment. Linked GPOs can also be used to apply settings to AD container objects that receive the linked settings through inheritance from another object.

◆ The steps involved in creating linked GPOs are as follows: The administrator creates a standard GPO with the configured settings for the end result he or she wishes to achieve. Unlike System Policies in Windows NT 4.0 that produced permanent changes in the Windows NT 4.0 machines, Windows 2000 GPOs apply only to the Windows 2000 computer while it is logged into the domain. When the Windows 2000 computer logs off the domain, the GPOs are removed from the machine.

◆ After the testing is completed, the next step is to determine what AD objects should be linked to the GPO. This is an important consideration because of the power of the GPOs to control the behavior of not only the users but also the computers for which they are implemented.

◆ GPOs use the principle of inheritance in AD to function. That is, a GPO must be assigned only once to a top-level object and then inheritance flows down to the children of that object. GPOs do not affect the peers of the object, only the children.

◆ One GPO can be linked to many AD objects (OUs, domains, sites, and so on), and one AD object can be linked to many GPOs. The administrator needs to consider the processing order for GPOs: local computer policies, local user policies, linked GPOs in the order of site–domain–OU, and unlinked GPOs in the order of site–domain–OU. As an administrator, you may also rank the respective GPOs to process in a specific order. AD administrators should avoid linking too many GPOs to objects because the processing of GPOs slows down the authentication to AD.

OBJECTIVES ON THE JOB

Linked GPOs can free the AD administrator from having to create the same GPO with the same settings many times in AD. The GPO must be created only once, and then linked to the objects in AD for administrative functionality.

PRACTICE TEST QUESTIONS

1. **You have inherited an AD implementation from another administrator. When you check the implementation, you find that many GPOs have been duplicated throughout the AD environment, and several have been duplicated incorrectly. What should be your first step to correct this situation?**
   a. Implement linked GPOs for this AD implementation.
   b. Remove all defective GPOs and re-create them correctly.
   c. Use the Linked GPO Checker tool in the SRK and allow it to adjust the GPOs as necessary.
   d. Use Visio to redesign your GPO implementation.

2. **Arrange the following linked GPOs in the correct processing order: Sites, Domains, Child Domains, Container Objects, OUs, Child OUs.**
   a. Sites, Domains, Child Domains, Container Objects, OUs, and Child OUs
   b. Sites, Domains, Container Objects, OUs, and Child OUs
   c. Domains, Child Domains, and Container Objects
   d. Container Objects, Sites, Child Domains, OUs, Child OUs, and Domains

3. **You have created a linked GPO for a remote site. The connection to this remote site is through a slow WAN. Why isn't this an effective connection?**
   a. The slow WAN will affect replication of the GPO.
   b. The slow WAN link will impact users when they log on to the network.
   c. If the WAN link breaks, the GPO and its functionality will no longer exist.
   d. If many users access a single GPO across a slow connection, there could be a negative impact.

4. **When logging into a Windows 2000 Active Directory forest from a child domain, you can inherit GPOs from a(n) _____.**
   a. site
   b. parent domain
   c. domain
   d. OU

5. **Linked GPOs cannot be used to control Windows NT 4.0 computers that belong to a Windows NT 4.0 domain in AD because:**
   a. there is no PDC to authenticate the Windows NT 4.0 clients.
   b. Windows NT 4.0 clients do not use AD GPOs.
   c. there is no AD security group for Windows NT 4.0.
   d. Windows NT 4.0 is restricted to only NTLM authentication.

1.5.5 Enable and configure auditing.

AUDITING YOUR NETWORK

UNDERSTANDING THE OBJECTIVE

An important AD administrator tool is auditing. Auditing allows you to record and document the use of your AD resources. You may configure auditing for objects or properties in AD, or for local resources on individual computers.

WHAT YOU REALLY NEED TO KNOW

◆ Auditing is an extremely valuable tool in Windows 2000. By using auditing, an administrator can track actual or attempted security breaches of their environment and you can require other details of AD or the local computer. These details include file and object access or attempts to change the system time.

◆ If implemented locally, you can require that resources to be audited reside only on NTFS volumes. If an administrator wants or needs to implement auditing on Windows 2000 partitions formatted with FAT, these partitions must be converted to NTFS. In addition, only an administrator or member of the administrators group can configure auditing; however, after auditing is enabled, administrators or server operators may view and work with the collected data.

◆ The tool for viewing collected auditing information is the Event Viewer. It contains sections for each type of information that the Event Viewer is responsible for collecting. The section to be used for viewing auditing information is the Security Log.

◆ When configuring auditing, you may track the success or failure of an action. You can also track both success and failure. This can be useful to determine attempted security breaches. Print devices may be audited to determine when printing is being done and by whom.

◆ As an administrator, you should resist the temptation to enable auditing on every resource and every object. Auditing impacts the performance of the computer for which it has been configured because of the amount of information being collected.

OBJECTIVES ON THE JOB

Auditing can help an administrator track access to resources and the use of resources in a network environment. Auditing information can also be collected for review and statistical analysis at a later date.

PRACTICE TEST QUESTIONS

1. _____ can track resource access on a Windows NT 4.0 computer in AD.
   a. Security logs
   b. Kerberos logs
   c. Auditing
   d. File and object access

2. Only _____ and members of the administrators group can access information collected by auditing.
   a. server operators
   b. backup operators
   c. audit operators
   d. users who work with server operators

3. If a Windows 2000 computer was initially installed with partitions formatted with FAT32, how can the administrator enable auditing for this machine?
   a. Reformat the partitions and then enable auditing.
   b. Back up and reformat the partitions.
   c. Enable auditing on the FAT32 partition.
   d. Convert the partition to NTFS, and then enable auditing.

4. You need to collect information that will tell you how frequently an application is being used. The setting you should configure in auditing is related to:
   a. application access
   b. application use
   c. file and object access
   d. object access

5. You are the administrator of a corporate environment running Windows 2000 AD. How can you allow the manager's user account access to auditing information?
   a. Re-create the user account as a power user on a Windows 2000 domain controller and add this account to the Event Viewer Permitted to use list. Then reboot the domain controller for the changes to take effect.
   b. Merge the user account into the local Event Viewer Users group. Have the user log off and log on to resynchronize the account.
   c. Add the user's account to the Server Operators group and have the user log off and log on to resynchronize the account.
   d. Enable the GPO Enable user view of auditing information setting. Add the user's account to this GPO and grant the Read permission for the GPO. Have the user log off and log on to the domain to resynchronize the account.

1.5.6 Monitor security by using the system security log file.

AUDITING YOUR NETWORK

UNDERSTANDING THE OBJECTIVE

Windows 2000 supports different techniques for saving and using auditing information, which you can use for monitoring and statistical purposes in your environment.

WHAT YOU REALLY NEED TO KNOW

◆ After you have enabled auditing, you will collect information in the Event Viewer. The amount of information collected can be quite large, so you probably should modify the Security Log configuration to different values than the default settings.

◆ The settings that you may want to change are the Log size settings. The first setting to modify is the Maximum log size. Because the default size is only 512K, you may decide to increase this size. Another setting to configure is When maximum log size is reached. This setting controls the behavior of the Event Viewer, and if not configured properly, it can cause the computer to lock up or shut down. The Overwrite events as needed setting will cause entries to be overwritten in the security log file as it fills up, something you may wish to avoid. The Overwrite events older than setting gives you more flexibility because the default setting is seven days. The range of values is from one day to 365 days. The Do not overwrite events (clear log file manually) setting can cause problems. When this setting is enabled and the log file fills up, the Event Viewer generates a message that it tried to write to the System Log. If the log file is full, it generates another message, which cannot be logged either because the log is filled up, and so on. If you use this setting, track the size of the log file, and clear it manually when it fills up.

◆ After information has been collected in the Event Viewer Security Log, it may be searched or filtered. The authorized auditing agent (administrator or server operator) may also save the auditing information in a variety of formats, including the .evt format for viewing in Event Viewer. The data also may be saved in a tab-delimited .txt file or as a comma-delimited .csv file. If the information is saved in the latter two formats, it may be imported to Microsoft Excel or Microsoft Access. These two tools allow statistical information to be extracted from the collected information and archived analysis.

◆ As the administrator, you may also need to dial in to your server to collect Security Log information. The Event Viewer tool supports this using a low-speed connection setting.

OBJECTIVES ON THE JOB

The information collected in the System Security Log file can be extremely useful for day-to-day administrative duties. You can monitor and analyze the auditing information you collect.

PRACTICE TEST QUESTIONS

1. You have just received an urgent call from a remote office in your environment. The domain controller, which is also the file server, is completely unresponsive. It has already crashed at least seven times (you have been told) and when the computer restarts, it crashes again. The only message that the computer displays is something about an error log. What might be the problem? (Choose all that apply.)
   a. The Event Viewer service is logging on with an incorrect password.
   b. A file in the path WINNT\SYSTEM32\CONFIG has been corrupted and cannot be opened by the Event Viewer.
   c. The configuration parameters for an Event Viewer log file are incorrect.
   d. An Event Viewer log file has filled up and is preventing the service from starting correctly.

2. Information generated by the Event Viewer can be saved in which formats? (Choose all that apply.)
   a. .rtf, .cpp, .pas, and .bas
   b. .doc, .cmd, and .wk3
   c. .txt, .csv, and .evt
   d. .wpd, .rpt, and .wp

3. The Event Viewer supports an administrator's ability to connect and download Event Viewer information over a telephone connection. If using this type of connectivity, you should:
   a. use a reliable phone connection.
   b. use the Low Speed Connection setting in the Event Viewer.
   c. configure the Remote Event Access local system policy.
   d. assign the Remote Event Access permission.

4. Which two tools allow statistical information to be extracted from collected information?
   a. Excel
   b. Access
   c. Microsoft Data Report
   d. Visio

5. If you have configured the policy "Do not overwrite events, clear log file manually" in the Security Log Properties dialog box, you must check the size of the log file manually because:
   a. you want to reduce fragmentation of the file.
   b. you want to track usage of the file.
   c. you want to determine at what rate the file fills up.
   d. the log file will make the computer stop when the log file reaches capacity, and the computer will be forced to reboot.

Section 2

Configuring, Administering, and Troubleshooting the Network Infrastructure

2.1 Troubleshoot routing. Diagnostic utilities include the tracert command, the ping command, and the ipconfig command.

CONNECTIVITY TOOLS

UNDERSTANDING THE OBJECTIVE

Because Windows 2000 uses the IP protocol as its primary network connectivity tool, the administrator has access to several IP-based connectivity/troubleshooting commands. Knowing how to properly use these commands and when to use them can greatly improve network functionality.

WHAT YOU REALLY NEED TO KNOW

◆ There are six different commands you should be aware of: arp, ipconfig, pathping, ping, route, and tracert. All must be used from a command prompt session in Windows 2000. Each command works on any version of Windows 2000; any user who can open a command prompt can use the commands.

◆ Although commands can be used to troubleshoot network connectivity issues for a local computer, no commands work remotely. It is impossible to use a command-line switch that would make the commands run on another computer.

◆ Of the six, only one command has potential as a hacking tool—ping. If configured correctly on multiple computers, ping can cause a **DoS** attack on your network.

◆ The route command could be used to reconfigure a static routing table for a server; however, the person attempting the reconfiguration would need either network access or physical access to the server. The arp command also has the potential for causing connectivity issues on a local computer with manually entered values. However, by default, values entered with the arp command remain in the ARP cache for only 10 minutes and then are aged out of the cache. Although permanent entries are allowed, *permanent* is defined as powered on. When the computer reboots, the cache is emptied. There is no support for permanent entries housed in the Windows Registry, but there is support for persistent entries in the routing table.

◆ The ipconfig command is a useful tool for many issues involving IP, particularly DHCP. The DHCP addresses on a DHCP client can be manually refreshed using ipconfig at the command prompt. An administrator could also use this script for more control over the refreshing.

OBJECTIVES ON THE JOB

The Windows 2000 administrator must remember that IP is not a single protocol, but is instead a suite of protocols, each with its own set of configuration and diagnostic commands. The commands are most commonly run from the command line and can be quite powerful, returning valuable information to the Windows 2000 administrator on the current state of the network environment. As an administrator, you need to understand which command to use in specific circumstances and what each command tells you about your network.

PRACTICE TEST QUESTIONS

1. **If you cannot implement RIP2 in your environment and must implement manual routing tables, which command should you use? (Choose all that apply.)**
   a. tracert
   b. rras
   c. route
   d. ipxroute

2. **The acronym PING stands for _____.**
   a. Packet InterNet Groper
   b. Packet Interface Gateway
   c. Protocol Interface Groper
   d. Packet Information Guard

3. **The _____ command can be used to reconfigure a static routing table for a server.**
   a. arp
   b. ping
   c. route
   d. dos

4. **Which of the following can be used to force registration with a Windows 2000 DDNS server?**
   a. ipconfig /registerdns
   b. arp -RR
   c. ping –a *server_name*
   d. dos /*hostname*

5. **The acronym ARP stands for _____.**
   a. Acquisition Registration Protocol
   b. Address Resolution Protocol
   c. Address Resolution Protocol
   d. Acquisition Release Protocol

6. **If you suspect problems with your routers in a routed network environment, as a general troubleshooting technique, what should you do?**
   a. Ping localhost, ping local IP address, ping default gateway, ping remote gateway, and ping remote system.
   b. Ping remote system, ping remote gateway, ping default gateway, ping local IP address, and ping localhost.
   c. Ping localhost, and ping remote gateway.
   d. Tracert localhost, tracert local IP address, tracert default gateway, tracert remote gateway, and tracert remote system.

2.1.1 Validate local computer configuration by using the ipconfig, arp, and route commands.

CHECKING YOUR LOCAL CONFIGURATION

UNDERSTANDING THE OBJECTIVE

To begin the process of connecting to your corporate network infrastructure, you must first verify the settings and parameters that support this connection. Three of the most common commands used for the verification process are ipconfig, arp, and route.

WHAT YOU REALLY NEED TO KNOW

◆ The ipconfig, arp, and route commands run from the command prompt in a Windows 2000 environment. The commands can be issued from a computer running either Windows 2000 Professional or Windows 2000 Server. If a user can access the command prompt or the Run command, then he or she can use these commands. While all three can disrupt the network functionality of the local computer only, the disruption is not permanent (in most cases) and will not affect remote computers.

◆ The ipconfig command is the IP configuration tool. The settings that it can configure are the status of the DHCP parameters, the registration of the local computer with a **DDNS** server (although it does not directly affect the DDNS zone), the flushing of the local DDNS resolver cache, and the modification of the DHCP class ID for the current computer. The tool also can be used to return all IP parameters for all IP connections, including modems, to a text file for archiving or later examination.

◆ The arp command allows the administrator to manipulate the ARP cache. It allows the mapping of a logical IP address against the physical MAC address of a **NIC**. The tool can be used to display the entire scope of the ARP cache information or the ARP cache for a specific network interface. The arp command can also delete entries from, or add entries to, the ARP cache. Entries added manually to the ARP cache are permanent in the sense that they are not aged out of the ARP cache as is normally done. However, they are lost when the computer restarts.

◆ The route command is used by the administrator to view and modify information in the routing table of Windows 2000. This tool also runs from the command prompt and can be used to report or modify the contents of the routing table. The output from the route command can be directed to a text file for later analysis. It can also be used to specify a persistent route, which is a route that will return to the routing table after a reboot of the computer.

OBJECTIVES ON THE JOB

The ipconfig, arp, and route commands help network administrators troubleshoot local network connectivity issues for clients in a Windows 2000 network environment. You should thoroughly familiarize yourself with these tools in Windows 2000.

PRACTICE TEST QUESTIONS

1. **As an administrator, you need to determine the contents of a user's Windows 2000 Professional local routing table. However, you want a printout because you can stay in the office for only a few minutes and then you have to leave. How can you produce a printout of the local routing table?**
   a. Expand the path WINNT\SYSTEM32\DRIVERS\ETC, right-click the file Route, and then choose the Print command to direct the output to the local printer.
   b. Click the Administrative Tools button and then select the Routing and Remote Access tool. When the tool opens, expand IP Routing and then right-click Static Routes. You will now see the static routing table.
   c. Open a command prompt, type the command route print > c:\route.txt, and then press the Enter key. Copy this file to a floppy disk or print the file from Notepad.
   d. Open the Registry and expand the path HKLM\SYSTEM\CurrentControlSet\Services\Routing. Print this section of the Registry.

2. **The arp command facilitates the mapping of a logical IP address against a physical _____ address.**
   a. cache
   b. NIC
   c. DDNS
   d. MAC

3. **How can you populate the ARP cache if it is empty? (Choose all that apply.)**
   a. Manually add the entries to the ARP cache.
   b. Use the ARP /add command to autoconfigure the cache.
   c. Ping the target computer.
   d. Use the IPCONFIG /arpcacherefresh command.

4. **To add entries to the static routing table, you must specify the _____ parameter.**
   a. metric
   b. network destination
   c. gateway
   d. netmask

5. **A _____ route is one that will return to the routing table after a reboot of the computer.**
   a. non-cached
   b. persistent
   c. NIC
   d. command-line

6. **The default value for the ArpCacheLife setting in the Registry is _____ minutes.**
   a. 10
   b. 8
   c. 4
   d. 2

2.1.2 Validate network connectivity by using the tracert, ping, and pathping commands.

VERIFYING YOUR NETWORK CONNECTIVITY

UNDERSTANDING THE OBJECTIVE

After you have verified your connectivity settings, you must verify the connectivity itself. Three commands are commonly used for this testing: tracert, ping, and pathping.

WHAT YOU REALLY NEED TO KNOW

◆ You can determine network connectivity with the tracert, ping, and pathping commands. They are run from the command prompt environment in Windows 2000. They will run on any version and for any user who has access to the command prompt. These tools are reporting tools only. They cannot be used to modify any settings.

◆ Use tracert if you suspect problems with your gateways. This command traces the path from the local computer through your routers and returns statistical information about the path. There are no optional switches to use and no configurable parameters required. If tracert cannot reach the target system name, you will receive an error message.

◆ The ping command uses ICMP, which is commonly blocked on network firewalls because it can be used to launch DoS attacks against Internet-connected servers. If the use of ping has not been blocked, it can be used to verify connectivity by IP. This command has additional command-line switches. You can ping the localhost, and then the target computer by IP address and then by name. If the target can be reached by IP address but not by name, you should begin looking at issues involving **DNS** and **WINS**.

◆ The pathping command combines the functionality of the tracert and ping commands. It cannot modify network connections, but it does use some command-line switches to modify the information for which it is searching. This command is particularly useful for testing **RSVP** connections and paths.

◆ You can configure all three commands to direct output to a text file for later analysis and examination.

OBJECTIVES ON THE JOB

An administrator should use the tracert, ping, and pathping commands whenever network connectivity issues are suspected. Each command returns a different set of information; pathping combines the functions of the other two.

PRACTICE TEST QUESTIONS

1. **You are using the ping command to troubleshoot a network connectivity issue in your environment. When you enter the target system name and press Enter, you receive an error message that tells you the destination is unreachable. What should you suspect is the cause of the problem? (Choose all that apply.)**
   a. an incorrect Cname stored in the BIND server
   b. an incorrect NetBIOS scope ID configuration
   c. an incorrect port used for the IP address when the ping command was issued
   d. incorrect gateway settings or a nonfunctional router

2. **When you use the tracert command, you receive a message that says it cannot resolve the target system name. What should you check next? (Choose all that apply.)**
   a. possible misconfigurations of DNS settings
   b. an empty gateway field
   c. neighboring computers to determine if they have connectivity
   d. whether you can ping the local router

3. **You should use the tracert command if you suspect problems with your _____. (Choose all that apply.)**
   a. gateways
   b. routers
   c. configuration paths
   d. connectivity prompts

4. **A common use of ping for troubleshooting is to ping the _____, and then the target computer by IP address and then by name.**
   a. DOS port
   b. localhost
   c. gateway
   d. path host

5. **The pathping command combines the functionality of _____ and ping.**
   a. RSVP
   b. Switch /A
   c. IP
   d. tracert

6. **If you need to collect statistical information about network packets lost in transmission, you should use the _____ command.**
   a. tracert
   b. ping
   c. pathping
   d. WINS start /A

2.2 Configure and troubleshoot TCP/IP on servers and client computers. Considerations include subnet masks, default gateways, network IDs, and broadcast addresses.

TCP/IP IMPLEMENTATION DETAILS

UNDERSTANDING THE OBJECTIVE

IP is the protocol of the Internet; however, it is not the simplest or easiest protocol to configure. To effectively support clients, the administrator must understand the different components involved in the IP configuration process.

WHAT YOU REALLY NEED TO KNOW

- ◆ If you use IP as an addressing scheme in your network, each network adapter must have a unique IP address. In addition, each adapter must also be configured with a correct subnet mask for that specific IP address. Your failure to provide a correct subnet mask for the client, or failure to provide a unique IP address for each network interface, will have serious consequences, such as an inability to connect to resources.

- ◆ The administrator supplies the IP address and subnet mask for clients. As an option, the administrator can supply a default gateway for network clients that do need connectivity outside their own subnet. The default gateway or router allows IP packets to reach destinations that are remote from the client. Computers need this information for remote connectivity with network resources. The subnet mask works in combination with the IP address to determine whether two IP addresses are local to each other. This determination cannot be made without first converting the IP addresses to binary format and examining them in conjunction with the subnet mask.

- ◆ Each IP address is composed of two parts, a network component and a host component. In addition, there are five classes of IP addresses: Class A, Class B, Class C, Class D, and Class E. The first three classes contain addresses used on both the public Internet and corporate intranets. Class D is the network multicast address range, and Class E is used for experimental purposes.

- ◆ Because an IP address has two components, IP can send broadcasts to all hosts on a subnet or to all subnets, depending on the structure of the broadcast packet. A broadcast to a particular subnet might look like 169.254.255.255. The 255 in the last two octets signifies a broadcast to that subnet. A broadcast can also be designated by the hexadecimal digit FF in each octet of the broadcast address. By replacing octets in the IP address, the IP protocol can control where broadcasts are sent.

OBJECTIVES ON THE JOB

IP has different parameters that must be configured for IP connectivity to occur. The misconfiguration of one parameter can disrupt network connectivity for one client or for an entire network. Thus, care must be used when configuring IP addressing parameters.

PRACTICE TEST QUESTIONS

1. **If you use IP as an addressing scheme in your network, each network adapter must have a unique IP _____.**
   - a. router location
   - b. format
   - c. gateway
   - d. address

2. **An IP address has two separate components: _____ and host.**
   - a. subnet
   - b. network
   - c. broadcast
   - d. scope

3. **The correct broadcast address for a default Class B address is _____.**
   - a. 255.255.0.0
   - b. *www.xxx.yyy*.255
   - c. 255.255.255.255
   - d. *www.xxx*.255.255

4. **The correct address for a broadcast to all attached networks is _____.**
   - a. 256.256.256.256
   - b. 255.255.255.255
   - c. *www*.255.255.255
   - d. 255.255.0.0

5. **Your default gateway address is your _____ address.**
   - a. NIC
   - b. formatted
   - c. router
   - d. gateway

6. **You have captured activity from your network into a Network Monitor capture file. You are analyzing the file contents and looking for unusual activity in the network. You have discovered a number of packets coming from one particular computer. The source address of the computer is always correct; however, the destination address is almost always FFFFFFFF. What type of address is this? (Choose all that apply.)**
   - a. It is an SAP broadcast from a NetWare 3.12 server.
   - b. It is a hexadecimal address.
   - c. It is a directed send to the Windows 2000 PDC Emulator FSMO role holder.
   - d. It is a broadcast address.

2.2.1 Configure client computer TCP/IP properties.

TCP/IP CONFIGURATION

UNDERSTANDING THE OBJECTIVE

Windows 2000 requires the TCP/IP protocol for AD to function. Other protocols can be installed to provide non-AD support to clients only, but AD must use TCP/IP. TCP/IP is a difficult protocol to configure manually, and there are many possibilities for error.

WHAT YOU REALLY NEED TO KNOW

◆ TCP/IP constitutes the backbone of the Internet. To use TCP/IP, you must configure the IP parameters, which consist of an IP address and a subnet mask. These two values are always required. You cannot configure one without the other.

◆ The IP address takes the form of a four-part numeric value shown as ***www.xxx.yyy.zzz***. This is the dotted-decimal representation, where each segment is an octet. There are four octets in each address.

◆ A numeric IP address is a shorthand representation of the actual IP address, which is a 32-bit binary number. An example of a 32-bit binary number would be 10000011.1101011.00000010.11001000. This number can be represented in dotted-decimal format as 131.107.2.200. A subnet value for this IP address could be 11111111.11111111.00000000.00000000, which in dotted-decimal format is 255.255.0.0. To properly implement IP in your network environment, you must understand and be proficient with the calculation of subnets.

◆ The matching part of the IP address is the subnet mask. The subnet mask allows the administrator to separate the network portion of the IP address from the host portion of the IP address. The values of 255 (all 1s in binary) block the network address. The remaining value is the host ID on the network.

◆ Windows 2000 computers support one IP address and a matching subnet address. You can multihome the computer, which means assigning more than one IP address to a computer. Logical multihoming is the assignment of many IP addresses against one NIC. Physical multihoming is the mapping of many IP addresses against many NICs.

◆ Additional IP configuration settings may be applied in Windows 2000. These settings include the addresses of DNS servers, the addresses of WINS servers, and the use of the local Lmhosts file.

OBJECTIVES ON THE JOB

Knowing how to use IP addresses and subnet masks is key to the operation of Windows 2000 AD and any IP-enabled network. You must be able to manually calculate IP addresses and subnet masks to properly configure your clients and AD for optimum operation.

PRACTICE TEST QUESTIONS

1. **To physically multihome a Windows 2000 Professional computer, you must configure it with _____. (Choose all that apply.)**
   a. the address of more than one NBNS server
   b. the address of more than one DNS server
   c. more than one NIC card
   d. more than one IP address

2. **To properly configure a Windows 2000 server for network connectivity with IP, you must supply a(n) _____.**
   a. WINS address and a subnet mask
   b. DNS address and an IP address
   c. WINS address and a DNS address
   d. IP address and a subnet mask
   e. WINS address and an IP address
   f. DNS address and a subnet address

3. **Windows 2000 requires the _____ protocol for AD to function.**
   a. Internet
   b. APIPA
   c. IP
   d. ROUTE

4. **In dotted-decimal representation, each segment is called a(n)_____.**
   a. 32-bit binary number
   b. octet
   c. parameter
   d. subnet mask

5. **The IP address takes the form of a(n) _____-part numeric value.**
   a. four
   b. eight
   c. sixteen
   d. two

6. **An IP address is a _____-bit binary number.**
   a. 32
   b. 16
   c. 8
   d. 4

7. **Which of the following is a valid IP address? (Choose all that apply.)**
   a. 00001101.01101110.00000011.11100010
   b. 11100000101111010000111111011111
   c. 131.107.256.200
   d. 127.10.10.200

2.2.2 Validate client computer network configuration by using the winipcfg, ipconfig, and arp commands.

IP CONFIGURATION VERIFICATION

UNDERSTANDING THE OBJECTIVE

Microsoft has given the network administrator different commands that can help verify a client's IP network connectivity. The winipcfg command is designed only for the Windows 9*x* and Windows ME environments. The ipconfig and arp commands can be used on the Windows 9*x*, Windows NT 4.0, and Windows 2000 platforms.

WHAT YOU REALLY NEED TO KNOW

◆ Three commands are available to assist you in determining IP configuration settings for Microsoft clients: winipcfg, ipconfig, and arp. The winipcfg command is usable only on the Windows 9*x* and Windows ME platforms. The ipconfig and arp commands function on Windows 2000 as well.

◆ The winipcfg command is a GUI tool. It cannot be used to alter IP settings, but it does allow users to determine their IP settings. The command also supports the release and renewal of DHCP information from the interface.

◆ The ipconfig command is a command-line tool. Its level of functionality is determined by the OS in use. On the Windows 9*x* and Windows ME platforms, it allows an administrator to view IP information, send the information to a batch file for viewing, and release and renew DHCP information for all adapters or for a specific adapter only.

◆ The ipconfig command on a Windows 2000 platform has more functionality. The administrator may view IP information for all adapters or only for a specific adapter, and may also release and renew DHCP information. However, the administrator may also use the command to force registration of the computer information with a DDNS server or display the contents of the local DDNS resolver cache. This cache may also be flushed using ipconfig. Additionally, DHCP User classes may be configured on a Windows 2000 computer using the ipconfig command.

◆ The arp command allows the Windows 2000 administrator to view and configure the ARP tables in Windows 9*x*, Windows ME, and Windows 2000. The command can be used to show the contents of the current ARP table, delete entries from the table, or add entries to the table. Entries in the ARP cache that have not been used for two minutes are removed from the cache. Entries that are being used can be renewed for up to 10 minutes. This is a configurable setting. Static entries added to the ARP cache are deleted when the computer powers off.

OBJECTIVES ON THE JOB

The winipcfg, ipconfig, and arp commands help the local administrator troubleshoot IP connectivity issues for IP-enabled clients.

PRACTICE TEST QUESTIONS

1. **Which of the following allows you to view IP configuration settings on a per-adapter basis? (Choose all that apply.)**
   a. ROUTE print
   b. IPCONFIG /network_adapter
   c. IPCONFIG /all
   d. WINIPCFG

2. **The ARP cache contains information about _____ mappings.**
   a. computer name-to-host name
   b. NetBIOS name-to-NetBIOS scope ID
   c. logical address-to-physical address
   d. IP address-to-subnet address

3. **The information returned by the use of the arp command is useful for determining the MAC address of a _____ that connects to an IP subnet.**
   a. video card
   b. gateway
   c. router
   d. NIC

4. **The winipcfg command is designed for use only in the Windows 9*x* and Windows _____ environments.**
   a. ME
   b. NT
   c. Server
   d. Advanced Server

5. **The ipconfig command allows an administrator to view IP information, send the information to a batch file for viewing, and release and renew _____ information for all adapters or for a specific adapter only.**
   a. DFS
   b. DNS
   c. DHCP
   d. EFS

6. **_____ entries added to the ARP cache are deleted when the computer powers off.**
   a. Static
   b. All
   c. Configured
   d. Dynamic

2.2.3 Validate client computer network connectivity by using the ping command.

PACKET INTERNET GROPER

UNDERSTANDING THE OBJECTIVE

Every system administrator should be well versed in using the ping command. It can return useful troubleshooting information to the administrator of a Windows 2000 domain or computer.

WHAT YOU REALLY NEED TO KNOW

◆ The ping command allows an administrator to use a single computer to check for IP connectivity in a network environment. For instance, the administrator can test for IP address connectivity or for functional name resolution.

◆ The ping command is used from a command prompt in Windows 2000. The most common use is to issue a command such as ping *computer_name* and then to press the Enter key. This sends ICMP packets out on the network to contact the computer designated by *computer_name*. You can also ping by IP address directly.

◆ If you suspect that your network has name resolution issues, you should use the ping command. Ping a target computer by name first. Then ping the same target computer by IP address. If pinging the name is unsuccessful but pinging by IP address is successful, you have narrowed your troubleshooting to a name resolution issue involving your DNS and/or WINS servers.

◆ The ping command also has several command-line switches that can enhance its usefulness. These switches allow the administrator to specify how many times to ping a target system or to ping the target until interrupted. Pinging can resolve IP addresses to hostnames. The command can also send a specific number of echo requests, instead of the default setting of four echos.

◆ Additional settings include a Do not fragment flag on the echo requests sent by ping, and a **TTL** and timestamp for echo packets being sent. The administrator can also configure a timeout duration for each echo reply.

◆ The blockage of ICMP packets at a firewall or proxy server can affect the use of the ping command. Because the ping command uses the ICMP protocol for its functionality, if this protocol is blocked, the command will not work. The administrator also must be aware that the ping command can be used to launch an attack against a network. This kind of attack is known as a DoS attack, and although it does no permanent harm to your data or servers, it does prevent them from responding to requests from clients.

OBJECTIVES ON THE JOB

Ping is a useful tool that allows the local administrator to verify connectivity with network resources and resolve name resolution issues in the network.

PRACTICE TEST QUESTIONS

1. **As an administrator, you are trying to troubleshoot some issues involving packets passing through your network. You are trying to determine which cable entering your 48-port switch is providing service to the computer on which you are working. Note that all 48 ports are filled. How can you determine which cable connects to the computer you are troubleshooting?**
   a. Use a network cable tester to track the suspected cabling to its source.
   b. Place a toner on the line and then trace the tone.
   c. Use the command ping IP_address –t to issue ICMP echos until interrupted.
   d. Visually trace the physical path of the cable.

2. **The _____ command can be used to troubleshoot name resolution problems.**
   a. DDNS
   b. GPOs
   c. APIPA
   d. ping

3. **You are trying to use the ping command for network troubleshooting on a Windows 2000 server. When you ping the localhost, you receive an error message that says the destination is unreachable. What should you do next? (Choose all that apply.)**
   a. Verify the correct entry in the local HOST file.
   b. Verify the correct entry in the DNS server.
   c. Verify the correct protocol name and assigned number in the PROTOCOL file.
   d. Verify that the gateway is configured.

4. **The ping command uses the _____ protocol for its functionality.**
   a. ICMP
   b. SSL
   c. DC
   d. CDFS

5. **The correct syntax for having the ping command resolve the hostname of a target system is _____.**
   a. ping 169.254.1.100 -a
   b. ping –a 169.254.1.100
   c. ping 169.254.1.100 /a
   d. ping 169.254.1.100/a

6. **The ping command can resolve IP addresses to _____.**
   a. NetBios names
   b. realms
   c. targets
   d. hostnames

2.3 Configure, administer, and troubleshoot DHCP on servers and client computers.

WINDOWS 2000 DHCP

UNDERSTANDING THE OBJECTIVE

DHCP is a crucial component of AD and an important component for Windows 2000 computers. DHCP is also the default IP configuration for Windows 2000 computers.

WHAT YOU REALLY NEED TO KNOW

◆ Using DHCP, an administrator can provide the IP address and subnet, the address of routers and DNS servers, and a variety of other configuration information for Windows 2000 and down-level clients.

◆ For a DHCP client that has never received DHCP addressing information, DHCP acquisition is a four-step process. An acronym to help you remember the four steps is **DORA**, which stands for DHCPDiscover, DHCPOffer, DHCPRequest, and DHCPAck. In DHCPDiscover, the client broadcasts on its local subnet for a DHCP server. Remember that at this point, the client does not have an IP address. DHCPOffer is the offer of a DHCP lease from a DHCP server. DCHPRequest is the request from the client to use the lease provided by the offering DHCP server. DHCPAck is the message from the DHCP server to the DHCP client confirming their assignment to the offered lease and furnishing the remainder of the lease configuration settings to the client. Each packet in the process is 342 bytes in size, for a total size of only 1,368 bytes. In a test lab environment, the entire process takes ¼ second.

◆ If the client is renewing a current DHCP lease, the process is simpler. Only the last two packets, DHCPRequest and DHCPAck, are involved. The first packet goes from the client to the server; the second packet goes from the server to the client. DHCP renewal depends on two Registry settings. The first one is T1. It marks the first lease renewal period and occurs at the 50 percent interval in the lease. The DHCP client attempts to contact the DHCP server that gave it the current lease. If the client cannot contact this server after several attempts, the client stops the renewal process. The next renewal attempt occurs 87.5 percent of the way through the lease. At this point, T2, the client begins the complete four-step process of obtaining DHCP service from any DHCP server that is listening. If Windows 2000, Windows 98, or Windows ME is being used, and if the DHCP client cannot contact a DHCP server, the client switches to autoconfiguration, called APIPA. It then selects an IP address from the private range of 169.254.*yyy.zzz*.

OBJECTIVES ON THE JOB

DHCP is an important service for maintaining a functioning IP environment. It can greatly simplify network administration and reduce the likelihood of IP misconfiguration.

PRACTICE TEST QUESTIONS

1. Time T1 represents the _____ percent interval for DHCP leases; time T2 represents the 87.5 percent interval for DHCP leases.
   - a. 25
   - b. 33
   - c. 40
   - d. 50

2. DHCP is a network technology that provides the automatic assignment of IP addressing information to DHCP _____.
   - a. routing tables
   - b. protocols
   - c. routers
   - d. clients

3. If a client is renewing a current DHCP lease, only _____ and DHCPAck are involved in the process.
   - a. DHCPRoute
   - b. DHCPRequest
   - c. DHCPGoto
   - d. DHCPReceive

4. If a Microsoft DHCP client receives several leases from several different DHCP servers, the client will always accept the _____ lease it receives from any server.
   - a. final
   - b. second
   - c. first
   - d. third

5. A DHCPAck is _____ bytes in size.
   - a. 1,369
   - b. 1,024
   - c. 16
   - d. 342

6. DHCP is an acronym for _____.
   - a. Distributed Host Configuration Protocol
   - b. Dynamic Hosted Client Packets
   - c. Dynamic Hardware Client Protocol
   - d. Dynamic Host Configuration Protocol

7. When a client begins the DHCP lease acquisition process and it has never had a DHCP lease before, it must complete four steps; each step is _____ bytes in size for a total size of 1,368 bytes.
   - a. 432
   - b. 435
   - c. 342
   - d. 341

2.3.1 Detect unauthorized DHCP servers on a network.

ROGUE DHCP SERVERS

UNDERSTANDING THE OBJECTIVE

AD provides for the authorization of DHCP servers in an AD environment. This reduces or eliminates issues concerning rogue DHCP servers, which are DHCP servers that were built and started by individuals other than the network administrators. These rogue servers may be configured with DHCP settings that can interfere with the functionality of your AD environment.

WHAT YOU REALLY NEED TO KNOW

◆ Windows 2000 DHCP servers in an AD environment must be authorized by the AD itself to function. Non-Windows 2000 DHCP servers, such as Windows NT 3.51, NT 4.0, or third-party DHCP solutions, do not require authorization to function in a Windows AD environment. Therefore, they can cause disruptions.

◆ Rogue DHCP servers are detected in the AD environment by using DHCPInform packets from other Windows 2000 DHCP servers or by detecting new, vendor-specific options from other Windows 2000 DHCP servers.

◆ When Windows 2000 DHCP servers start, they broadcast the DHCPInform packet to locate the AD Enterprise root where other DHCP servers should be located. When other Windows 2000 DHCP servers receive the DHCPInform packet, they respond with a DHCPACK packet that acknowledges the first message and contains information about the AD enterprise services root. The DHCP server that is starting can collect a list of DHCP servers in AD that are authorized to start and provide the service.

◆ If no other AD-enabled DHCP servers are on the returned list and AD is not available, the DHCP server can start and provide services to clients. The DHCP server continues to check every five minutes to determine if a connection to an AD Enterprise is available and, if so, whether the server is on the list of authorized servers. If both conditions are met, the server continues to run.

◆ If the DHCP server finds that the AD Enterprise has not authorized the server, it stops the DHCP service and will not respond to client requests for DHCP. These steps apply only to Windows 2000 DHCP servers. Down-level and third-party DHCP implementations do not support or recognize the concept of DHCP server authorization in AD, which may cause problems in your AD environment.

OBJECTIVES ON THE JOB

Windows 2000 supports several Microsoft-specific enhancements to commonly available network services, including the authorization of Windows 2000 DHCP servers through AD. Using the DHCP snap-in, an administrator can control the Windows 2000 DHCP servers in an environment and reduce the frequency of misassignment of DHCP information to AD clients.

PRACTICE TEST QUESTIONS

1. DHCP_____ is a DHCP packet type that is 342 bytes in size.
   - a. Inform
   - b. Install
   - c. Internet
   - d. Authorize

2. AD provides for the authorization of _____ servers in an AD environment.
   - a. TTL
   - b. UNC
   - c. ADSI
   - d. DHCP

3. When contacted by a Windows 2000 DHCP server that is starting up, other Windows 2000 DHCP servers will respond to the incoming DHCPInform packet with a _____ packet.
   - a. magic cookie
   - b. DHCPNack
   - c. DHCPMagicCookie
   - d. DHCPAck

4. Rogue DHCP _____ are detected in the AD environment by using DHCPInform packets.
   - a. NICs
   - b. gateways
   - c. routers
   - d. servers

5. Members of the _____ group can authorize Windows 2000 DHCP servers in AD.
   - a. Domain Admins
   - b. Forest Admins
   - c. Schema Admins
   - d. Enterprise Admins

6. Reducing the occurrence of rogue DHCP servers in your AD environment is an important task because rogue DHCP servers could cause _____. (Choose all that apply.)
   - a. incorrect gateway assignment
   - b. faulty application of EFS permissions through incorrect DNS assignment
   - c. the inability of client computers to communicate even though they are on the same subnet
   - d. incorrect or nonexistent client leases

2.3.2 Configure authorization of DHCP servers.

ENABLING DHCP SERVERS

UNDERSTANDING THE OBJECTIVE

Windows 2000 DHCP servers must be authorized before they can respond to requests for services from DHCP clients. Only Windows 2000 DHCP servers support the concept of authorization in AD to respond to requests.

WHAT YOU REALLY NEED TO KNOW

◆ The default configuration for IP in Windows 2000 is DHCP. To support this configuration, Windows 2000 provides a DHCP server with improved functionality. One new feature is the requirement that Windows 2000 DHCP servers be authorized through AD before they respond to DHCP requests.

◆ For Windows 2000 DHCP servers to respond correctly, they must be installed on either a Windows 2000 domain controller or a Windows 2000 member server that belongs to an AD environment. Failure to meet these conditions prevents the DHCP service from responding correctly to requests.

◆ The server hosting the DHCP Server service must have a statically configured IP address on at least one network interface. The DHCP server can support multiple network interfaces.

◆ After the DHCP Server service has been installed and configured, the administrator must open the DHCP Management console and right-click the DHCP server to be authorized. Next, he or she must select the Authorize option and supply either an IP address or a hostname for the server hosting DHCP. He or she then must click the Add button to authorize the service. Only a member of the Enterprise Administrators group can authorize DHCP servers in AD.

◆ After the DHCP server has been authorized, it is available to service DHCP requests. It will also add its name to the list of authorized DHCP servers in the directory. Each DHCP server that starts will broadcast to other DHCP servers to obtain this list and determine if it has been authorized to start its DHCP Server service.

◆ It is important to remember that only the Windows 2000 DHCP servers in your enterprise must be authorized in AD. Down-level DHCP servers or third-party DHCP servers are not required to be authorized in AD. However, it's possible that these unauthorized DHCP servers may complicate your network environment by providing incorrect DHCP information to your network DHCP clients.

OBJECTIVES ON THE JOB

Windows 2000 DHCP provides the AD administrator with a tool that can control Windows 2000 DHCP servers and reduce or eliminate the possibility of rogue DHCP servers in the network environment. Previous versions of Windows domains did not have this control.

PRACTICE TEST QUESTIONS

1. Windows 2000 DHCP servers can be authorized in AD only by members of the
_____ group.
    a. Account Operators
    b. Server Operators
    c. Domain Administrators
    d. Enterprise Administrators

2. Windows 2000 DHCP servers must be _____ before they can
respond to requests for services from DHCP clients.
    a. rebooted
    b. configured
    c. authorized
    d. formatted

3. The default configuration for IP in Windows 2000 is _____.
    a. DDNs
    b. DNS
    c. TCP/IP
    d. DHCP

4. The packet sent out by a Windows 2000 DHCP server that is booting is a
_____ packet.
    a. DHCPInform
    b. DHCPAuthorize
    c. DHCPNAck
    d. DHCPConsent

5. The server hosting the DHCP Server service must have a statically configured
IP address on at least one _____.
    a. request condition
    b. router
    c. interface
    d. hexadecimal address

6. DHCP servers can be installed on a _____. (Choose all that apply.)
    a. DNS server
    b. domain controller
    c. WINS server
    d. member server

2.3.3 Configure client computers to use dynamic IP addressing.

CLIENT DHCP CONFIGURATION

UNDERSTANDING THE OBJECTIVE

Because the default IP configuration in Windows 2000 is a DHCP configuration, you need to understand how to configure clients for this protocol.

WHAT YOU REALLY NEED TO KNOW

◆ Windows 2000 servers and Windows 2000 Professional computers use DHCP by default. Extra configuration steps must be performed if the administrator wants to build the computers with static IP configurations. After the computers have been built, they run seamlessly with DHCP in your network environment. In addition, most Windows 2000 servers that host subsidiary services, including domain controllers (with certain exceptions), can run in a Windows 2000 network using DHCP.

◆ Windows 2000 DHCP configuration allows the administrator to enable DHCP for either the IP address/subnet mask or the DNS information or both. This allows the administrator great flexibility in the assignment of IP information for their clients.

◆ Another new feature of the Windows 2000 implementation of DHCP is the concept of classes. DHCP now supports either vendor classes or user classes. The vendor class allows the administrator to assign IP addressing information based on the identity of the manufacturer of the computer's NIC. The user class is a variable that the administrator can create on local clients to designate a particular attribute of a computer class.

◆ Down-level clients can also use Windows 2000 DHCP, although they cannot utilize the advanced settings that this new DHCP server provides. Non-Microsoft clients and clients that require the BOOTP protocol are also supported by the Windows 2000 DHCP server.

◆ As an additional planning implementation for the administrator, you should know that the default lease interval is now eight days. Also, if a Windows 2000 DHCP client cannot contact a DHCP server, the client will use APIPA and select an IP address from the private class B range of 169.254.0.0. This allows DHCP clients to communicate with each other, but not with computers not configured by APIPA. Microsoft clients that support APIPA are Windows 98, Windows ME, and Windows 2000.

OBJECTIVES ON THE JOB

Windows 2000 DHCP provides the network administrator with some powerful configuration tools, including vendor and user classes and simple configuration. When combined with the concept of authorized DHCP servers, Windows 2000 gives the administrator many advantages over other forms of DHCP for AD clients.

PRACTICE TEST QUESTIONS

1. Windows 2000 servers and Windows 2000 Professional computers use
   _____ by default.
   - a. NNTP
   - b. SSL
   - c. PNP
   - d. DHCP

2. As the administrator of a small company, you want to optimize the network
   connectivity of your client computers. Ideally, you want your desktop clients to
   receive one set of DHCP configuration settings and your laptop clients to receive a
   different set of settings. To achieve this functionality, you could implement
   _____. (Choose all that apply.)
   - a. BOOTP
   - b. user classes
   - c. vendor mappings
   - d. vendor classes

3. DHCP now supports vendor classes and _____ classes.
   - a. user
   - b. admin
   - c. usenet
   - d. subnet

4. The DHCP lease process is a four-step process if the client has never had a DHCP
   lease before. The four DHCP packets are _____.
   - a. DHCPInform, DHCPRequest, DHCPAck, and DHCPOffer
   - b. DHCPDiscover, DHCPOffer, DHCPRelease, and DHCPAck
   - c. DHCPDiscover, DHCPOffer, DHCPRequest, and DHCPAck
   - d. DHCPRelease, DHCPDecline, DHCPOffer, and DHCPRenew

5. Most Windows 2000 servers that host _____ services, including
   domain controllers (with certain exceptions), can run in a Windows 2000 network
   using DHCP.
   - a. implemented
   - b. configured
   - c. supplemental
   - d. subsidiary

6. The range for an APIPA address is _____.
   - a. 254.169.0.0
   - b. 169.254.0.0
   - c. 192.168.1.0
   - d. 131.107.0.0

2.3.4 Configure DHCP server properties.

CONFIGURING THE DHCP SERVER SERVICE

UNDERSTANDING THE OBJECTIVE

Before the Windows 2000 DHCP server can provide services to clients, it must be configured. Once configured, the server will support the AD network environment and clients.

WHAT YOU REALLY NEED TO KNOW

◆ Windows 2000 DHCP server is compatible with all current **RFCs** that define and delineate DHCP operation and performance. It can support any Windows 2000 client, as well as any down-level or third-party DHCP client. The Windows 2000 DHCP server has 76 separate scope options available for address management. The DHCP management tool allows the management of multiple DHCP servers from one console.

◆ The DHCP server must be installed before it can be configured. The installation is performed through the Add/Remove Programs and Add/Remove Windows Components tools. Also, the computer hosting the DCHP server must use static IP addresses. After the DHCP server is installed, it is recommended that you install the latest service pack for Windows 2000, and then allow the DHCP server to reboot.

◆ After the server has rebooted, the administrator can configure user and vendor classes and predefined options for different kinds of clients. He or she can also create different kinds of scopes.

◆ Other configuration settings for the server are DHCP logging configurations and DNS settings. A new capability of the DHCP server is its integration with DNS, which allows the DHCP server to update DNS mappings for the clients. The default setting is to allow the clients to update their own forward lookup information while the DHCP server updates the reverse lookup information. This behavior can be changed to provide more functionality to the down-level clients by allowing the DHCP server to update DNS entries for those down-level clients.

◆ Other configuration settings include configuring conflict attempts for the client lease process and configuring the location of the audit log file, the DHCP database path, and the network interface bindings.

◆ As a final step in configuring your DHCP server, you must remember that DHCP servers do not replicate among themselves. Therefore, to protect your network, you need to provide some kind of fault configuration, either another DHCP server or a good tape backup of the DHCP database.

OBJECTIVES ON THE JOB

After the DHCP server is configured, you may begin creating the DHCP scopes that will provide automatic IP address assignment for your DHCP clients in a Windows 2000 AD environment. Using the new DHCP server, you can achieve maximum functionality and optimization for your clients.

PRACTICE TEST QUESTIONS

1. By default, the Windows 2000 DHCP server updates the DNS information for the client _____.
   - a. only when renewing the DHCP lease at time T1
   - b. only when the client issues the command ipconfig /registerdns
   - c. only if the client requests it
   - d. never, unless the Registry setting UpdateClientDNS is added to the Registry as a type D_WORD with a value of 1

2. Windows 2000 allows the administrator to manage multiple DHCP servers from one DHCP _____.
   - a. console
   - b. domain
   - c. router
   - d. interface

3. Windows 2000 allows the administrator to configure up to _____ different kinds of option classes for different kinds of DHCP clients.
   - a. 3
   - b. 4
   - c. 5
   - d. 2

4. A person who can administer a DHCP server is a member of the _____ group in Windows 2000.
   - a. Enterprise Administrators
   - b. DHCP Admins
   - c. Domain Admins
   - d. Server Operators

5. A computer hosting a DCHP server must use _____ IP addresses.
   - a. static
   - b. formatted
   - c. dotted-subnet
   - d. APIPA-approved

6. A new capability of the DHCP server is its integration with DNS, which allows the DHCP server to update DNS _____ for the clients.
   - a. configurations
   - b. services
   - c. mappings
   - d. host files

2.3.5 Create and configure a DHCP scope.

PROVIDING DHCP FOR THE CLIENTS

UNDERSTANDING THE OBJECTIVE

After a DHCP server is installed and configured, you can begin enabling DHCP for your clients. To provide this support, you create a DHCP scope that contains the addresses to assign to your clients.

WHAT YOU REALLY NEED TO KNOW

◆ A DHCP scope is a database of addresses that you want to make available to your clients. A scope may contain only one IP address or it may contain an entire subnet. Microsoft recommends that a Windows 2000 DHCP server hold no more than 2,000 individual scopes, each containing a collection of available DHCP addresses.

◆ The process of creating a new scope is managed by the New Scope Wizard in Windows 2000. This tool prompts you for all the information needed to create a new scope, such as the name of the scope, the starting and ending IP addresses, and the length of the subnet mask. The wizard also prompts you to enter any exclusions, either as a single address or as a block of addresses. The next configuration is the lease interval, which, by default, is eight days. The range is from 1 minute to 999 days. You are next prompted to configure common scope options such as the default gateway, the DNS server information, and the WINS server information. The last step in the wizard is to activate the scope. The scope may be deactivated when desired.

◆ The configuration of the multicast scope is similar, except it has a default lease interval of 30 days and has no additional options such as DNS or WINS.

◆ DHCP reservations allow you to map a specific DHCP address against a specific MAC address for a client. This guarantees that the client always receives the same IP address. The DHCP options can be applied to the DHCP server, the DHCP scope, or to and individual reservation or client.

◆ Because you are using DHCP for IP address assignment, you can be flexible when managing your available leases. Because the DHCP servers do not replicate, it is important to distribute your leases for redundancy. Microsoft recommends a 25/75 split, with 25 percent on one server and 75 percent on another. For performance reasons, you might want to exclude excess leases, if any, from the scope. Excluded leases can be added to your address pool at a later date. As for lease durations, a short lease period is recommended if the number of available leases approximately equals the number of clients; a longer lease is recommended if you have more leases than clients.

OBJECTIVES ON THE JOB

A DHCP scope allows you to provide automatic IP addressing to your network clients. The DHCP service in Windows 2000 can provide DHCP service for any client requiring DHCP, even non-Microsoft clients. As administrator, you will configure and implement the service.

PRACTICE TEST QUESTIONS

1. **The most common settings for a DHCP scope are _____. (Choose all that apply.)**
   a. Option 003 Router
   b. Option 047 NetBIOS Scope ID
   c. Option 046 WINS/NBT Node Type
   d. Option 008 Cookie Servers

2. **The maximum duration for a DHCP lease is _____.**
   a. over 2½ years
   b. 30 days
   c. indefinite
   d. 6 months

3. **The minimum duration for a DHCP lease is _____.**
   a. 1 day
   b. 4 hours
   c. 1 minute
   d. 10 minutes

4. **A multicast scope has a default _____ interval of 30 days.**
   a. service
   b. lease
   c. server
   d. address life

5. **DHCP reservations allow you to map a specific DHCP address against a specific MAC address for a _____.**
   a. gateway
   b. server
   c. client
   d. router

6. **A DHCP scope allows you to provide automatic _____ addressing to your network clients.**
   a. IP
   b. TCP/IP
   c. DFS
   d. DNS

2.4 Configure, administer, and troubleshoot DNS.

USES WITHIN WINDOWS 2000

UNDERSTANDING THE OBJECTIVE

Windows 2000 was designed to use DNS as its name resolution service. Previous Microsoft operating systems used WINS for name resolution. If you are planning an implementation of Windows 2000, you must understand how to implement DNS into your environment.

WHAT YOU REALLY NEED TO KNOW

◆ DNS is the name resolution service used on the Internet. It is also the name resolution implemented in Windows 2000 for use by Windows 2000 clients. DNS is a well understood and dependable service, and the Microsoft implementation is compliant with the most current RFCs defining DNS.

◆ The version of DNS implemented in Windows 2000 is DDNS. DDNS supports name registration by the clients themselves; the DNS administrator is not required to manually create DNS entries. The Windows 2000 DHCP server can assist in this process by registering the **PTR** information with the DNS server for DHCP clients. Also, the DHCP server can be configured to register the forward lookup information for down-level clients with the DNS server.

◆ The Windows 2000 DNS server also integrates with AD by supporting a new form of DNS that is exclusive to the Microsoft environment. The new DNS service is called AD Integrated, and it eliminates one of the standard DNS problems, which is the single point of failure. AD Integrated moves the information contained in the standard DNS zone into the AD itself. This accomplishes several tasks; one of the most important is the elimination of the single point of failure for DNS. AD Integrated distributes the DNS database file to all Windows 2000 domain controllers in AD. This allows AD to manage the replication and security of the DNS zone database files.

◆ Another improvement in Windows 2000 DDNS is the Microsoft implementation of an RFC called **IXFR**. When a standard DNS server transfers the zone database file, the entire file is replicated. IXFR replicates only those DNS records that have changed. This reduces the amount of bandwidth used by the DNS servers. The clients using DNS also register into DNS services running on the computers, particularly the services on the domain controllers. The services being registered are **SRV** records, and they allow DNS clients to locate services in the network, such as Global Catalog servers and domain controllers. Many other SRV records also register in this fashion with DNS.

OBJECTIVES ON THE JOB

The new implementation of DNS found in Windows 2000 was designed to provide the optimal support and performance for AD. It uses the latest RFC standards for DNS implementation to provide a secure integration with the AD and the highest level of support.

PRACTICE TEST QUESTIONS

1. SRV records allow a client to query Windows 2000 DDNS _____ to locate AD services.
   a. routers
   b. servers
   c. gateways
   d. interfaces

2. SRV records hosted on a Windows NT 4.0 DNS server must be entered as _____ records.
   a. Cname
   b. MX
   c. A
   d. PTR

3. DNS is the second generation of what service?
   a. Lmhosts
   b. Hosts
   c. WINS
   d. NBNS

4. Windows 2000 DNS can be configured as a(n) _____ server. (Choose all that apply.)
   a. caching only
   b. standard secondary
   c. AD Integrated
   d. standard primary

5. When installing AD onto a Windows 2000 server, DC PROMO will install a(n) _____ DNS server.
   a. standard primary
   b. AD Integrated
   c. AD caching only
   d. master server

6. An AD integrated DNS implementation removes the _____.
   a. latency of zone transfer data
   b. high zone transfer bandwidth usage
   c. single point of failure for the DNS primary server
   d. lack of zone transfer security

7. You are planning a rollout of Windows 2000 AD and must be certain that only specified servers can replicate DNS zone file information to your DNS servers. What is the easiest way to implement this requirement? (Choose all that apply.)
   a. Employ IPSec to verify the integrity of your zone files.
   b. Configure digital signatures for the DNS servers to use when they perform a zone transfer.
   c. Implement secure updates on the DNS servers.
   d. Configure the Zone Transfer option to replicate only to specified servers.

2.4.1 Configure DNS server properties.

CONFIGURING THE DNS SERVER

UNDERSTANDING THE OBJECTIVE

DNS is required for AD to be installed correctly. It is the name resolution service for not only the Internet, but also for your AD implementation.

WHAT YOU REALLY NEED TO KNOW

♦ The version of DNS in Windows 2000 is known as DDNS. Unlike previous versions of DNS, the DDNS server does not require that an administrator manually add entries to the DNS database. DDNS allows the client computers and the DHCP server to register the hostname to IP address mapping information with DNS. This greatly simplifies the name resolution process in Windows 2000 AD.

♦ Windows 2000 DNS can be configured in two separate modes. The first mode is as a standard primary DNS server. The second mode is called AD Integrated. A standard primary DNS server maintains a single copy of its DNS database on one computer. If the primary DNS server fails, it is impossible to make updates to the DNS database. AD Integrated moves the DNS database from one single DNS server and places in into the AD. This has significant advantages for your AD implementation. The first benefit is the removal of the primary DNS server as the single point of failure. Instead, the DNS database is now distributed on, and accessible from, all domain controllers for that particular domain. A second, more important benefit is the application of AD security on top of your DNS database file. This allows the administrator to protect the DNS information with the more rigorous AD security model.

♦ The administrator can also install different kinds of DNS servers in the environment. If using standard DNS primary servers, the administrator can install DNS secondary servers. The secondary servers contain read-only copies of the DNS database obtained from a DNS primary server. Another kind of DNS server is the DNS caching-only server. This server does not maintain a DNS database file on its hard drive. Instead, it maintains the DNS records in a memory cache. This has the advantage of eliminating transfers of the DNS database to the caching-only server; however, it also means that if this server reboots, it loses all its DNS information and must rebuild its resolution cache.

♦ The DNS console allows you to monitor and control many DNS servers from one DNS console. From this console, you can clear the DNS cache information and establish settings for controlling the scavenging of stale resource records from the database.

OBJECTIVES ON THE JOB

DNS is the name resolution tool for Windows 2000 computers and AD. It is crucial to AD. If you do not supply the address of a DNS server during the installation of AD, you will be prompted to allow AD itself to install and configure a DNS server.

PRACTICE TEST QUESTIONS

1. _____ is required for AD to be installed correctly.
   - a. DNS
   - b. EFS
   - c. GPO
   - d. DDNS

2. The version of DNS in Windows 2000 is known as _____.
   - a. IIS
   - b. DDNS
   - c. DFS
   - d. SSL

3. An AD Integrated DNS server keeps its database on a Windows 2000 _____ computer.
   - a. PDC emulator
   - b. AD domain controller
   - c. DNS master server
   - d. DNS caching only server

4. DNS servers map _____ names against IP addresses.
   - a. NetBIOS
   - b. node
   - c. station
   - d. host

5. A standard _____ DNS server maintains the master copy of its DNS database on one computer.
   - a. resolution
   - b. primary
   - c. secondary
   - d. tertiary

6. As an administrator, you want to avoid a zone transfer to one of your DNS servers located at a remote office. To do so, you should implement a(n) _____ DNS server.
   - a. master
   - b. secondary
   - c. AD Integrated
   - d. caching only

7. The configuration of a _____ allows a DNS server to resolve hostnames of clients for which it has no record in its internal database.
   - a. standard secondary file
   - b. forwarder
   - c. root hints file
   - d. BOOT file

2.4.2 Manage DNS database records such as CNAME, A, and PTR.

FREQUENTLY USED DNS NAME RECORD TYPES

UNDERSTANDING THE OBJECTIVE

After a DNS server has been installed, you can use it for mapping hostnames against IP addresses in your network. There are many different address types in the DNS database, but some will be used more frequently than others.

WHAT YOU REALLY NEED TO KNOW

◆ When you are ready to start adding entries to your DNS database, you must understand the types of records that can be added. There are 19 different record types that exist in the Windows 2000 DNS database. The DNS administrator also has the ability to create new record types as necessary.

◆ The CNAME record type is the canonical name, or alias, for the hostname. The CNAME record type allows the administrator to create multiple aliases for a single hostname/IP address setting. An administrator does not have to reveal the actual hostnames of their servers. Administrators need only configure a CNAME for the server in DNS and allow clients trying to connect to use the alias of the server, instead of the actual name of the server. This kind of mapping can be extremely useful for building virtual Web servers on a single IIS server. Instead of using multiple servers, the administrator can simply create the CNAME records and allow DNS to direct these incoming requests to the correct computer. A CNAME consists of the alias to be created and the **FQDN** against which the alias is to be mapped.

◆ The A record is the basic DNS record type. To create an A record, you must supply a host name and an IP address. For manually created entries, the IP address should be static. For entries created either by the client or by the DHCP server, the IP address information will be supplied to the DNS server. The same host name and a different IP address are supported, as is the creation of records having the same host name and IP address, but having different capitalization. Identical names but with different uses of capitalization may be seen by certain types of DNS servers (BIND) as different computers, even though they may both use the same IP address.

◆ The third common DNS record type is the PTR record. The PTR is also known as the Reverse lookup record. When performing a standard DNS name resolution, the DNS server is queried for the IP address that maps against a specific host name. The PTR does exactly the opposite. The DNS server is queried for the host name of the IP address that was just presented for resolution. The DHCP server creates the Reverse lookup automatically when a DHCP address is leased to clients. The PTR record can also be created manually when A records are created in the DNS database.

OBJECTIVES ON THE JOB

The DNS server has the CNAME, A, and PTR record types, which are commonly used in a DNS-enabled network environment. They should be familiar to every AD administrator.

PRACTICE TEST QUESTIONS

1. After a DNS server has been installed, you can begin to use it for mapping
   _____.
   - a. leases
   - b. databases
   - c. records
   - d. hostnames

2. By default, when a DHCP client receives a DHCP lease, the _____
   information is updated by the DHCP server on the DNS server.
   - a. DHCP
   - b. PTR
   - c. PTR
   - d. CNAME

3. The A record in DNS, by default, can be created by _____.
   - a. a manual process or by Active Directory
   - b. the DHCP server or by WINS lookup
   - c. a caching only server or by a standard secondary server
   - d. the client computer or by the administrator

4. The A record in Windows 2000 DNS is for IP version _____.
   - a. 6
   - b. 5
   - c. 4
   - d. 3

5. The definition of CNAME in Windows 2000 _____ and the definition
   of CNAME in BIND are the same.
   - a. DDNS
   - b. AD
   - c. CDFS
   - d. DNS

6. You are building several Web sites to be hosted on the same IIS 5.0 Web server.
   You want a separate name assigned to each Web site, and you do not want to
   reveal the actual name of the Web server to the Internet. What technologies would
   help you achieve this goal? (Choose all that apply.)
   - a. virtual servers with custom header pages
   - b. Internet Security and Acceleration Server
   - c. DNS CNAME
   - d. multihoming

7. A(n) _____ record is the most basic type of DNS record.
   - a. D
   - b. C
   - c. B
   - d. A

2.4.3 Create and configure DNS zones.

ENABLING DNS

UNDERSTANDING THE OBJECTIVE

DNS servers provide name resolution through DNS zones. The zones contain the hostname to IP address mappings for the DNS clients. You must understand the concept of DNS zones to effectively implement DNS in your environment.

WHAT YOU REALLY NEED TO KNOW

◆ A DNS zone is an administrative function within DNS. The zone separates one group of addresses from another group for administrative purposes. For example, a bank may decide to create several DNS zones internally. One zone would contain the auto loan department while another zone might contain the home loan department. Zones divide DNS information along company departments or areas of responsibility.

◆ There are two main types of zones in DNS: the forward lookup zone and the reverse lookup zone. The forward lookup zone is used in the conventional manner; a client attempts a look up of a client hostname to an IP address. The reverse lookup zone allows a client to provide an IP address and obtain a hostname out of the zone. Each type of zone is created independently from the other. A DNS server must always have a forward lookup zone; however, the reverse lookup zone is optional. Another difference in the two types of zones is the names used. By default, the name of the forward lookup zone is the name of the DNS domain that it supports. The default name of the reverse lookup zone is derived from taking the network IP address, reversing it, and then appending a text string to it. As an example, the reverse lookup zone for 192.168.1.0 would appear as 0.1.168.192.in-addr.arpa.

◆ Windows 2000 DNS features a wizard-based tool that walks the administrator through the process of creating both forward and reverse lookup zones on the DNS server. To complete the wizard, you will need to know whether you want to create a standard primary, standard secondary, or AD Integrated zone. You will then provide a name, if you are using a forward lookup zone. You can supply a network IP address or name for a reverse lookup zone. After creating the zone file, you can add entries to it.

◆ Other configuration settings for the DNS zones include choosing either unsecured dynamic updates or secure dynamic updates. Another setting is the configuration of WINS lookup and zone transfers. If you have configured WINS lookup and have BIND servers in your infrastructure, be sure to disable the replication of WINS lookup information to these BIND servers. The same configuration settings that can be adjusted for the forward lookup zones can also be adjusted for the reverse lookup zones.

OBJECTIVES ON THE JOB

Windows 2000 DNS is one of the most important tools for the AD administrator. You must thoroughly understand how to configure the DNS service to respond to client requests.

PRACTICE TEST QUESTIONS

1. DNS servers provide name resolution through DNS lookups made to
   _____.
   - a. routers
   - b. zones
   - c. printer drivers
   - d. gateway sections

2. If you want to control how computers update their DNS information to guard
   against imposters, you should configure DNS for _____ updates.
   - a. dynamic
   - b. secure
   - c. IPSec
   - d. DDNS secure

3. If you have a mixed environment of Windows NT 4.0 clients and Windows 2000
   clients, you should enable the _____ service on the DNS server to
   assist name resolution requests from Windows 2000 computers that are attempting
   to locate Windows NT 4.0 computers.
   - a. Lmhosts lookup
   - b. Local hosts file
   - c. WINS lookup
   - d. WINS-R lookup

4. An AD administrator needs to distribute the administrative responsibility for parts
   of the DNS environment. How can this be accomplished?
   - a. Create a separate DNS server in each part of the infrastructure with records for
     only that section of the environment.
   - b. Design a subnetted environment and implement Answer A.
   - c. Set up DNS zones.
   - d. Implement NetBIOS scope IDs.

5. If you are using standard secondary DNS servers, you need to configure zone
   transfers to these servers. What configuration options do you have for configuring
   these settings? (Choose all that apply.)
   - a. to any server
   - b. to replication partners only
   - c. only to servers listed on the Name Servers tab
   - d. only to the implemented servers

6. The name of the person responsible for a DNS server can be found on which tab in
   the Zone Properties dialog box?
   - a. General
   - b. Start of Authority
   - c. Name Servers
   - d. WINS

2.5 Troubleshoot name resolution on client computers. Considerations include WINS, DNS, NetBIOS, the Hosts file, and the Lmhosts file.

WINDOWS 2000 NAME RESOLUTION

UNDERSTANDING THE OBJECTIVE

Windows 2000 provides different techniques for name resolution. For hostname resolution, the administrator may configure DNS and Hosts files. For NetBIOS resolution, the administrator may configure WINS and Lmhosts files. All these techniques also are available for supporting down-level clients. The administrator also has troubleshooting tools available.

WHAT YOU REALLY NEED TO KNOW

◆ Windows 2000 depends on the DNS service for name resolution of Windows 2000 clients. However, down-level clients primarily depend on WINS for name resolution. As the administrator of a Windows 2000 environment, you must understand the operation of both services and how to troubleshoot them.

◆ WINS and DDNS are very similar in function. Both are dynamic services that allow the clients to register with each service (this must be configured in DNS). Each service registers services running on client computers into its database for use in name registration requests. DNS is used for hostname-to-IP address resolution, while WINS is used for NetBIOS name-to-IP-address resolution. The administrator must remember that in a Windows NT 4.0 environment, the NetBIOS name is almost always the hostname. Windows NT 4.0 requires WINS for name resolution. Windows 2000 requires DNS for name resolution. Windows NT 4.0 can be configured to use DNS, and Windows 2000 can be configured to use WINS.

◆ The administrator also has two manually configured alternatives to DNS and WINS that can be enabled on a computer-by-computer basis. As a local replacement for DNS, you may implement and configure a Hosts file. This will provide hostname resolution. You can also configure the Lmhosts file for NetBIOS name resolution. The two files are similar in function and construction, but have several important differences in implementation.

◆ Finally, you have an assortment of troubleshooting tools you can use to manage name resolution deficiencies in your network. The ipconfig command is a common tool with which every administrator should already be thoroughly familiar. The nbsstat command is used for troubleshooting and displaying NetBIOS information. The nslookup command is used with your DNS servers. The netdiag command is a powerful tool for detailing many different aspects of your local network environment.

OBJECTIVES ON THE JOB

One of the most important duties of the Windows 2000 administrator is to maintain name resolution in a mixed environment of Windows 2000 and down-level clients. Different tools exist for providing and troubleshooting the resolution.

PRACTICE TEST QUESTIONS

1. For hostname resolution, the administrator can configure DNS and
   _____ files.
   - a. replicated
   - b. resolved
   - c. Lmhosts
   - d. Hosts

2. Windows 2000 depends on the DNS service for name resolution of Windows 2000
   _____.
   - a. clients
   - b. servers
   - c. interfaces
   - d. services

3. When configuring your network to support Windows 95 clients, you must provide
   the _____ name resolution service.
   - a. WINS
   - b. DNS
   - c. DHCP
   - d. NBNS

4. If you have a small group of users running Windows 2000 in a remote office and
   you do not want to place a Standard Secondary DNS server in the office, what
   technique can you use for name resolution? (Choose all that apply.)
   - a. preloading the NetBIOS name cache
   - b. creating a local Hosts file
   - c. placing an AD Integrated DNS server in the site
   - d. placing a DNS caching-only server in the site

5. To support name resolution of Windows 2000 hostnames from Windows NT 4.0
   computers that are configured only with the address of a WINS server, what setting
   should you enable on the WINS server?
   - a. The WINS server should be configured to register with a DNS server.
   - b. The WINS server should be multihomed and each network interface should be
     configured with the address of the WINS server.
   - c. The WINS server should be configured for DNS lookup and configured with the
     address of an authoritative DNS server for that domain.
   - d. The WINS server should be configured to implement an Lmhosts file.

6. If you need to determine the IP address of the client computer's configured DHCP
   server, what command should you use?
   - a. nbtstat
   - b. ipconfig
   - c. nslookup
   - d. netdiag

2.5.1 Configure client computer name resolution properties.

LOCAL NAME RESOLUTION METHODS

UNDERSTANDING THE OBJECTIVE

Windows 2000 clients can use DDNS or WINS for name resolution. A DHCP server can supply both settings or the client can be configured statically with the addresses of DDNS or WINS servers.

WHAT YOU REALLY NEED TO KNOW

◆ All Microsoft operating systems from Windows 95 forward have supported the Lmhosts and Hosts files. These two files are holdovers from the pre-DNS, pre-WINS days of the early Internet. Both files can be used for local name resolution; however, they must be configured before they can be used.

◆ The Lmhosts and Hosts files are located in the path \WINNTSYSTEM32\DRIVERS\ETC. The files do not have extensions attached, and it is important that you do not add extensions to the files if you work with them. Files with extensions will not be used by the operating system. Also, if you decide to use the two files, you must be certain that they are saved as ASCII text and not as UNICODE. The EDIT tool is a good tool for creating and modifying these two files because it can save files only as ASCII text.

◆ The Lmhosts file can take the place of or supplement a WINS server. It contains the mappings of NetBIOS computer names to IP addresses. The Lmhosts file is also programmatic because it allows the administrator to enter up to 100 mappings for NetBIOS names and then preload those entries into the NetBIOS name cache on the local computer. The administrator can also enter mappings for domain controllers or other computers. The sample Lmhosts file on every Microsoft OS contains information on how to configure these files. Name resolution using Lmhosts is faster because the computer attempting the resolution can check for a mapping locally.

◆ Another file that can be used for name resolution is the Hosts file. This file is similar to the Lmhosts file; however, it is simpler in format. In addition, unlike the Lmhosts file, Hosts is not programmatic. The Hosts file will, however, allow the administrator to enter hostname-to-IP-address mappings and NetBIOS names-to-IP-address mappings.

◆ You must remember that if these files are configured, they will override name resolution from either the DNS or WINS servers. If you experience name resolution issues with DNS or WINS, you may want to determine if these two files have been configured.

OBJECTIVES ON THE JOB

If you must configure name resolution for a client who may not have a constant network connection or who travels frequently, consider using the Lmhosts and Hosts files.

PRACTICE TEST QUESTIONS

1. The Hosts file can work in conjunction with _____ in a Windows 2000 environment. (Choose all that apply.)
   a. DHCP
   b. WINS
   c. DNS
   d. RRAS

2. You have created an Lmhosts file for your network clients. You checked all the mappings and you know they are correct. However, the file is not working and you need to resolve the problem. What should you check? (Choose all that apply.)
   a. Whether the file has an extension attached to it.
   b. Whether the path to the file to verify it is correct.
   c. Whether the file was created in Word and saved as a Word document.
   d. Whether the file was saved in ASCII format.

3. The Hosts file can contain entries mapping NetBIOS _____ to IP addresses.
   a. clients
   b. ports
   c. interfaces
   d. names

4. The Lmhosts file must be saved as _____ text.
   a. Winn32
   b. Binary
   c. UNICODE
   d. ASCII

5. The Lmhosts file allows you to preload up to _____ entries in the NetBIOS name cache in Windows 2000.
   a. 250
   b. 50
   c. 150
   d. 100

6. The correct syntax for preloading an entry from the Lmhosts file into the NetBIOS name cache is:
   a. *NetBIOS name; IP address; #Pre*
   b. *#PRE NetBIOS name; IP address*
   c. *IP address; #PRE; Netbios name*
   d. *IP address; Netbios name; #PRE*

7. The syntax for placing an entry into the Hosts file is _____.
   a. *FQDN, IP address*
   b. *Remark, FQDN, IP*
   c. *IP address; hostname*
   d. *hostname; IP*

2.5.2 Troubleshoot name resolution problems by using the nbtstat, ipconfig, nslookup, and netdiag commands.

NAME-RESOLUTION TROUBLESHOOTING TOOLS

UNDERSTANDING THE OBJECTIVE

Tools exist in Windows 2000 to assist you in troubleshooting name-resolution issues in your network infrastructure. These are all command-line utilities and can be be scripted for use in automated processes.

WHAT YOU REALLY NEED TO KNOW

♦ The nbstat command shows you the status of your current IP connections and can also display protocol statistics about those connections. You can add several command-line switches after the nbstat command. With nbstat, you can release a client name registration with the WINS server and then refresh the registration.

♦ The ipconfig command can also be used to troubleshoot name-resolution issues. The ipconfig command allows you to view current IP settings, either for every connected adapter or by a specific adapter name. After you view the information, ipconfig allows you to perform some troubleshooting. You may release and renew DHCP leases for all DHCP-enabled adapters or you may release and renew a specific adapter. The ipconfig command also allows the tool user to flush the DNS resolver cache as needed and, as a separate function, allows use of the /registerdns switch, which forces registration of the computer's hostname and IP address with the designated DNS server.

♦ The nslookup command is a powerful tool for an administrator dealing with DNS servers. The nslookup command has a fairly lengthy list of command-line switches that can be used for troubleshooting DNS. These switches allow the administrator to perform tasks ranging from a simple name lookup against DNS to more complex queries against the DNS server or servers. The nslookup command allows the administrator to choose which DNS server to query and also allows that DNS server to be selected as the primary DNS server. The nslookup command can also be used to return, either to the screen or to a file, a list of all records in the database.

♦ The netdiag command is a powerful tool that allows extensive testing of your network infrastructure components. There are 25 separate tests that can be run, ranging from a test of your browser service to a test of your WAN configuration. The netdiag command will return diagnostic information, including the processor type and installed hotfixes. Many command-line options are available. One option, the /v switch (verbose), returns detailed information concerning the status of all protocols running on the system.

OBJECTIVES ON THE JOB

The nbstat, ipconfig, nslookup, and netdiag commands help resolve name-resolution issues. Each one returns a different set of information that the administrator can use to troubleshoot name resolution in the network environment.

PRACTICE TEST QUESTIONS

1. **What command allows the administrator to test Kerberos for proper operation?**
   a. nbtstat
   b. nslookup
   c. ipconfig
   d. netdiag

2. **You need to produce a listing of all records contained in the DNS zone of a child domain. What command should you use?**
   a. nbstat
   b. nslookup
   c. ipconfig
   d. netdiag

3. **If you need to force reregistration with your WINS server, what tool should you use?**
   a. nbtstat
   b. nslookup
   c. ipconfig
   d. netdiag

4. **You have a computer that is physically multihomed with five network interfaces. Each network interface uses DHCP for its IP addressing information. You must refresh the DHCP lease on a specific card, yet you do not want to release the other four leases. What command should you use?**
   a. nbtstat
   b. nslookup
   c. ipconfig
   d. netdiag

5. **You have a Windows 2000 server that has had several hot fixes installed, but no one in your office remembers which ones were installed. What command will show a list of installed hot fixes?**
   a. nbtstat
   b. nslookup
   c. ipconfig
   d. netdiag

6. **You want to purge the local DNS resolver cache on a Windows 2000 Professional computer. What command should you use to accomplish this?**
   a. nbtstat
   b. nslookup
   c. ipconfig
   d. netdiag

7. **The nbtstat command shows you the status of your current _____ connections.**
   a. IP
   b. NetBIOS
   c. DNS
   d. DDNS

2.5.3 Create and configure a Hosts file for troubleshooting name resolution problems.

THE HOSTS FILE EXPLAINED

UNDERSTANDING THE OBJECTIVE

The Hosts file is a useful, easy-to-create tool. Before DNS existed, the Hosts file was used for hostname-to-IP-address translation and mapping. Since the advent of DNS, the Hosts file can be used for Hostname resolution when a DNS server is unavailable.

WHAT YOU REALLY NEED TO KNOW

◆ The Hosts file is a text file that contains hostname/FQDN-to-IP-address mappings. It allows the administrator to create a local version of what is basically a simple DNS server, with the restriction that Hosts file entries must be created manually. The Hosts file can introduce problems into your network, because of issues involving the creation of the file, and name/IP conflicts caused by the use of the Hosts file itself.

◆ There are constraints associated with the creation of the Hosts file. The Hosts file in Windows 2000 must always be saved to this path: \%SYSTEMROOT%\SYSTEM32\DRIVERS\ETC. The file must never be saved with an extension of any kind. An extension will render the file unusable. The file must be saved as ASCII text. If it is saved as any other file format, including UNICODE, the file will be unusable. The Windows Notepad tool can be used to create the Hosts file; however, for more consistent results, use the Edit.exe tool in Windows 2000. You should do this because Notepad can save files as ASCII or as UNICODE, while the EDIT tool understands only ASCII; UNICODE is not possible.

◆ After you decide how to create the file, you must collect the information to be placed in the file itself. You need the hostnames or FQDNs of computers to be placed in the Hosts file. Using the Hosts file does not restrict you to Windows 2000 computers. The records you are adding are A records.

◆ When you have the computer information, begin entering it. The syntax is this: *IP Address hostname comment.* At least one blank space must separate each value. The Hosts file will support CNAME records as well as standard A records. If you need to make two entries using different cases, this is also supported. The Hosts file will support the use of NetBIOS names and IP addresses for name resolution. This is important because, in a Microsoft environment, the NetBIOS name is almost always the Hostname. This simplifies the overhead. Be aware that a Hosts file will be read before a DNS server will be queried. This may cause name-resolution issues in your network.

OBJECTIVES ON THE JOB

A Hosts file provides a small version of DNS on the local computers that have been configured to use it. Using a Hosts file should not disrupt your network.

PRACTICE TEST QUESTIONS

1. **The Hosts file _____.**
   a. contains hostname/FQDN-to-NIC-address mappings
   b. can contain canonical entries
   c. cannot contain manual entries
   d. is never saved to the SystemDriver folder

2. **The Hosts file in Windows 2000 must always be saved to the path _____.**
   a. \%SYSTEMROOT%\DRIVERS\SYSTEM32\ETC
   b. \%SYSTEMROOT%\SYSTEM32\DRIVERS\ETC
   c. \%SYSTEMROOT%\DRIVERS\ETC
   d. \SYSTEMROOT\SYSTEM32\DRIVERS\ETC

3. **The Hosts file is the original version of what network service?**
   a. WINS
   b. DNS
   c. DHCP
   d. NBNS

4. **When creating a Hosts file, only computers that use the _____ protocol can be included.**
   a. NetBIOS
   b. IPX/SPX
   c. IP
   d. DLC

5. **You have created a Hosts file on a user's computer. The file does not work. You have checked the path to the file and the contents of the file and have verified that the file does not have an extension. What should you check next?**
   a. whether the user has the correct IP subnet information
   b. whether the Hosts file was not saved as ASCII text
   c. whether the user has been configured through the Registry to not use a Hosts file
   d. whether DHCP settings are overriding the contents of the Hosts file

6. **The default entry for every Hosts file is _____ and _____.**
   a. local name, IP address
   b. IP address, local name
   c. loopback address, localhost
   d. loopback address, hostname

2.5.4 Create and configure an Lmhosts file for troubleshooting name resolution problems.

THE HOSTS FILE EXPLAINED

UNDERSTANDING THE OBJECTIVE

Before WINS existed, the Lmhosts file was used for NetBIOS name-to-IP-address translation and mapping. The Lmhosts file can be a useful tool and is easy to create.

WHAT YOU REALLY NEED TO KNOW

- ◆ The Lmhosts file is functionally similar to the Hosts file; however, there are important differences. The similarities are the methods of creation and the rules governing file types and file extensions. The differences in the two files occur because the Lmhosts file is programmatic, and because, although the Hosts file can contain NetBIOS names in addition to host names, the Lmhosts file is restricted to NetBIOS names only.

- ◆ The process of creating the Lmhosts file and its location on the computer is exactly the same as for the Hosts file. However, the Lmhosts file gives an administrator increased control over the entries in the file. Microsoft has placed a sample Lmhosts file in the ETC directory. Create your file as a new file. Do not use the sample file to create your actual Lmhosts file. The Lmhosts file is read from top to bottom, and the sample file contains several lines of commented text, which slows down the reading of the file.

- ◆ The Lmhosts file can be used to preload the local NetBIOS name cache with up to 100 entries. These entries should be placed at the bottom of the Lmhosts file so that they are not reread into the name cache every time a lookup is performed. The command for preloading is #PRE. All programming commands in the Lmhosts file are case sensitive. Another useful command in the Lmhosts file is #DOM. This command designates a domain controller for the local computer. The two commands can be used together as #PRE #DOM. This will preload a specific domain controller into the local NetBIOS name cache.

- ◆ The Lmhosts file can also hold commands that will redirect the computer to a centrally based network Lmhosts file. For an administrator, this means that you would not need 500 separate copies of the Lmhosts file. You would need only a few copies on network-accessible computers, perhaps domain controllers, and instructions in the local version of the Lmhosts file to find those copies for NetBIOS name resolution. The Lmhosts file also supports the use of special characters to designate computers holding specific resources in your environment, such as special application servers or other computer types.

OBJECTIVES ON THE JOB

The Lmhosts file fulfills the same purpose as the Hosts file. It provides a local alternative to your network-based DNS and WINS name-resolution technologies.

PRACTICE TEST QUESTIONS

1. **The Lmhosts file _____.**
   a. is case sensitive
   b. is non-programmatic
   c. can contain host names
   d. duplicates the Hosts file

2. **The Lmhosts file is restricted to only _____ names.**
   a. Fat32
   b. NetBIOS
   c. hexadecimal
   d. PNP

3. **The Lmhosts file is the original version of what network service?**
   a. WINS
   b. DNS
   c. DHCP
   d. NBNS

4. **When creating an Lmhosts file, what additional functionality can you include? (Choose all that apply.)**
   a. a preloaded NetBIOS name cache
   b. designated special purpose application servers
   c. designated DNS computers
   d. preloaded DLC hosts

5. **You have created an Lmhosts file on a user's computer. The user is reporting problems with slow resource access. You have checked the contents of the Lmhosts file, the extension on the file, and the file type. What should you check next?**
   a. that the file was saved to the correct path
   b. that you created a new Lmhosts file and did not use the template
   c. that the user has the Enable Lmhosts lookup feature enabled in the IP properties on the WINS tab
   d. that the #BEGIN_ALTERNATE section is correct

6. **The default entry for every Lmhosts file is _____.**
   a. local name and IP address
   b. IP address and NetBIOS name
   c. loopback address and localhost
   d. none of the above; there are no defaults

7. **The command in the Lmhosts file to use a network-based Lmhosts file is _____.**
   a. #BEGIN_ALTERNATE
   b. #SEEK_NETWORK
   c. CNAME DNS_SERVER SERVERNAME
   d. Such a command does not exist.

Section 3

Managing, Securing, and Troubleshooting Servers and Client Computers

3.1 Install and configure server and client computer hardware.

CONFIGURING HARDWARE

UNDERSTANDING THE OBJECTIVE

Unlike previous versions of the Windows NT platform, enhancements and modifications to the basic Windows 2000 operating system support a wider range of hardware devices. One of the most significant improvements is the addition of a **PnP** component. Also, Microsoft has implemented other additions and improvements to basic hardware support to markedly improve the overall computing experience and to lower **TCO** for the administrator.

WHAT YOU REALLY NEED TO KNOW

- ◆ The configuration of hardware on a Windows 2000 computer, either the Server or Professional version, can be very simple if the hardware to be installed supports the PnP standard. Slight problems may be encountered on the Server platform because it was not designed to support the range of hardware options that the Professional platform supports.
- ◆ The first step in installing hardware on a Windows 2000 computer is to use the Windows 2000 hardware qualifier tool to ascertain the hardware is supported by the operating system. After the hardware qualifier tool has returned its report, you should check the hardware compatibility list to make certain that the hardware qualifier is returning accurate results.
- ◆ The Device Manager is the primary tool that administrators use to configure hardware devices on Windows 2000. This tool was designed to be accessible only by the administrator or members of the Administrators group. It can also be accessed by a non-administrator using the "Run as" function in Windows 2000. However, this person must know the administrator password.
- ◆ Another improvement to the Windows 2000 platform is the use of digitally signed drivers for the hardware devices installed on Windows 2000. As an administrator, you can configure different levels of blocking for unsigned device drivers. This setting can also be implemented as a GPO in AD. This protection of the device drivers extends to a protected cache on Windows 2000 computers where uncorrupted copies of the system DLLs are held.
- ◆ Windows 2000 has several tools to troubleshoot the problem of unsigned drivers being installed into the operating system. One of them, the File Signature Verification tool, can search the operating system for unsigned drivers. Another tool can detect corruption of the kernel drivers in the operating system.
- ◆ A significant advantage of Windows 2000 over previous NT versions is that it fully supports the PnP architecture that was introduced with Windows 98. For you, as an administrator, this means that device installation is now simplified because the operating system itself can detect most newly installed hardware and load the correct drivers to use this hardware.

OBJECTIVES ON THE JOB

Windows 2000 provides the most comprehensive support to date of any Microsoft OS in terms of protecting key operating system files and supporting the installation of device drivers. The new PnP support provides more options for users and administrators in terms of hardware that can be installed to enhance the computing environment. Also, the implementation of digitally signed and tested DLLs allows the administrator to control DLL installations in the environment.

PRACTICE TEST QUESTIONS

1. **To protect the Windows 2000 operating system from untested and potentially unsafe device drivers, Microsoft has developed the process of driver _____. (Choose all that apply.)**
   - a. testing
   - b. certification
   - c. inspection
   - d. replacement

2. **Microsoft has developed a program that applies _____ to drivers that are approved for use on Windows 2000.**
   - a. antivirus protection
   - b. driver integrity checks
   - c. digital signatures
   - d. 128-bit encryption

3. **Windows 2000 features an implementation of _____.**
   - a. virtual device drivers
   - b. the El Torito specification
   - c. Windows 98 VXXD
   - d. PnP

4. **As an administrator, you can restrict the installation of unsigned DLLs by using _____. (Choose all that apply.)**
   - a. local policies
   - b. Device Manager
   - c. AD policies
   - d. Driver Manager

5. **Only drivers signed by _____ can be installed in Windows 2000.**
   - a. independent software vendors
   - b. Microsoft
   - c. the CertSign utility
   - d. 3DES encryption

6. **Before building a new Windows 2000 server, you should perform some preliminary steps to support your hardware devices. Besides obtaining the appropriate drivers, you should also consult the _____.**
   - a. Microsoft TechNet site for hardware problems
   - b. Windows 2000 Hardware Qualifier tool
   - c. manufacturer's Web site FAQs
   - d. instruction manual of the device

7. **Using a local security policy for installing drivers, Windows 2000 can be configured with the _____ option. (Choose all that apply.)**
   - a. Ignore
   - b. Block
   - c. Verify
   - d. Warn

3.1.1 Verify hardware compatibility by using the qualifier tools.

HARDWARE DISCOVERY

UNDERSTANDING THE OBJECTIVE

After you decide to update your servers and client computers to Windows 2000, you must determine if they can support the installation of Windows 2000.

WHAT YOU REALLY NEED TO KNOW

◆ Windows 2000 has very specific hardware requirements regarding which CPUs are supported and the amount of physical RAM available on each system. In addition, you must check your peripheral devices—network adapters, video cards, CD-ROM drives, and other physical components—to determine their compatibility with the Windows 2000 platform. Microsoft has published an **HCL** for the administrator who wants to upgrade systems. These guidelines indicate minimum hardware requirements.

◆ If you plan to upgrade computers that already have an operating system, along with applications and data on the hard drives, you need to perform additional planning and testing before actually installing Windows 2000 in your production environment. Fortunately, Microsoft has provided a Web site and a tool to assist you.

◆ The Web site is the Microsoft Hardware Compatibility Web site, located at *http://windows.microsoft.com/windows2000/reskit/webresources*. There are two versions of this Web site: one for Windows 2000 Professional and one for Windows 2000 Server. The site is a database of hardware that is supported on the Windows 2000 platform. If your device is listed on the Web site, Windows 2000 will recognize and use the device. If the device is not listed, it is not supported and it may not function using Windows 2000. However, you may be able to download drivers from the manufacturer's Web site. A version of the HCL is located on the installation media for Windows 2000, but it may be outdated.

◆ After you have checked the HCL, you may use a hardware-testing tool to generate a report on compatible hardware on the machine you are installing. The tool can be started by using the standard installation file for Windows 2000, WINNT32, and it is launched using the /checkupgradeonly command-line switch. This tool runs from inside the OS currently on the computer to be upgraded and checks for potential hardware and software problems. There are four sections tested for compatibility. They are MS-DOS Configuration, Plug and Play Hardware, Software Incompatible with Windows 2000, and Software to Reinstall.

◆ The use of the HCL and the /checkupgradeonly command-line switch on the Windows 2000 installation media should tell the administrator whether particular computers will support Windows 2000. Additional compatibility tools are available from Microsoft. You should also consult the Windows 2000 Professional and Server Resource Kits to determine the correct upgrade paths from the older OSs to Windows 2000.

OBJECTIVES ON THE JOB

To effectively install Windows 2000, you must determine if your computer hardware will support the OS. You should be completely familiar with these requirements before you begin upgrading your equipment. If you are in a production environment, you should build a test lab and experiment with and test different installation techniques and hardware combinations.

PRACTICE TEST QUESTIONS

1. **Windows 2000 can be installed as an upgrade on which of the following operating systems? (Choose all that apply.)**
   a. Windows NT 3.5
   b. Windows ME
   c. Windows NT 4.0 Enterprise Server
   d. Windows 98

2. **Which of the following is not a separate Windows 2000 platform?**
   a. Windows 2000 Professional
   b. Windows 2000 Server
   c. Windows 2000 Advanced Server
   d. Windows 2000 Terminal Server

3. **The /checkupgradeonly command-line switch is run with which executable?**
   a. WINNT.EXE.
   b. SETUP.COM
   c. INSTALL.BAT
   d. WINNT32.EXE

4. **The HCL is on the Support CD that comes with every copy of Windows 2000 Server. However, this copy of the HCL should generally not be used because _____. (Choose all that apply.)**
   a. it is specifically for hardware made in the United States, and not hardware manufactured in other countries
   b. the hardware listed on this HCL version is not production equipment, but only development and test equipment
   c. this HCL version is current only for the date that the CD was created and might be out of date
   d. it does not cover the Terminal Server and Advanced Server OSs

5. **_____ provides links to Microsoft Web sites that can help with hardware and software issues.**
   a. /checkupgradeonly
   b. HCL
   c. Windows Upgrade
   d. OS Upgrade

6. **/checkupgradeonly can be used with _____.**
   a. WINNT32.EXE
   b. WINNT.EXE
   c. SETUP32.exe
   d. WINNT32.EXE /b

7. **You have decided to upgrade your Windows NT 3.51 domain controller to Windows 2000 Server. The domain controller has applications and data stored on it. How should you check for compatibility with Windows 2000? (Choose all that apply.)**
   a. Consult the Windows NT 3.51 Resource Kit for upgrade options.
   b. Consult the Windows 2000 Resource Kit for upgrade options.
   c. Use WINNT.EXE /checkupgradeonly.
   d. Use WINNT32.EXE /checkupgradeonly.

3.1.2 Configure driver signing options.

INSTALLING DRIVERS

UNDERSTANDING THE OBJECTIVE

Installing untested hardware drivers into a Microsoft operating system can cause problems. In the past, an administrator had to spend a great amount of time dealing with these drivers. With Windows 2000, Microsoft has implemented a new management technique that allows the administrator to control the introduction of unknown and potentially damaging device drivers.

WHAT YOU REALLY NEED TO KNOW

- ◆ Driver signing was introduced to prevent users from installing untested and potentially damaging drivers from various sources because those drivers might negatively impact the Windows 2000 operating system. All drivers written by Microsoft for Windows 2000 have been tested and verified as safe to use with the operating system. Also, any third-party software company or developer that wants to obtain and use the Windows 2000 branding on their product must submit the drivers to Microsoft for verification. If Microsoft determines that the drivers are safe for use with Windows 2000, it digitally signs the driver and returns it to the developer for inclusion in their application.

- ◆ This testing process gives you, as the administrator, peace of mind in knowing that Microsoft-branded drivers are safe for Windows 2000. You can also check driver files from third-party vendors that may have declined or neglected to provide these driver files to Microsoft for testing. Using the 'Driver Signing Options' in the Windows 2000 operating system, you can control, on a machine-by-machine basis or as a GPO in AD, the computer's behavior when an attempted installation of an unsigned driver is detected. Based on the configuration of three settings, you may allow unrestricted driver installations, warn about unsigned drivers but allow Microsoft-signed drivers, or prohibit all unsigned drivers.

- ◆ Three settings are used for configuring driver signing. The first setting is Ignore. This allows the installation of all drivers regardless of the signature on the file. This is obviously the least desirable option. The second setting is Warn. This setting causes a warning message to appear when someone attempts to install an unsigned driver. The user may choose to continue the process or stop the installation. The third setting and the one that will probably appeal to most administrators is Block. This setting blocks the installation of unsigned drivers on the Windows 2000 platform. If applied as a GPO in AD, this can be a powerful and far-reaching option. With this setting configured, only drivers signed by Microsoft will be allowed to install.

- ◆ The ability to control drivers and the existence of a GPO that restricts access to only specific Web sites for file downloads can help to reduce your TCO. You will have a lower incidence of operating system corruption caused by unauthorized software installations and their accompanying drivers.

OBJECTIVES ON THE JOB

This new ability to block the installation of unsigned drivers can be an important management technique for the Windows 2000 administrator. You now can prevent your clients from browsing the Internet and downloading and installing unsigned and potentially unsafe applications, which could damage the OS or cause a virus infection.

PRACTICE TEST QUESTIONS

1. The digital signatures attached to Microsoft-signed drivers are an example of what technology?
   - a. PKI
   - b. EFS
   - c. IPSec
   - d. SSL

2. If the computer device driver signing settings have been set to _____, the client still can install unsigned drivers. (Choose all that apply.)
   - a. Warn
   - b. Verify
   - c. Ignore
   - d. Permit

3. A device driver signing setting of _____ blocks all drivers from being installed. (Choose all that apply.)
   - a. Deny
   - b. Block
   - c. None
   - d. No Access

4. A client calls your help desk to complain about an issue encountered while downloading files from a Web site. While performing the download, the client was prompted many times about installing drivers. The client wants the computer configured to stop these prompts. Where can you configure these settings? (Choose all that apply.)
   - a. Control Panel\Network
   - b. My Computer\Manage
   - c. My Computer\Properties\Hardware tab
   - d. Control Panel\System

5. Even DLLs created by Microsoft will prompt the user for _____ if the computer has been so configured.
   - a. permission
   - b. path
   - c. the installation directory
   - d. account

6. DLL is an acronym for _____.
   - a. Distributed Logical Layer
   - b. Dynamic Link Layer
   - c. Dynamic Link Library
   - d. Dynamic Linked Library

7. What action may cause the Driver Warning dialog box to appear for a client? (Choose all that apply.)
   - a. changing the IP address
   - b. copying files
   - c. installing a new print device
   - d. installing a digital camera

OBJECTIVES

3.1.3 Verify digital signatures on existing driver files.

DIGITAL FILE SIGNATURE VERIFICATION

UNDERSTANDING THE OBJECTIVE

Windows 2000 provides the administrator with a tool to verify the authenticity of drivers used on the Windows 2000 platform. This tool looks for the digital signatures that Microsoft provided to third-party software developers as part of the Windows 2000 Application Certification process. The digital signatures attached to these files prove that these files have been tested and certified for use on the Windows 2000 platform.

WHAT YOU REALLY NEED TO KNOW

- ◆ The tool used to check for the validity of digital signatures is **sigverif**. It is located in the SYSTEM32 directory on any Windows 2000 computer and is launched from the Run line. This tool checks the digital signatures of all drivers on the system. When launched, it opens to a small GUI window on the desktop. The tool can run in a remote session using Terminal Server, provided the appropriate permissions for the Terminal Server account have been specified.
- ◆ The tool has three basic functions. First, it views the certificates attached to each file to check for signs of tampering since the file was certified. Second, the tool allows the administrator to search for signed files in a specific location. Third, the tool allows the administrator to search for unsigned files in a specific location.
- ◆ The sigverif tool also features an Advanced tab, which allows the administrator to configure logging options and the level of search to conduct. The available search levels include either a complete search of the entire machine or a search against a specific location of the machine.
- ◆ The information that the sigverif tool checks consists of the filename, the modification date, the version number, the signed status, and the location of the file. When the search concludes, a Signature Verification Results box is placed on the desktop of the computer. This box shows the total number of files searched and the number of signed files, unsigned files, and files not scanned. It also shows the administrator the files on the system that have not been digitally signed. The tool also produces a log file that the administrator can view to verify the signature status of drivers on the system.
- ◆ The sigverif tool is used in combination with Windows 2000 Signature Checking, which the administrator can enable using the driver signing options. The DLL files that are checked in this process encompass the drivers needed for all hardware components on a Windows 2000 computer and can be broken down into these categories: hard disk controller, keyboard, modem, mouse, multimedia device, network adapters, printers, SCSI adapters, smart card readers, and video displays.

OBJECTIVES ON THE JOB

The ability to verify the digital signatures attached to installed drivers on the Windows 2000 platform can help you maintain Windows 2000 computers. You can verify that only drivers tested by Microsoft are installed on the system. You also can look for files without Microsoft signatures and determine what devices they support. Using this tool to detect and report on unauthorized drivers can help support your corporate environment because you can maintain tighter control on the activities of your supported users and on any software they may attempt to install on their computers.

PRACTICE TEST QUESTIONS

1. Windows 2000 drivers on the _____ need to be signed, even though Microsoft provided these files.
   - a. Microsoft Web site
   - b. installation media
   - c. application installation media
   - d. computer

2. The sigverif tool has _____ that will modify the operation of the tool.
   - a. different modes of operation
   - b. several command line switches
   - c. a GUI version
   - d. a DOS version

3. The sigverif tool can be used in conjunction with _____ options.
   - a. configured driver signing
   - b. AD GPOs
   - c. IP
   - d. Kerberos

4. If you suspect that some drivers have been corrupted and that their digital signatures are damaged, you should _____.
   - a. run the Driver Verifier to check for errors in the kernel-mode drivers
   - b. delete the drivers and manually reinstall the files
   - c. run the sigverif tool in certificate repair mode to rebuild the certificates
   - d. none of the above

5. The _____ tool can be configured to run during the system startup process and is used to verify driver signing.
   - a. Signer
   - b. sigverif
   - c. Verifier
   - d. Driver Signer

6. As an administrator, you want to run the sigverif tool on your Windows 2000 servers using a Terminal Server session. How can you do this? (Choose all that apply.)
   - a. Add the EnableRemoteSIGVERIFScan entry as a D_WORD type to the Registry of the server to be checked.
   - b. Assign the TsInternetUser account to the Domain Admins account in AD Users and Computers.
   - c. Remotely run the sigverif tool.
   - d. Open a Terminal Server session with the remote server and use the tool.

7. The WHQL program was established by Microsoft to _____.
   - a. verify the integrity of SYS files
   - b. test drivers that application developers have written for use with Windows 2000
   - c. test Registry settings required to apply new device drivers
   - d. apply digital signatures to approved device drivers for Windows 2000

3.1.4 Configure operating system support for legacy hardware devices.

LEGACY HARDWARE IMPLEMENTATIONS

UNDERSTANDING THE OBJECTIVE

One of the many operating system improvements in Windows 2000 is its ability to use PnP hardware. Windows 9x users previously enjoyed this feature, but it was unavailable to Windows NT 4.0 users. If you install new hardware that supports the PnP functionality, you usually don't need to manually configure these devices. However, if you have older hardware to install or use, you may be required to configure the devices for support under Windows 2000.

WHAT YOU REALLY NEED TO KNOW

◆ There are several techniques that an administrator can use to enable legacy hardware support in Windows 2000. Probably the simplest method is to perform an in-place upgrade of the operating system. This means starting with a Windows NT 4.0 computer and upgrading the OS to Windows 2000. This process upgrades the OS but does not remove directories. If the device ran under Windows NT 4.0, it should (with a few exceptions) continue to run under Windows 2000.

◆ If you cannot perform the in-place upgrade and a completely new installation is required, you still have options. You should consult the Web site for the manufacturer of the device and search for any documentation dealing with legacy hardware. If this process doesn't help, your next option is to configure the device manually.

◆ Several tools exist for manual configuration. The first tool to consider should be the Add/Remove Hardware Wizard located in the Control Panel. It attempts an automated installation of the hardware. It's best to let Windows automatically detect devices, but the administrator also can select devices from a list. When this latter option is used, the administrator has more flexibility in choosing the correct device.

◆ The next best option would be to use the Device Manager in the Computer Management console. To use the Device Manager, you must be logged on as an administrator or as a member of the Administrators group. The next step is to open Device Manager and begin the installation. If the installation completes but the device does not function, you might have to manually configure the device settings using Device Manager. You can adjust the **IRQ**, the **DMA**, the I/O port addresses, and the memory ranges for hardware devices. The Device Manager will alert you to settings that conflict with other settings on the system.

◆ Part of your task as a systems administrator is to enable legacy hardware support for downlevel operating systems, not just Windows 2000. You therefore must know and understand which Microsoft operating systems support which kinds of hardware. Remember that while Windows 98 and Windows ME can support USB devices, Windows 95 and Windows NT 4.0 cannot.

OBJECTIVES ON THE JOB

The support of legacy hardware on Windows 2000 can be a complex task. However, if you understand basic hardware configuration principles and settings and understand how to use the Device Manager to configure these settings, you should be successful in enabling these devices.

PRACTICE TEST QUESTIONS

1. Hardware settings that may need to be reconfigured for legacy devices include the _____ settings. (Choose all that apply.)
   a. IRQ
   b. ECP
   c. DMA
   d. CMOS

2. **Legacy hardware can include _____.**
   a. print devices
   b. external drives
   c. PCMIA cards
   d. MMF hard drives

3. Installation of legacy hardware for _____ may be possible using Windows 95 PnP drivers.
   a. Windows 2000
   b. Windows NT 4.0
   c. Windows ME
   d. Windows MS DOS

4. **Windows _____ supports a simple form of PnP.**
   a. MS DOS
   b. 95
   c. NT 4.0
   d. CE

5. **PnP allows the OS to configure hardware settings for PnP devices. What is the primary hardware component that PnP supplants?**
   a. CMOS configuration
   b. hardware jumpers
   c. FlashBIOS updates
   d. motherboard jumper configuration

6. One of the options in the _____ allows the administrator to update drivers.
   a. Computer Management snap-in
   b. Control Panel/System tab
   c. System/Advanced Settings tab
   d. Device Manager console

7. **You receive a call at your help desk from a user who is trying to install a new device in a Windows 2000 Professional computer. The user cannot run the Device Manager tool. How can you allow the user to run the Device Manager while still logged on?**
   a. Have the user open Device Manager from the Run line using the switch /u.
   b. Have the user run the Device Manager using the Runas command.
   c. Have the user log off as a user and log on as a local administrator.
   d. Have the user call their local administrator for support.

3.2 Troubleshoot starting servers and client computers. Tools and methodologies include Safe Mode, Recovery Console, and parallel installations.

STARTING, RECOVERING, AND RESTORING

UNDERSTANDING THE OBJECTIVE

Windows 2000 provides the administrator new capabilities to log the startup of Windows 2000 computers. The Windows 2000 OS also provides the administrator new capabilities to recover the system in the event of a catastrophic failure. The administrator can use Safe Mode, the Recovery Console, and parallel installation.

WHAT YOU REALLY NEED TO KNOW

- ♦ Windows 2000 provides new tools that did not exist under Windows NT 4.0. To monitor the startup process, Windows 2000 now supports a startup log file and a Safe Mode boot option, something that Windows 9x has provided since its inception.
- ♦ The Safe Mode boot option provides the user and the administrator different start options, including a VGA start mode, a Safe Mode without network support, and a Console Mode for troubleshooting at the command prompt without loading the GUI interface. If you must support devices in a Safe Mode boot session that are not normally part of this process, you can add those components to the Registry settings that control the Safe Mode boot settings.
- ♦ Another capability of the Windows 2000 OS is the Recovery Console. This tool, which does not install by default, allows the administrator to boot from the Windows 2000 installation media and run a Windows 2000 session directly from the CD. After the Recovery Console session has been started, the administrator can manipulate files and folders, copy files from removable media to the hard drive, or copy files from the hard drive to removable media. Using the Recovery Console, the administrator can attempt the recovery of a failed Windows 2000 installation. The Recovery Console can also be used on a Windows NT 4.0 installation.
- ♦ The administrator can also consider a parallel installation of Windows 2000 as a recovery tool. The success of this technique depends on the feasibility of installing a second copy of Windows 2000 onto the failed installation and accessing the required files and folders from the new installation of the OS. The parallel installation can access all files and folders except for those resources protected with EFS.
- ♦ As always, the key to recovering any system lies in having complete, up-to-date system backups of the OS and important data on the system. The administrator should also know the different methods required to restore systems using backups from the OS, including the methods and data from the AD itself.
- ♦ The administrator must also remember that only specific Microsoft operating systems support the Safe Mode boot process. Windows 95, Windows 98, Windows ME, and Windows 2000 do support the Safe Mode boot process. Windows NT 4.0 does not support this ability. That is one reason why the emergency repair process may be used more frequently on the Windows NT 4.0 platform.

OBJECTIVES ON THE JOB

An important job for the administrator is troubleshooting the startup of Windows 2000 computers. This can be accomplished using the Safe Mode boot process, the Recovery Console, or other tools in Windows 2000. The administrator can also use tools for performing a system restore.

PRACTICE TEST QUESTIONS

1. The Windows 2000 _____ can be used to recover a failed Windows NT 4.0 installation.
   - a. Recovery Console CD
   - b. Winnt32.exe tool
   - c. OS Recovery tool
   - d. emergency repair process

2. The Recovery Console is _____ by default on a Windows 2000 Professional platform, and is an optional installation on Windows 2000 Server.
   - a. secured
   - b. disabled
   - c. not installed
   - d. restricted to use only by the administrator

3. To perform a parallel installation on a Windows 2000 platform, the user must have _____ if the computer belongs to a Windows 2000 AD domain.
   - a. local administrator permissions
   - b. the Recover System GPO assignment
   - c. Enterprise Admin membership
   - d. the Install OS GPO permission

4. If a Windows 2000 server has been configured as an Enterprise Root CA, the administrator must use the _____ command to back up the CA database.
   - a. backup/system state
   - b. backup/CA
   - c. cabackup
   - d. ntbackup /ca /s

5. To use the VGA troubleshooting process in a Windows 2000 startup, the _____ mode should be used.
   - a. Safe Mode/Base Video
   - b. Base Video
   - c. Safe Mode/VGA
   - d. Safe Mode/Video Troubleshooting

6. To fine-tune the Safe Mode boot process, the administrator can add additional services by using the _____ tool.
   - a. Safe Mode editing
   - b. REGEDIT32
   - c. REGEDT32
   - d. Notepad with the SAFEBOOT.INI

3.2.1 Interpret the startup log file.

SYSTEM STARTUP TROUBLESHOOTING

UNDERSTANDING THE OBJECTIVE

A new feature of Windows 2000 is the ability to create a log file during the startup process if Windows 2000 will not start correctly. This did not exist in Windows NT 4.0 and is an important new tool for administrators trying to troubleshoot Windows 2000 startup problems.

WHAT YOU REALLY NEED TO KNOW

◆ If a Windows 2000 computer does not start correctly, the administrator can start the machine in Safe Mode for troubleshooting purposes. Safe Mode can be toggled by pressing F8 during the system start. After this key is pressed, the user is presented with several startup options, including the option to Enable Boot Logging.

◆ After Boot Logging is enabled, the machine continues to start and records the load status of all files required by the operating system for startup as the files attempt to load on the system. After the system starts, the log file is saved to the %systemroot% directory under the name **Ntbtlog.txt**. It can be viewed using any text editor and is approximately 10-15 KB in size. The Ntbtlog.txt file is created every time Safe Mode is selected for starting the computer.

◆ The Ntbtlog.txt file can be used several different ways. The simplest method is to use the Safe Mode on a nearby computer and then compare the two log files, looking for differences. This could also be combined with the Resource Kit DRIVERS tool, which will create a list showing all drivers currently loaded on the system.

◆ After the information from the Ntbtlog.txt file has been generated, it must be interpreted. The log file is simple in format, consisting of only two columns. The first column shows the load status of the file, and the second column shows the path (in some cases) of the loaded files. As you examine the first entries of the Ntbtlog.txt file, you will see that the first file recorded as loading on the system is NTOSKRNL.EXE. Files loaded before this file are not recorded in the log.

◆ The Ntbtlog.txt file is a standard text file. As such, it can be imported into Excel or Access for data analysis or archiving. If a new hardware device were installed on the system and now the computer either no longer boots or crashes while booting, the use of the Ntbtlog.txt file might help in troubleshooting.

◆ Windows NT 4.0 also supports the /SOS switch, which can be installed into the Boot.ini file for use when the computer starts up. This switch lists the drivers being loaded on the system by NTDETECT.COM. Windows 2000 supports this option automatically when the Safe Mode – Boot option is enabled on the computer. The checked build of the NTDETECT.COM file is another troubleshooting tool administrators can use. This tool is available on the installation media as NTDETECT.CHK. This file shows the processing of NTDETECT as it discovers system hardware. To use the file, replace the standard version of NTDETECT.COM with this new tool and rename the file from NTDETECT.CHK to NTDETECT.COM.

OBJECTIVES ON THE JOB

Microsoft allows the computer's user, not just the administrator, to record in a log file the required files for a system start in Windows 2000. With this information and the information from other utilities, the administrator can see which files did and did not load during the Windows 2000 startup process. This data can also be collected for archiving or analysis.

PRACTICE TEST QUESTIONS

1. The Ntbtlog.txt file begins collecting information when the _____ file loads.
   - a. BOOTSEC.DOS
   - b. NTDETECT.COM
   - c. NTBOOTDD.SYS
   - d. NTOSKRNL.EXE

2. The Ntbtlog.txt file is saved as a _____ formatted file.
   - a. txt
   - b. wpd
   - c. mdb
   - d. xls

3. You press the _____ to enter Safe Mode.
   - a. Alt key
   - b. F10 key
   - c. F8 key
   - d. CTRL+F8 keys

4. The Ntbtlog.txt file can be enabled remotely by using what process?
   - a. Terminal Server
   - b. SystemStateDataLog in the Registry
   - c. The System Console tool
   - d. None of the above

5. When a Windows 2000 computer is booted into _____, system startup is much faster because only essential services are being loaded.
   - a. Safe Mode Boot – Networking Only
   - b. VGA Mode
   - c. Safe Mode Boot
   - d. Non-network mode

6. To boot a Windows NT 4.0 computer into the Safe Mode Boot option, you must _____.
   - a. use the F8 function key to begin the process
   - b. use the Windows NT 4.0 boot disk to begin the process
   - c. select the F8 Safe Mode Boot – Troubleshooting
   - d. none of the above

7. A client has just installed a legacy hardware device and now the computer no longer boots. What technique could this client use to begin the troubleshooting process? (Choose all that apply.)
   - a. Restart the computer and use the Shift+F8 combination to select the Last Known Good Configuration.
   - b. Restart the computer and use the Shift key to bypass the normal load of system files, and then boot using the Recovery Console Mode.
   - c. Boot the computer from the installation CD and perform the emergency repair process.
   - d. Boot the computer, use the F8 key to bring up the Start Menu options, and then select the fourth entry on the list.

3.2.2 Repair an operating system by using various startup options.

SYSTEM STARTUP OPTIONS

UNDERSTANDING THE OBJECTIVE

Because Windows 2000 supports a Safe Mode boot option, the administrator has several choices available for starting a Windows 2000 computer if problems develop before the desktop is delivered. You use F8 to access all options.

WHAT YOU REALLY NEED TO KNOW

◆ There are nine options available for booting any Windows 2000 computer. One of these is available only for Windows 2000 domain controllers. The other eight are available for all versions of Windows 2000.

◆ All options are available without using the emergency repair process. In addition, the options are available to any user sitting at the local machine. The nine different options are: Safe Mode, Safe Mode with Networking, Safe Mode w/Command Prompt, Enable Boot Logging, Enable VGA Mode, Last Known Good Configuration, Directory Services Restore Mode, Debugging Mode, and Boot Normally. Each of these modes has specific functionality.

◆ The three Safe Mode options have a similar basic operation. The differences are found in the levels of networking support implemented and in the user interface provided. The normal Safe Mode boots without any network support and uses the standard desktop (although only in low-resolution 16-color mode). The networking option enables the network interface to allow a connection to AD for more advanced troubleshooting. The command prompt option disables the standard GUI interface and replaces it with the command prompt environment.

◆ The boot logging option records a log file created at startup to determine what files are loaded during this session. The default behavior of Windows 2000 is to create this file anytime a Safe Mode boot option is selected. The VGA mode uses a standard 16-color VGA display setting for problems with video drivers. The debugging mode is an advanced mode for capturing debug information during **BSOD** events. This information can be transmitted to Microsoft technical support as it is generated, or the file can be saved to transmit at a later time.

◆ The last setting, Directory Services Restore Mode, is available only on Windows 2000 domain controllers and is used for performing restorations to AD. When this mode is used, the AD database is off-line and can be treated as any other large file would be (with special precautions, however, because of what it represents). All options, except for the Boot Normally option, may cause the machine to boot considerably slower because the disk caching driver support is not enabled.

◆ Windows NT 4.0 and Windows 2000 can also be repaired by using a boot disk. This disk contains a small version of the operating system that is sufficient to allow the operating system to start and function normally from the computer hard disk. Once the computer has started, you will have complete access to the normal desktop and tools.

OBJECTIVES ON THE JOB

Microsoft operating systems support several different boot options administrators can use to troubleshoot the boot process. Windows 95 and Windows 98 support processes that are specific to these operating systems. Windows NT 4.0 and Windows 2000 also support boot options that are similar to one another.

PRACTICE TEST QUESTIONS

1. When troubleshooting a system crash on a Windows NT 4.0 system, _____ mode should be selected only if a pair of null modem cables is available.
   - a. Debugging
   - b. Crash Dump
   - c. System Recovery
   - d. Direct Connect

2. The Enable VGA Mode is most commonly used to troubleshoot problems with _____. (Choose all that apply.)
   - a. screen resolution
   - b. color depth
   - c. recovery of the desktop
   - d. alignment

3. A client has just installed a new video card and drivers, and the computer will not start correctly. How can the user attempt to repair the system?
   - a. Press F8 and then choose Safe Mode with Command Prompt.
   - b. Press F8 and then choose Debugging Mode.
   - c. Press F8 and then choose Last Known Good Configuration.
   - d. Press F8 and then choose Enable VGA Mode.

4. _____ mode can be used on any Windows 2000 computer to perform an Authoritative Restore of AD.
   - a. System Restore
   - b. AD Rebuild
   - c. AD Restore
   - d. AD Recovery

5. Any user of a _____ computer can select any of the startup options listed on the Safe Mode menu. (Choose all that apply.)
   - a. Windows NT 4.0
   - b. Windows 95
   - c. Windows 98
   - d. Windows 2000

6. You have a brand new computer and the hardware that is required to run the computer. However, the hardware does not appear on the list of required system drivers for a Safe Mode boot. How can you start your computer and have the OS recognize the required hardware during a Safe Mode boot?
   - a. Rebuild the computer and press F6 to install additional drivers during the initial OS configuration phase.
   - b. Edit the Registry to include the required hardware devices under the Safe Mode startup options.
   - c. Boot the computer from the installation media and begin the repair process to install the required drivers into the OS.
   - d. Use the Safe Mode option of Safe Mode with Command Prompt and load the drivers manually.

7. The Safe Mode option boots a Windows 2000 computer with _____.
   - a. complete support for all installed hardware
   - b. only minimal hardware support for all installed hardware
   - c. no support for any external hardware
   - d. only minimal hardware support, except for network adapter cards

3.2.3 Repair an operating system by using the Recovery Console.

WINDOWS 2000 RECOVERY CONSOLE

UNDERSTANDING THE OBJECTIVE

Microsoft has provided the Recovery Console tool in Windows 2000 to allow limited access to the operating system and files, regardless of which file system installed the operating system. It is not necessary to have a bootable hard drive to use the tool because it can be run directly from the CD installation media.

WHAT YOU REALLY NEED TO KNOW

◆ The Recovery Console is a command-shell environment that is totally separate from the command prompt in the OS. When the Recovery Console is running, you have access to only the %Systemroot% folder, the %Windir% folder, and %Systemroot%\Cmdcons (if installed). You can access parent folders and all child objects only. By default, you cannot access other partitions or folders unless you use the set command. In addition, before you can access any of the partitions or folders listed above, you must log on with the administrator's password. If the computer belongs to an AD domain, this last step can be made automatic through the use of a GPO setting or by using the Local Security Configuration and Analysis tool settings.

◆ After you have accessed the Recovery Console and logged in, you can perform administrative functions on the above noted system folders. You can also start and stop services running on the machine, map drives, create and remove directories, and perform other functions. You should have experience with the DOS operating system and be comfortable with the command-line environment to use this tool.

◆ The Recovery Console does not install by default on a Windows 2000 computer. The normal procedure to gain access is to start the computer using the Windows 2000 installation media and then select the Emergency Repair\Recovery Console option. This path starts the actual Recovery Console session. The Recovery Console can be installed into the OS after the fact by starting the OS normally and then, after logging on, entering this command: cd_drive\I386\winnt32.exe /cmdcons. You then will be prompted to install the installation media to complete the installation.

◆ The Recovery Console provides the same functionality on a Windows NT 4.0 computer as it does on a Windows 2000 computer. Obviously, you cannot replace sections of the operating system from the Windows 2000 CD; however, you could mount the CD or a floppy disk and gain access to files directly if file replacement is necessary.

◆ Windows 2000 supports the Recovery Console; however, Windows NT 4.0 does not have an equivalent tool. A Windows NT 4.0 computer must be booted from the Windows 2000 CD to allow a Recovery Console to run in a Windows NT 4.0 environment.

OBJECTIVES ON THE JOB

The Windows 2000 Recovery Console is an important addition to the Windows 2000 administrator's tool kit. Using this tool affords extensive flexibility in your recovery techniques.

PRACTICE TEST QUESTIONS

1. A client's installation of Windows NT 4.0 has been corrupted by a virus infection. The ticket must be dispatched to a local administrator for resolution. The local administrator might use which tools to resolve the client's problem? (Choose all that apply.)
   - a. Windows 2000 boot disks
   - b. Windows NT 4.0 boot disks
   - c. Windows 2000 installation CD
   - d. Windows NT 4.0 installation CD

2. By default, an administrator has access to the _____ folders.
   - a. WINNT and SYSTEM32
   - b. %SYSTEMROOT% and CD-ROM
   - c. %SYSTEMROOT% and %WINDIR%
   - d. %OS2LIBPATH% and SYSTEM32

3. In the Recovery Console, you can use the _____ command to check the hard drive for errors.
   - a. scandisk /f
   - b. checkdisk /f
   - c. chkdsk /f
   - d. chkdsk

4. By default, you cannot access a floppy disk from the Recovery Console until you issue the _____ command.
   - a. mount /dev/fd0 /A.
   - b. set floppy=a:
   - c. mount floppy=a:
   - d. The floppy disk is already enabled when you use the Recovery Console.

5. You cannot install the Recovery Console onto a Windows 2000 Server using mirrored partitions until you _____ the mirror.
   - a. break
   - b. replace
   - c. replicate
   - d. synchronize

6. The Recovery Console can be used to write a new _____ to the appropriate media.
   - a. disk partition
   - b. digital signature
   - c. MFT
   - d. MBR

3.2.4 Recover data from a hard disk in the event that the operating system will not start.

DATA RECOVERY TECHNIQUES

UNDERSTANDING THE OBJECTIVE

Inevitably, your computers will crash at one point or another. This is a fact of life. However, there are specific techniques that can be used in Windows 2000 to recover crashed systems. You may not get a complete recovery of the operating systems, but you might at least recover the data on the hard drives.

WHAT YOU REALLY NEED TO KNOW

- ◆ Several different techniques exist for recovering data from a hard drive failure. The administrator can optimize these procedures and improve the success rate if the administrator has proactively planned for this circumstance.

- ◆ When developing a data recovery plan for your network, you should know what type of information must be restored and from what type of Windows 2000 platform it is being restored. This information shapes your data restoration technique and implementation. The recovery of information from a Windows 2000 Professional computer is vastly different than the recovery of the AD database from a domain controller.

- ◆ For the actual recovery process, your first step is to restart the system and enable boot logging. Determine if the system will start and then view the log file. If this is not successful, restart the system using the F8 Safe Mode boot option. Recall that this starts the system with minimal drivers loaded. Use the Drivers tool from the Resource Kit to obtain a list of all loaded drivers, and compare this listing to the contents of the Bootlog file. Identify and then correct any differences.

- ◆ If the OS will not start (as in the case of severe virus infections or permanent corruption of key system files), but the data on the system must be recovered, you can install a parallel installation of the OS. In this second installation of the OS, be careful *not* to format the partition when prompted. This second installation may require third-party tools if free space does not exist on the partition. After it is installed, you will have access to all the files on the non-operative OS *except* for any data protected by EFS.

- ◆ You should also be certain that your users are creating their **ERDs**. If they are Windows 2000 clients, these disks are created using the Backup tool. If they are Windows NT 4.0 clients, the disks are created using the rdisk command. Remember that only an administrator can use the /s switch with the rdisk command.

OBJECTIVES ON THE JOB

If you have prepared in advance and if you understand the different techniques available to you, you should have only minimal difficulty recovering data from crashed systems.

PRACTICE TEST QUESTIONS

1. If you are planning to store backup tapes offsite, a commonly accepted minimum distance is _____ miles from the source of the backup.
   - a. 100
   - b. 75
   - c. 25
   - d. 50

2. To create an ERD in Windows 2000, you must use the _____.
   - a. command prompt and rdisk /s
   - b. command prompt and rdisk
   - c. Backup tool and the Emergency Repair Disk
   - d. command prompt and the NTBACKUP.EXE file

3. John calls your help desk to open a trouble ticket. His computer crashed and he is trying to restart it. He has an ERD and is trying to boot the system from it. So far he has been unsuccessful. John knows that his files are stored on a network file server somewhere, but he doesn't know the location. Why can't John use the ERD to boot his computer?
   - a. The ERD must be used from the Recovery Console.
   - b. The ERD requires the use of the systems administrator password.
   - c. The ERD must be created with the /s command-line switch to transfer the system files to the disk.
   - d. The ERD is not bootable.

4. A parallel installation involves _____.
   - a. formatting the drive and reinstalling Windows 2000
   - b. formatting the drive and installing Windows NT 4.0
   - c. installing Windows 2000 in a new partition or empty folder
   - d. installing Windows 2000 on another computer, and then using a null modem cable to connect and transfer files

5. To back up the Registry information in Windows 2000, you should run _____. (Choose all that apply.)
   - a. REGBACK
   - b. REGDMP
   - c. Backup
   - d. NTBACKUP

3.2.5 Restore an operating system and data from a backup.

RECOVERING THE SYSTEM

UNDERSTANDING THE OBJECTIVE

After the system has crashed, you must recover it. The recovery technique for a Windows 2000 Professional system differs from that for a Windows 2000 Server system, which in turn differs from that for a Windows 2000 domain controller. Each machine runs with its own level of services, and each has important details to consider when performing a system restore.

WHAT YOU REALLY NEED TO KNOW

- ◆ Several conditions must be met before you can attempt a Windows 2000 restoration. First, the person performing the restore must be a member of the Administrators or Backup Operators group. The system also must be stable enough to accept the restored system files. If the computer crashed because of an unstable driver or other file, and if this file was part of the backup, the restore process will restore this problem file as well.
- ◆ You also must decide on the type of restoration to be performed. If the computer is a Windows 2000 Professional computer, then most likely only data has to be restored. However, if the computer is a member server or domain controller, you must restore services and databases as well as data. You might need to include an authoritative restore of the AD itself.
- ◆ When performing a system restore that was created using the Windows 2000 Backup utility, the administrator has an option to perform a complete system restoration or to restore only selected files and folders contained in the backup itself. The part of the backup set that contains the complete listing of all backed up files and folders is called the catalog; it can be accessed in a manner similar to accessing any other partition or folder in Explorer. The catalog may be expanded to allow the selection of the entire catalog or you can select only specific files and folders. When the restore is performed, remember that the files contained in the backup will overwrite the files on the restore point.
- ◆ If you need to restore the AD, you have to determine the precise kind of restore to be accomplished. The Non-Authoritative restore process calls for the restoration of the AD database using a recent backup, and then allowing normal, AD synchronization and replication to bring the domain controller up to date with its peer domain controllers. The Authoritative restore begins as a Non-Authoritative restore and then uses additional steps to mark its copy of the AD as the authoritative copy for the AD environment. This forces all other domain controllers to accept this machine as having the master copy of the AD database and signals these other domain controllers to accept only AD information from this particular domain controller.
- ◆ Windows NT 4.0 uses a simple tape restoration technique for rebuilding its computing domain infrastructure. In this technique, the Windows NT 4.0 operating system is rebuilt from the installation media and all relevant service packs and hot fixes must be installed before making an attempt to recover the domain installation. After the operating system has been restored to its level of functionality prior to the system crash, a backup utility may be used to restore critical Registry settings

OBJECTIVES ON THE JOB

Different techniques exist for restoring data from Windows 2000 computers. The most important parts of the restore process will be permissions, current backups, and stable computers.

PRACTICE TEST QUESTIONS

1. Only the _____ group is authorized to perform a system restore. (Choose all that apply.)
   - a. Power Users
   - b. Restore Operators
   - c. Backup Operators
   - d. Administrators

2. A Non-Authoritative restore is used to return the _____ service to operational status.
   - a. WINS
   - b. AD
   - c. CA
   - d. Kerberos

3. An Authoritative Restore is used on a Windows 2000 _____ domain controller. (Choose all that apply.)
   - a. Professional
   - b. Server
   - c. Advanced Server
   - d. Datacenter Server

4. A(n) _____ backup solution can be used to restore the AD.
   - a. remote
   - b. third-party
   - c. unscripted
   - d. unattended

5. The Windows NT 4.0 restore process allows the administrator to restore _____. (Choose all that apply.)
   - a. Registry files
   - b. applications
   - c. Certificate Server settings
   - d. system state information

6. The Windows 2000 restore process can be used _____.
   - a. remotely
   - b. only locally
   - c. through a Terminal Server session
   - d. through a Telnet session

7. A user has performed a system state backup and installed a new application that corrupted the OS. The user rebuilt the system and installed the OS, which is now running. The user has attempted to restore the system state data several times, but the data is always restored with all NTFS file permissions missing. What is causing the problem? (Choose all that apply.)
   - a. The system needs the most recent Windows 2000 service pack.
   - b. The most recent Windows 2000 Professional service pack is not installed.
   - c. The partition is formatted with FAT and not NTFS.
   - d. The partition has been formatted with NTFS.

3.3 Monitor and troubleshoot server health and performance. Tools include System Monitor, Event Viewer, and Task Manager.

A HEALTHY SERVER

UNDERSTANDING THE OBJECTIVE

Part of your daily duties will be to maintain your servers, whether they are Windows NT 4.0 servers or Windows 2000 servers. From an architecture standpoint, both systems have many commonalities; however, they are different enough to require some special considerations in their day-to-day care.

WHAT YOU REALLY NEED TO KNOW

◆ Windows NT 4.0 and Windows 2000 support graphical diagnostic utilities that can be used to collect a variety of information about the status and health of the operating system, applications, and services. Windows NT 4.0 uses a utility named Performance Monitor, while Windows 2000 uses an MMC snap-in called System Console. Both tools support the collection of crucial, system-wide information in a real-time graphical monitored format. They also feature a text-based version of the real-time mode, a logging utility, and a system alert tool. Both tools can also work remotely to collect data about remote computers using a network connection.

◆ The System Console tool from Windows 2000 supports advanced data collection methods and additional tools for collecting data from network resources. Performance Monitor is included in the Windows 2000 Server Resource Kit.

◆ Both platforms support Task Manager, which is a small, robust, system monitoring tool. Task Manager does not collect or even recognize the level of data that the first two tools can; however, it also doesn't need extensive configuration to work.

◆ Another diagnostic tool that is available on both platforms is the Event Viewer. This tool collects what are essentially activity logs from the OS and key services. The Event Viewer in Windows 2000 is the more robust tool, and it gathers more information about the operating system and services than does the Windows NT 4.0 version. However, the information collected and the interface where this information is viewed are substantially the same on both platforms.

◆ An important task for any administrator is the removal or disabling of unnecessary services. Unneeded protocols may be the worst offenders, followed by services that provide no useful functionality. For example, if a site uses only IP for network connectivity and you have no clients that require the IPX/SPX protocol, why should NWLink remain loaded on your servers?

OBJECTIVES ON THE JOB

Monitoring your servers is an important part of your daily function as a Windows administrator. You must optimize and fine-tune both platforms to preserve their functionality.

PRACTICE TEST QUESTIONS

1. **One of the differences between Task Manager and Performance Monitor on the Windows NT 4.0 platform is _____. (Choose all that apply.)**
   a. Task Manager can be used to launch new tasks, while Performance Monitor cannot
   b. Performance Monitor can track NBT usage, while Task Manager cannot
   c. Task Manager can be used only by the local system administrator, while any user can launch Performance Monitor
   d. Task Manager can be used to collect application statistics and send them to Microsoft Access for analysis, while Performance Monitor cannot

2. **In a network environment where all clients and servers use appropriate versions of Windows 2000 only, which of the following would be unnecessary services? (Choose all that apply.)**
   a. IP
   b. TFTP
   c. NBT
   d. AppleTalk

3. **A client has a legacy application that was written for a specific business need. After converting the network infrastructure to Windows 2000, this application no longer functions. The client informed you that the application used to run on a dedicated Windows NT 4.0 server and that previously, all Windows NT 4.0 and Windows 98 clients could access this application. What tool could you use to begin an evaluation of why this application no longer functions?**
   a. Performance Monitor
   b. Task Manager
   c. System Console
   d. Network Manager

4. **A user has called your help desk with some questions about the performance of her computer, which is running Windows 2000 Professional. Which tool could you use to gather information about the situation?**
   a. System Console/Log view
   b. System Console/Report view
   c. System Console/Alert view
   d. Event Viewer

5. **In a purely Windows NT 4.0 environment without Internet connectivity, _____ is an unnecessary service that could be removed or decommissioned.**
   a. DHCP
   b. WINS
   c. RRAS
   d. DNS

OBJECTIVES

3.3.1 Monitor and interpret real-time performance by using System Monitor and Task Manager.

REAL-TIME PERFORMANCE

UNDERSTANDING THE OBJECTIVE

As an administrator of Windows 2000, you may need to collect real-time information about the performance of your system. For instance, if you have just installed a new Ethernet card, how can you gauge its performance? By using System Monitor, of course.

WHAT YOU REALLY NEED TO KNOW

◆ The most basic tool used for monitoring the health of a Windows 2000 computer is Task Manager. The Task Manager can be started by right-clicking the taskbar and clicking Task Manager, or by typing taskmgr.exe on the Run line.

◆ Task Manager allows the user to view a list of applications and processes that are running. It also allows the user to view key system performance data, such as the total usage of physical RAM and PAGEFILE. Task Manager can be used to terminate applications that have become nonresponsive or to start new applications by using the New Task button. Task Manager can also be removed as part of a GPO configuration in AD. Task Manager does function in a Terminal Server session, but it has no remote administrative capabilities.

◆ System Monitor is a full-featured tool that supports monitoring the Windows 2000 computer. The System Monitor can be started in several different ways. One method is to type perfmon at the Run line. Another method is to click the Performance icon in the local Administrative Tools listing. By default, no objects are enabled for monitoring when the tool opens.

◆ The System Monitor watches system workload units returned by objects, which are associated with counters and instances in the System Monitor setup and configuration. The objects are part of the OS and computer, and they include the Processor, Physical Memory, or WINS Server objects. Each object has an associated list of counters. The WINS Server object list counter includes Failed Queries/sec or Unique Conflicts/sec. In addition, each object may have multiple instances, such as the object PhysicalDisk in a system with more than one physical hard drive.

◆ System Monitor works remotely. Remote usage is preferred because running an instance of System Monitor on a computer impacts the performance of that computer and can skew any data tracking that is being performed. System Monitor will work in different views as well. The administrator can choose from the Standard graph view, the Report view, and the Alert view. It also supports data logging for extended recording of data. Once collected, the data can be manipulated for viewing and exported to applications such as Access, Excel, or Word for formatting or analysis.

OBJECTIVES ON THE JOB

The Task Manager tool is simple and intuitive to use and should present no problems to the average user. System Console is a more complex tool that requires configuration.

PRACTICE TEST QUESTIONS

1. **To collect information about the number of users currently connected anonymously to your FTP server, you should use the _____ tool.**
   - a. Internet Information Services snap-in
   - b. Task Manager
   - c. Network Monitor
   - d. System Monitor
   - e. FTP Monitor

2. **Only the local administrator or a user with _____ can use Task Manager.**
   - a. at least Power User permissions
   - b. Task Manager local permissions
   - c. the AD GPO Use Task Manager
   - d. local logon permissions

3. **The Task Manager can be removed through the use of a(n) _____.**
   - a. Registry hack
   - b. AD GPO
   - c. setting to delete the file Taskman.com
   - d. local security policy.

4. **You are collecting system statistics on a new computer model that your employer might purchase in quantity. Which tool allows you to collect and analyze the required data? (Choose all that apply.)**
   - a. PowerPoint
   - b. System Console/Log View
   - c. System Console/Graph View
   - d. Access
   - e. Task Manager
   - f. Excel

5. **Because the System Console uses ActiveX controls, System Console views can be inserted into _____ using FrontPage.**
   - a. Visio sheets
   - b. Word documents
   - c. Web pages
   - d. Trellix pages

6. **The default view in System Console is the Graph View. What other graphical view can be used in System Monitor?**
   - a. Logarithmic
   - b. Polar
   - c. Histogram
   - d. Scattered XY Plots

7. **Information collected by the Task Manager can be exported to _____ for analysis at a later date.**
   - a. applications
   - b. Windows Management Instrumentation
   - c. Excel
   - d. none of the above

3.3.2 Configure and manage System Monitor alerts and logging.

ADVANCED SYSTEM MONITOR USAGE

UNDERSTANDING THE OBJECTIVE

System Monitor has capabilities which are advanced beyond the normal collection of data for instant viewing. System Monitor can also be configured to collect information in a log file format and can be configured with specific events enabled as alerts. The log view allows the administrator to record long-term system usage information, and then collect, archive, and analyze this information. The alert view supports the configuration of specific system events to be continuously monitored and actions that can be taken when the criteria for the event are matched.

WHAT YOU REALLY NEED TO KNOW

- ◆ The System Console supports the creation of detailed log files, which are used by the administrator for statistical analysis of computers and servers. When configured to generate a log, the System Console collects all available data from selected counters and selected instances associated with the particular object being logged.
- ◆ The administrator can choose between two different types of recorded logs in System Console. The first log type is a **counter log**. Counter logs record information detailing hardware resources and system services. Counter logs also record all information about the selected objects for later analysis. A new log reporting tool has been created for Windows 2000—the **trace log**. Trace logs track event activity and allow an administrator to generate correlations between services running on the computer and the impact of those services on the computer system. Trace logs are tracked from start to finish, unlike counter logs, which are sampled at determined rates.
- ◆ Counter logs must be configured by choosing a local or remote machine to monitor. Next, a list of specific object counters and instances to monitor and the data-sampling rate, which defaults to 15 seconds, must be generated. The sampling rate is configurable in terms of seconds, minutes, hours, and days. Additional settings include the location of the log files, the default name assignment, the type of file to be generated (CSV, TSV, and so on), any relevant comments, and the maximum log file size. You also must configure the settings for log file startup and log file shutdown. You can use an optional command-line setting to execute when the log file stops collecting data. The trace log is similar to the counter log, except that it logs only network services.
- ◆ The System Console supports the Alert object, which allows an administrator to configure specific objects/counters for System Console to monitor. The Alerts object in System Console can be configured to monitor counters on either the local computer or remote computers. Unlike the Windows NT 4.0 tool, which supported only one specific object per alert session, the Windows 2000 System Console supports multiple objects occurring on multiple machines from the same instance. This allows the administrator to configure one System Console Alert view with many objects, each with its own alert criterion. However, only one sampling rate may be selected. If different sampling rates are required, the administrator must open and configure separate System Console Alert events with specific configuration settings.

OBJECTIVES ON THE JOB

The System Console allows the administrator to collect data on services currently running on the computer, and to also configure alerts for specific events occurring on the computers.

PRACTICE TEST QUESTIONS

1. When using the _____ view in System Console, the administrator cannot configure multiple events in a single alert view, and each event cannot have a separate time sampling interval configured.
    a. System Alert
    b. Alert
    c. Alert Monitor
    d. System Monitor

2. The System Console supports two different kinds of log file files. The _____ log file is used to track events occurring on the system.
    a. Statistical
    b. Event
    c. Counter
    d. Trace
    e. Performance
    f. System

3. When configuring a Counter Log, you must configure _____. (Choose all that apply.)
    a. counters
    b. objects
    c. sampling rates
    d. security settings
    e. pause log settings
    f. stop log settings

4. When an alert is added to the _____, the administrator can enable the ability to send a network message to a specific individual.
    a. System Console
    b. Command Console
    c. Alert Monitor
    d. Monitor queue

5. System Console logs should not be collected on the machine being logged because _____.
    a. the data will not be collected correctly
    b. the creation of the data log will impact the performance of the computer
    c. system logs collected locally cannot access protected local resources
    d. local system log collection needs elevated security permissions, which are only available remotely

6. When configuring counter logs in System Console, you should select the _____ log file type if you want continuous collection of log information.
    a. CSV
    b. Binary File
    c. TSV
    d. Binary Circular File

7. System Console Alert logs can be monitored only on _____.
    a. Windows 2000 Server
    b. Windows NT 4.0 Server
    c. Windows ME
    d. NTFS partitions

3.3.3 Diagnose server health problems by using Event Viewer

EVENT VIEWER AND SERVER HEALTH

UNDERSTANDING THE OBJECTIVE

Event Viewer is a tool found in the Administrative Tools on every Windows 2000 computer. The Event Viewer can return detailed information about events occurring on the system. On a Windows 2000 server, the Event Viewer tool will show information about specific services installed on the computer.

WHAT YOU REALLY NEED TO KNOW

◆ The Event Viewer is a tool that collects system and service events in Windows 2000. On a Windows 2000 domain controller, you may encounter these Event Viewer logs: Application, Security, System, Directory Service, DNS Server, and File Replication Service. The first three are found on all Windows 2000 computers. The last three are found only on servers. Events recorded in the Event Viewer are shown with one of five possible icons. One icon indicates an informational event. Another icon represents a warning event and the third event icon indicates an error event. The other two icons, a padlock and a key, are found in the Security log and represent a failed audit and a successful audit, respectively.

◆ The Event Viewer log view displays eight columns of data: Type, Date, Time, Source, Category, Event, User, and Computer. These columns can be sorted by double-clicking the column headings. All Event Viewer logs have the same column settings and options. Additional settings for each log include the ability to save the log files as a specific data type, to open previously saved log files, and to clear the log files.

◆ Event Viewer log files can be saved for later analysis by using the Event Viewer or by saving to a specific format, such as in an .evt file for viewing in Event Viewer or in .txt and .csv delimited files, which can be imported into applications such as Word, Excel, or Access. If the files are opened in Access, the administrator can use the Wizard in Access to create a database of Event Viewer log objects.

◆ After selecting an event to view, double-click the event. The Event Properties view opens to show information specific to this event. You will see the date, time, and type of the event, along with the user who generated the event, the computer that recorded the event, and the source of the event. You will also see the category for the event and an event ID number. If you have access to the Windows 2000 Server Resource Kit, you can perform a lookup on the event ID numbers to determine causes for the message.

◆ In Event Properties view, you can also see a description of the event. This contains the exact text of the generated error message. In some instances, it may be possible to copy this message into either the Server Resource Kit search engine or TechNet.

◆ Beyond showing just local data, the Event Viewer can also connect to remote computers. This allows the administrator to access remote servers and determine what events may be occurring on those computers. This connectivity does not require that any additional services be installed on either computer.

OBJECTIVES ON THE JOB

The Windows 2000 Event Viewer can make available to the administrator a great deal of diagnostic information concerning the health of their servers. In addition to normal events, special events can be recorded to identify problems with servers and related services.

PRACTICE TEST QUESTIONS

1. As an administrator, you suspect that problems exist on your DNS server, which is located in an office across town. What tool could you use to check the status of your DNS server? (Choose all that apply.)
   a. NSLOOKUP
   b. DNS snap-in
   c. Event Viewer
   d. Remote Console
   e. NET SHOW DNS

2. Which tool can be used to check the status of the File Replication Service? (Choose all that apply.)
   a. File Monitor
   b. Replication Monitor
   c. REPADMIN
   d. Event Viewer/File Replication Service

3. Where could you obtain the status of the replication link created by the KCC?
   a. Event Viewer/File Replication Service
   b. Event Viewer/Directory Service
   c. REPADMIN
   d. Event Viewer/System Log

4. Data collected by the Event Viewer can be exported to _____ or Excel for warehousing and analysis.
   a. System Console
   b. Access
   c. Microsoft Works
   d. ADSI Edit

5. The default size of the Event Viewer log file is _____ KB.
   a. 256
   b. 512
   c. 1024
   d. 2048

6. Event Viewer log files can be saved in which file format? (Choose all that apply.)
   a. *.evt
   b. *.txt
   c. *.csv
   d. *.mdb

7. The default behavior of Windows 2000 Server is to _____ if the Security log fills up and will not write more events.
   a. shut down
   b. send an alert
   c. notify the administrator
   d. notify a Windows 2000 server via secure RPC

OBJECTIVES

3.3.4 Identify and disable unnecessary operating system services.

SERVER OPTIMIZATION

UNDERSTANDING THE OBJECTIVE

As a Windows 2000 administrator, you can optimize your servers by disabling and/or removing unnecessary services.

WHAT YOU REALLY NEED TO KNOW

◆ As the first step in your optimization process, you must identify those services running that perform no useful function on the computer. If you are running Windows 2000 Server as a domain controller, you must use TCP/IP as your network protocol. However, do you have additional protocols installed on the system? If so, are they needed by clients in your environment?

◆ To determine if supplemental protocols are being used, configure a System Console log to collect information about these additional protocols. If no protocol activity is detected after a reasonable amount of time, remove them.

◆ Is this computer a domain controller? If so, does it have DNS, WINS, or DHCP installed? If so, why? How many separate installations of these subsidiary services are running in your infrastructure? You need at least one instance of each service per site. Two would be better in terms of fault tolerance. Remove other instances unless a valid need exists for them.

◆ Are your servers using high-density (32-bit) screen colors? If so, replace these with the lowest density screen colors. Servers don't require 16 million colors on the monitor. Are the OpenGL screen servers running on critical machines? Remove these because of the impact on the processor to drive them.

◆ Check the Windows 2000 Professional computers for the presence of the Speech Recognition tools. These can visibly affect system performance and cause erratic behavior while running. If you support clients who require the speech tools, make certain to provide high-quality headsets and microphones. You may need to move these individuals to a private office for the speech tools to work consistently.

◆ Dynamic update during installation can download new patches or components if Internet access is available. However, this may affect network performance and lead to inconsistencies regarding client computer builds and configurations and builds in a corporate environment. You might want to consider a GPO to limit or restrict the use of the Windows Update feature.

◆ To improve performance on all computers, you can consider disabling the CD Autorun feature. Autorun periodically queries the CD drive looking for media. This can interrupt the processor while it is performing more important work. While obviously not critical on newer systems, it may be a performance factor on marginal Windows 2000 computers.

OBJECTIVES ON THE JOB

As a Windows 2000 administrator, you must optimize the performance of your computers. You may be fortunate enough to have an infrastructure comprising the latest computers with the best performance. However, you may also have the opposite environment, with many computers that perform only marginally well with Windows 2000.

PRACTICE TEST QUESTIONS

1. A client calls your help desk to complain about a Windows 2000 computer that is acting erratically. Among the complaints are slow speed, long pauses while working with applications, and erratic behavior of certain applications, such as Outlook and Word. Also, the user says that every time a loud car goes by, the computer reacts. What should you suspect is the source of the problem? (Choose all that apply.)
   a. a bad power supply
   b. a defective hard drive
   c. a loose power cable
   d. a badly fragmented hard drive
   e. the Speech tools are installed

2. Your corporate network seems to have an excessively high degree of bandwidth utilization. You have collected network data in a System Console log file and have been analyzing the results. You notice a great deal of multicast traffic present in the data. What tool could you use to further isolate the source of this traffic?
   a. PerfMon
   b. NetMon
   c. ReplMon
   d. IPSecMon

3. Assume that you have resolved the issue in Question 2. The culprits of the additional multicast traffic are your six WINS servers. Why are they generating so much multicast traffic?
   a. Six NetMeeting sessions are being run in your network.
   b. You have too many WINS clients.
   c. All six WINS servers have been configured to autoreplicate with each other.
   d. The WINS database on one WINS server is corrupt, and this affects the other five WINS servers.

4. Network users are calling your help desk to complain about the accessibility of one of your Windows 2000 file servers. You ask a local administrator to check the server and then report to you on its condition. The local administrator reports that nothing is wrong, and that moving the mouse stopped the 3D Pipes screen saver and made file access normal again. What should you suspect is the cause of the problem?
   a. intermittent router connectivity caused by overfragmentation of IP packets
   b. IP frozen-screen syndrome
   c. excessive processor overhead generated by the OpenGL screen saver
   d. excessive paging caused by insufficient RAM on the server

5. Your company's Windows 2000 Professional computers were originally built using RIS with an image of a model machine. They should all be identical to one another. You are receiving an increasing number of service calls, however, which indicate that many computers have been modified by some process. What should you suspect is the cause of the problem? GPOs are in place to control application installation by the users.
   a. Local administrators are changing machines by adding components.
   b. The Windows Update feature is running automatically.
   c. Users are logging on as administrators and installing applications.
   d. Your clients have a new virus infection on their computers.

3.4 Install and manage Windows 2000 updates. Updates include service packs, hot fixes, and security hot fixes.

UPDATING WINDOWS 2000

UNDERSTANDING THE OBJECTIVE

Windows 2000, like any other operating system, must be updated from time to time. Anomalies present in the operating system also may need to be addressed. The tools used by Windows 2000 to address these issues are service packs and hot fixes.

WHAT YOU REALLY NEED TO KNOW

◆ Service packs, as implemented by Microsoft for Windows 2000, contain updated files needed by the operating system. However, service packs also contain files that install additional functionality for the operating system. Service packs are generic across the Windows 2000 Professional and Server platforms. It is not necessary to obtain one version for servers and another for workstations.

◆ Service packs can be downloaded directly from the public Microsoft Web site or ordered for a nominal fee from Microsoft. If you subscribe to Microsoft TechNet, you will receive service packs for all Microsoft products as part of that subscription. In terms of functionality, there is a difference between service packs on CD and service packs downloaded from the Internet. The Internet download consists of only the service pack file. No optional tools or components are included with this version, unlike the version that is available on CD. The CD version not only contains the service pack executable itself, but also contains additional files for optional components and tools that can be installed into Windows 2000.

◆ While service packs have replacement files and Registry fixes designed to keep the operating system and services up-to-date, a hot fix tool is designed to patch or repair one specific service or feature at a time. A service pack may be well over 100 MB in size, while a hot fix may be under 1 MB. Service packs can be installed on any Windows 2000 platform, while a hot fix is intended for specific versions of the operating system with specific service packs installed on that operating system.

◆ Service packs are cumulative; hot fixes are not. A hot fix commonly is included in the next released service pack if it is considered applicable to the majority of Windows 2000 installations. A hot fix should not be installed unless the computer exhibits the specific problem the hot fix was designed to remedy.

◆ Another issue with service packs and hot fixes is the limited ability to uninstall both tools. Neither can be readily uninstalled after they have been applied to the computer. If you do uninstall them, you run the risk of damaging the operating system.

OBJECTIVES ON THE JOB

Service packs and hot fixes constitute the primary method that you will use to apply updates to the Windows 2000 operating system. Service packs are issued on a regular basis and can be safely applied to any Windows 2000 computer; hot fixes are problem-specific.

PRACTICE TEST QUESTIONS

1. A Windows 2000 service pack can be installed on a Windows 2000 _____ server. (Choose all that apply.)
   a. Cluster
   b. DataCenter
   c. Microsoft Operations Manager
   d. Cookie

2. You are working on a help desk when a user calls to open a trouble ticket. Acting on the advice of a friend, the user went to the Microsoft Web site and searched for, found, and installed all available hot fixes. Now the computer won't start. What can be done to help this user? (Choose all that apply.)
   a. Verify Internet connectivity and reestablish connectivity to the update site.
   b. Schedule an appointment for a technician to go to their work site and rebuild the computer after trying to recover the data files.
   c. Walk the user through booting the computer using the Safe Mode boot process, and then attempt to uninstall all hot fixes using Control Panel/Add and Remove Programs.
   d. Walk the user through performing a parallel installation of Windows 2000 on this computer to recover the data.

3. You support a small company that has 100 employees who all use Windows NT 4.0 Workstation. The office manager asks you to create a process to use the Windows Update feature to apply operating system updates to these machines as an automated process. How would you implement this? (Choose all that apply.)
   a. Verify Internet connectivity for all clients and configure the Windows Update feature to run automatically without user intervention.
   b. Make certain the company firewall will support and allow a connection to the Microsoft Update Site.
   c. Configure an AD GPO to support this process.
   d. All of the above
   e. None of the above

4. The process to remove a Windows 2000 service pack depends on the use of the _____.
   a. correct version of the service pack
   b. Uninstall service pack switch when first installing the service pack
   c. checked build version of the service pack
   d. Uninstall version of the service pack

5. Your Windows NT 4.0 DNS server is acting erratically. Host records are disappearing after they've been added and you cannot perform zone transfers to your BIND secondary servers. Also, recursive lookups seem to be failing. Which Windows NT 4.0 service pack implemented support for SRV records on the Windows NT 4.0 DNS server?
   a. Service Pack 3
   b. Service Pack 4
   c. Service Pack 5
   d. Service Pack 6

3.4.1 Update an installation source by using slipstreaming.

AUTOMATING INSTALLATION OF SERVICE PACKS

UNDERSTANDING THE OBJECTIVE

If you are an experienced user of a Microsoft operating system, then you are familiar with service packs. The installation of service packs into a Windows operating system is a necessary and vital part of your day-to-day administration. Windows 2000 now provides enhanced functionality for this process through the use of a new technology called slipstreaming.

WHAT YOU REALLY NEED TO KNOW

- ◆ Service packs contain the most current drivers, system files, executables, and Registry fixes for the Windows 2000 OS. All Microsoft operating systems from Windows 95 forward have service packs available at the Microsoft Web site for free download. Additional products such as Exchange and SQL Server also have their own service packs. The service pack should be installed whenever new applications or services are added to the computer. They should also be reinstalled when new hardware devices are attached to the computer. Also, the installation of a service pack may resolve computer issues such as incorrect drivers, outdated system files, or new Registry settings that were enabled after the Windows 2000 product was released to market.

- ◆ Windows 2000 service packs can be very large in size, frequently 100 MB or more. You may be reluctant to involve your users in the process of reapplying the service packs. Another problem involves building a new computer with the base OS and then being required to install the most current service pack to bring the OS up to current standards.

- ◆ The solution to these problems is the slipstream process. **Slipstreaming** allows an administrator to unpack the most recent service pack files into a network-based installation **sharepoint**, and then replace the files from the installation media with the replacement files from the service pack. It must be noted, however, that the slipstreaming technology is available only for the Windows 2000 platform and cannot be used for any downlevel platforms. These older systems need the service packs installed and refreshed using other techniques.

- ◆ To implement slipstreaming in your environment, you must use the update.exe /slip command in the directory that contains the installation media that you want to update. After the command is used, installation of the OS proceeds normally without the use of additional switches or commands.

- ◆ Windows 2000 service packs are cumulative. That is, successive service packs contain all the functionality of previously released service packs, plus additional functionality. Therefore it is not necessary to apply all service packs to your client and server computers; only the most recent service pack is needed.

OBJECTIVES ON THE JOB

Service packs and their use with Microsoft operating systems are a fact of life. All operating systems use service packs to update, refresh, and fix operating system components. One of your normally scheduled tasks as a Windows administrator is to maintain the status of the service packs on all the computers that you support. You must assure that the most recent service packs are applied to the correct platform and the correct applications. By enforcing this policy, you will maintain your Microsoft Windows platforms in the most up-to-date level of functionality.

PRACTICE TEST QUESTIONS

1. Service packs are available for Windows 2000 Server and _____.
   a. Windows NT 4.0 Workstation
   b. MS DOS 6.22
   c. Windows NT 4.0 Terminal Server
   d. all of the above

2. The _____ version of a service pack is required to begin a Windows 2000 debug session for Microsoft Technical support.
   a. latest
   b. MSDN
   c. debug
   d. checked build

3. Your help desk has just received a call from a user who decided to update the service pack on a Windows NT 4.0 Workstation computer with NT 4.0 Service Pack 6. After the computer rebooted, the user discovered that the third-party e-mail client no longer functioned, so the user installed Service Pack 5 as a solution. Now the user reports several problems on the computer, ranging from no network connectivity to a nonfunctional installation of Internet Explorer. As the help desk technician, what should you tell the client?
   a. Reinstall the service pack, but this time use Service Pack 6a.
   b. Install Service Pack 4, and then reinstall service packs 5, 6, and 6a, in that order.
   c. Reinstall Service Pack 6 followed by Service Pack 6a, and then reinstall Internet Explorer.
   d. A recovery of the computer is impossible because the operating system has been damaged. Please back up all of your data; the computer must be rebuilt.

4. You have been given the job to build a team Web server using a Windows NT 4.0 member server. You want to install IIS 4.0 on this server to provide services. However, the server currently is configured with Service Pack 3 for Windows NT 4.0. What process should you use to accomplish this task?
   a. Reinstall Service Pack 3, install IIS 4.0, and then install Service Pack 6a.
   b. Install Service Pack 6 and then install IIS 4.0.
   c. Install IIS 4.0 and nothing else.
   d. Install Service Pack 4, install Service Pack 6, and then install IIS 4.0.

5. You support a client with a business reason to use MS-DOS 6.22. The client wants to have the DOSShell application installed on the computer. Where can you get this application?
   a. the Windows 95 service pack
   b. the MS DOS service pack
   c. the Windows NT 4.0 Support Tools folder on the Windows TechNet CD version of the Windows NT 4.0 service pack
   d. as a downloadable feature from the MS DOS service pack located at *www.microsoft.com*

3.4.2 Apply and reapply service packs and hot fixes.

ADDITIONAL SERVICE PACK ISSUES

UNDERSTANDING THE OBJECTIVE

If you have already installed the operating system and must apply the latest service pack or hot fix as part of your normal infrastructure maintenance, you need to know what techniques are available to you. You also need to know how many times a service pack can be reinstalled and any guidelines that govern the hot fixes you want to use.

WHAT YOU REALLY NEED TO KNOW

- ◆ Most Microsoft operating systems and applications have service packs. There is a service pack for MS Office 2000 and for Exchange Server 5.5. All Microsoft operating systems from MS-DOS 6.22 forward have service packs. Service packs are available as free downloads from Microsoft. They are intended to serve as a repository for fixes to the application or operating system, and should be applied to assure maximum functionality of these components. Service packs are usually scheduled with some regularity and can be applied by all users of the intended application or operating system (with sufficient security permissions).
- ◆ Hot fixes are considerably smaller than service packs. While service packs address general issues and have been tested for installation of the appropriate application or platform, hot fixes address specific issues and never address more than one issue at a time. Hot fixes have not been tested for all platforms and should be applied only to specific platforms or applications for specific reasons. A service pack can be applied as many times as necessary, while a hot fix should be applied only once, and then only if you are experiencing the problem the hot fix was designed to address. An additional issue for hot fixes is that they are service pack-specific. That is, the hot fix will frequently advise that a specific version of a service pack must be installed prior to applying the hot fix.
- ◆ Service packs can be applied to the system in several different ways. Service packs are available from the public Microsoft Web site and can be downloaded from there, although for Windows 2000, these are reduced-functionality service packs. The full-function service packs are available only on CD. Service packs are also a normal part of the Microsoft TechNet subscription service. Hot fixes are also available from the Microsoft Web site and can be downloaded for use later or stored on a network file share or other media.
- ◆ Before using either a service pack or a hot fix, you must close all open applications, because these applications may be using files that the service pack or hot fix is trying to replace. After the applications are closed, the installation of the service pack or hot fix may proceed.

OBJECTIVES ON THE JOB

A smart administrator knows that service packs and hot fixes can be used to update key files and services running on a Microsoft operating system or to update Microsoft applications. Service packs are available as free downloads directly from Microsoft, or they can be obtained on a CD for a small fee which covers the cost of copying the CD. Service packs are also available as part of Microsoft subscription services, such as the TechNet or MSDN Subscriber services. Hot fixes are available only from the Microsoft Web site and should be used only if the problem the hot fix addresses currently exists. Also, Windows 2000 operating system service packs can be made part of a GPO update process.

PRACTICE TEST QUESTIONS

1. How many service packs are available for Microsoft Windows NT 4.0?
   a. 1
   b. 3
   c. 5
   d. 7

2. While service packs for Windows NT 4.0 were released on an as-needed basis, Microsoft has committed to releasing service packs for Windows 2000 every _____ months.
   a. 3
   b. 6
   c. 12
   d. 4

3. Hot fixes should be installed _____.
   a. as they are made available, regardless of whether the system exhibits the problem the hot fix addresses
   b. only if a problem is detected with the operating system that is not addressed by the most recent service pack, and then only after reading the installation instructions for the hot fix
   c. only after installing the most recent service pack
   d. only after other hot fixes are removed from the system

4. Periodically, the _____ Web site should be checked for updates to related applications.
   a. SMS
   b. IIS
   c. Office
   d. Exchange

5. A client calls to report a computer problem following the installation of a new application that was downloaded from the Internet. What should you suggest as a first step in the resolution process?
   a. Uninstall the application.
   b. Reinstall the operating system.
   c. Search for a possible hot fix and install it.
   d. Reinstall the latest service pack.

6. Your help desk receives a call from a client who is experiencing frequent GPF error messages in Windows NT 4.0. What specific troubleshooting solution does TechNet suggest to eliminate this problem on this platform?
   a. Reinstall the operating system, and this time remove support for the 8.3 file-naming convention.
   b. Install the GPF hot fix for Windows NT 4.0.
   c. Apply the GPF/Registry hot fix and reboot.
   d. Reinstall the most recent service pack.

7. You have installed SMS version 2.0 on your Windows 2000 server, but the Network Monitor tool is not functioning correctly. You know you need to install a service pack to fix the problem. Which service pack should you install?
   a. the most recent Windows 2000 service pack
   b. the Network Monitor hot fix
   c. the most recent SMS service pack
   d. the SMS hot fix

3.4.3 Verify service pack and hot fix installation.

SERVICE PACK AND HOT FIX VERIFICATION

UNDERSTANDING THE OBJECTIVE

One characteristic of service packs and hot fixes is that each is numbered. Service packs are cumulative, while hot fixes are specific. Service packs may be reapplied, while hot fixes are applied only once. Service packs do not require specific hot fixes, but hot fixes do require specific service packs. You must determine which service packs and hot fixes have been installed on a system.

WHAT YOU REALLY NEED TO KNOW

♦ Service packs are specific for applications and operating systems. Service packs are also numbered, and they are cumulative. Service packs always report their version information to either the operating system or the application for which the service pack was designed. Service packs also exist for Microsoft applications. These can be installed by going to the Microsoft Office Web site and selecting the appropriate service pack. Third-party applications may also have service packs available.

♦ Hot fixes are specific for issues involving applications, services, or operating systems. They are not cumulative and do not necessarily report their version information to the application or operating system for which they were installed. They are numbered however, and usually are included in the next service pack.

♦ One tool that can be used to determine service pack versions, along with a wealth of other information about the operating system, is **Winmsd**. This is the Windows diagnostic tool. It opens a GUI interface that shows hardware resources, components, and software environment and Internet settings. Clicking the System Summary options will show the currently installed service pack. It does not show the list of installed hot fixes, however.

♦ To see the list of installed hot fixes, use the Add or Remove Programs applet in the Control Panel. This applet shows all installed hot fixes on the system and the names of the hot fixes. An advantage to using this approach is that you can remove hot fixes from the system using the same interface. Note that service packs cannot be removed using this tool.

♦ Another method that can be used to determine the status of service packs and hot fixes from a single interface is the **Netdiag** tool. Netdiag is not part of the normal installation for Windows 2000. To use this tool, you must have installed either the Windows 2000 Server Resource Kit or the Windows 2000 Server Support Tools. It is not possible to simply copy the file from one computer to another; it must be installed. After it has been installed, open a command prompt and type netdiag. The tool takes a while to test the system and collect information. However, after approximately one minute, it returns the current service pack version and all installed hot fixes.

OBJECTIVES ON THE JOB

Verifying the versions of currently installed service packs and hot fixes is important to maintain the proper operation of your supported servers, workstations, and applications. Service packs and hot fixes can be installed for many Microsoft applications and for all operating systems. Several tools can be used to determine service pack versions for operating systems. The About option on the Help menu for Microsoft applications lists the service packs that have been installed.

PRACTICE TEST QUESTIONS

1. Service packs are available for _____. (Choose all that apply.)
   a. Windows 98
   b. Office 2000
   c. Exchange 5.5
   d. Active Directory

2. You want to determine what hot fixes are installed on a Windows 2000 computer. Which tool will show this information?
   a. Control Panel/Add Remove Programs
   b. Windows Update/Show installed updates
   c. the resource kit tool ShowHotfixes
   d. Winmsd

3. To determine which service pack is installed on Office 2000 components, you should _____.
   a. click Control Panel/Add Remove Programs
   b. use the Help menu in any Office component
   c. use the Netdiag tool from a command prompt
   d. use the Service Pack Helper tool from the Office Resource Kit

4. What tool can be used to discover the list of installed hot fixes for Windows 2000?
   a. Server Manager
   b. System Console
   c. Control Panel/Services
   d. Netdiag

5. A client has called with a problem. The client decided to update a Windows 2000 Professional computer by installing all available hot fixes on the system. The computer did not have any service packs installed, but did have a complement of applications and data. The computer now will not boot at all. What went wrong? (Choose all that apply.)
   a. The Server Manager was corrupted.
   b. They failed to install the latest service pack prior to installing the hot fixes.
   c. They installed all available hot fixes manually instead of using the Windows Update tool.
   d. They installed the hot fixes while not logged on as an administrator.

6. Your Windows NT 4.0 WINS server is exhibiting some unusual behavior. You have tried repeatedly to delete entries from the WINS database, but these deleted entries keep showing up in the database. You have checked the replication partners for this WINS server and they have the same problem. What is the solution? (Choose all that apply.)
   a. Break the replication link between the WINS servers and delete the entries manually on all WINS servers at once.
   b. Install Windows NT 4.0 Service Pack 3.
   c. Add the WINSManDel entry to the Registry as a D_WORD with a setting of 1.
   d. Install Windows NT 4.0 Service Pack 4.

OBJECTIVES

3.4.4 Remove service packs and hot fixes.

UNINSTALLING SERVICE PACKS AND HOT FIXES

UNDERSTANDING THE OBJECTIVE

Service packs and hot fixes are not like normal applications. They have specific constraints on their installation, and they have very specific constraints on any attempts to uninstall them. Service packs and hot fixes do more than copy files and drivers. They also apply functional changes and updates to the Registry settings of both the operating system and any applications targeted by the service pack or hot fix. Changes to the Registry are not reversible. Attempts to uninstall service packs or hot fixes may, and probably will, render the system unstable. Service packs cannot be completely removed from a Microsoft operating system or application. The situation for hot fixes is similar; attempting to uninstall them may render the system unstable.

WHAT YOU REALLY NEED TO KNOW

◆ When installing service packs for the operating system, you will be prompted to select the option to support the uninstallation of the service pack. If you select the uninstall option, a folder named $NTServicepackUninstall$ will be created in the %SYSTEMROOT% folder. The created folder contains the files from the current installation of Windows 2000 that will be replaced by the service pack installation. However, only one Uninstall folder is created by the service pack installation; each successive service pack uses the same Uninstall folder for its files.

◆ The files that are backed up for an automated restore by one operating system service pack installation are overwritten by the next installation. Therefore, to attempt to uninstall a service pack, you must first copy the service pack Uninstall folder to a different location, preferably not on the computer that will have the service pack installed. After this folder is copied, you can install the desired service pack. Hot fixes do not prompt you to create this Uninstall directory. They simply replace files without user intervention.

◆ The ability to uninstall a service pack depends entirely on whether the option to back up files for a service pack uninstall was selected. Successful removal of a service pack and the availability of the tools required to remove the service pack can happen only when the uninstall option has been selected. If the uninstall option was selected, then two techniques exist. The first technique is to use the Add and Remove Programs applet in Control Panel. Once the Remove option is selected, follow the instructions. The other method is to use the **spuninst** command-line tool, which is located at %systemroot%\$NtServicePackUninstall$\. Type the spuninst command, and then reboot the computer to remove the service pack. Note that this is a technique only for the Windows 2000 service pack, not other operating systems.

◆ Hot fixes can be uninstalled using the Add and Remove Programs applet in Settings/Control Panel. However, removing a hot fix can introduce system instability and render the computer unusable. Make certain to thoroughly back up your system before attempting to uninstall a hot fix.

OBJECTIVES ON THE JOB

Service packs and hot fixes permanently change the systems on which they are installed. They replace key operating system files and device drivers with newer versions. Service packs will, and hot fixes might modify or supplement the Registry.

PRACTICE TEST QUESTIONS

1. The proper procedure to remove a hot fix is to _____.
   a. manually clean the Registry and reboot the computer
   b. use the hot fix uninstall tool
   c. use the Control Panel/Add and Remove Programs applet
   d. go to the Windows hot fix link at *www.servicepacks.microsoft.com*

2. Service packs can be removed by using the _____. (Choose all that apply.)
   a. Control Panel/Add and Remove Programs applet
   b. RegClean utility
   c. spuninst utility
   d. manual Registry cleaning process

3. The proper method for removing a service pack from an application such as Microsoft Office 2000 is _____.
   a. to use Control Panel/Add and Remove Programs to remove the service pack from the application
   b. to remove the application and then reinstall the application
   c. to use the Rollback Service Pack utility in the Control Panel
   d. none of the above

4. A hot fix can be removed from a Windows 2000 computer by using the _____ utility.
   a. hot fix uninstall
   b. Rmhotfix command line
   c. Control Panel/Add and Remove Programs
   d. hot fix rollback

5. Last week from the Microsoft Web site, a user installed a hot fix on a computer. Now the computer is not running correctly. The user wants the correct procedure to uninstall this hot fix. What should you tell the user?
   a. You must determine if the user selected the option to create an uninstall directory for the hot fix first. If the user created this directory, then the user may proceed directly to the uninstall option for the hot fix.
   b. The hot fix can be removed without difficulty using the Control Panel/Add and Remove Programs applet.
   c. Hot fixes cannot be removed. You will schedule an appointment for a technician to come out and rebuild the computer.
   d. The user needs to download another hot fix in order to remove this hot fix from the system.

6. To uninstall a Windows 2000 service pack, you must select the Uninstall option during the original installation process. The service pack will then create a special directory to hold the files that were replaced during the service pack installation. The name and location of this directory folder is _____.
   a. C:\WINNT\UNINSTALL
   b. %SYSTEMROOT%\UNINSTALL
   c. %systemroot%\$NtServicePackUninstall$\
   d. %systemroot%\%windir%\$NtServicePackUninstall$\

Section 4

Configuring, Managing, Securing, and Troubleshooting Active Directory Organizational Units and Group Policy

4.1 Create, manage, and troubleshoot User and Group objects in Active Directory.

USER AND GROUP MANAGEMENT

UNDERSTANDING THE OBJECTIVE

If you are migrating from a Windows NT 4.0 environment to a Windows 2000 environment, you know that an NT 4.0 domain holds information about users and groups only. You are also aware that you may populate only a limited amount of user information into the NT 4.0 accounts. With AD, however, you now can have user accounts that are populated with a great variety of data that can be placed in the information store for each user.

WHAT YOU REALLY NEED TO KNOW

◆ To begin populating your AD environment, you must first create user accounts. You can also create, in advance, computer accounts for the machines that will join your AD environment. These computer accounts can be created when the computers are joined to the AD domain during the build process. User accounts and computer accounts may be created using a scripted approach with a variety of scripting techniques, or they may be created manually.

◆ Just as your AD environment will hold a population of users and their accounts, so too will it contain a population of groups for the AD environment. Some of these groups will exist by default in the AD environment when it is created; as the administrator, you can create others to provide enhanced functionality and control for and of your supported users. All user accounts begin with the basic User type, while several different types of Groups exist: Local, Domain Local, Global, and Universal. Of these, the Universal Group will be found only in a Windows 2000 Native Mode environment. Also, the functionality of the Domain Local Group will differ between a domain in Mixed mode and a domain in Native mode.

◆ After the user account has been created, it must be configured. By default, there are 55 separate data fields to populate in the attribute list for each AD user. Additional attributes can be enabled. You either add them to the AD Schema directly or you enable attributes that exist in the Schema, yet have not been activated.

◆ After the users and their accounts have been created, you may need to search for specific attributes of a specific user. You also may need to locate other information contained within the AD itself. The Find tool will locate these resources for you and allow you to manipulate or alter them when located.

◆ Another user management feature is the ability to create and use template accounts, which, in turn, are used to create common classes of user accounts. As an alternative to the scripted creation of user accounts, templates provide great flexibility and control.

OBJECTIVES ON THE JOB

User and Group management is an important part of your daily Windows 2000 AD management. AD provides various tools to facilitate this part of your administrative duties.

PRACTICE TEST QUESTIONS

1. **If your Windows 2000 AD domain is in Mixed Mode, which Group type does not exist in your domain? (Choose all that apply.)**
   a. Local Group
   b. Domain Local Group
   c. Global Group
   d. Universal Group

2. **Users in Windows 2000 can belong to a maximum of _____ groups.**
   a. 2048
   b. 1023
   c. 512
   d. 1024

3. **By default, all users in the AD belong to the _____ Group.**
   a. Domain Users
   b. Network Configuration Users
   c. Users
   d. Everyone

4. **As an administrator, you must locate a user's Generational Suffix in the AD. Which tool should you use?**
   a. ADSI
   b. LDP
   c. Find
   d. Search

5. **One of the default attributes in the AD is the _____ value.**
   a. Team Members
   b. Managed By
   c. UNIX Realm
   d. Context

6. **You are the administrator for a child domain in a Windows 2000 AD forest. You need to locate a user whose account lives in a peer domain. You are able to connect to this other domain because of what AD feature?**
   a. DDNS name resolution
   b. AD transitive trusts
   c. Kerberos trusts
   d. SRV records and the Global Catalog

4.1.1 Create and configure user and computer accounts for new and existing users.

BASIC USER ACCOUNT MANAGEMENT

UNDERSTANDING THE OBJECTIVE

In a Windows NT 4.0 domain environment or a Windows 2000 AD domain, all users and their computers require accounts for full access to the resources hosted in the domain. Although Windows NT 4.0 and Windows 2000 require different tools to create the user and computer accounts, the desired goal and the end result are the same.

WHAT YOU REALLY NEED TO KNOW

◆ Windows NT 4.0 domain user accounts are created using a tool called User Manager for Domains. This simple GUI tool supports the creation and configuration of user accounts. With this tool, the administrator can create a single user account, assign a password, and configure other account-related settings, such as the expiration date of the account and whether the user can change his or her own password. This tool exists on Windows NT 4.0 domain controllers and Windows 2000 domain controllers and is accessed by typing the command usrmgr in the Run box.

◆ Just as every user requires a user account, every computer requires a computer account. Windows NT 4.0 computer accounts are created with Server Manager. This tool is started by typing srvmgr in the Run box. Although the tool was intended for use with Windows NT 4.0 computers (workstations and servers), Windows 2000 computers (running either Professional or Server) will also appear in the interface and can be minimally managed. This tool allows computer accounts to be created for Windows NT 4.0 computers and provides management functions such as creating and deleting shares and starting and stopping services on both platforms. Functions that are not supported on Windows 2000 will return an error message stating this lack of support.

◆ Windows 2000 users and computers are managed from a tool called Active Directory Users and Computers. This is an **MMC** snap-in tool that supports many levels of functionality, from creating and deleting accounts, to organizing the entire AD forest and/or domain. Creating a user in Windows 2000 is more involved because the administrator must decide where to place these accounts prior to the actual account creation. For instance, should the new user be placed into the Users container object, or should the user instead be placed into a newly created OU somewhere in the AD? What about the user's computer? Should that be placed into the default Computer OU or into another special purpose OU in AD?

OBJECTIVES ON THE JOB

Creating accounts for users and computers is an important part of the daily administration of either a Windows NT 4.0 or Windows 2000 AD domain.

PRACTICE TEST QUESTIONS

1. **By default, newly created AD user accounts are placed _____.**
   a. in the User's OU
   b. in the User's container
   c. where specified by the administrator
   d. where specified by the domain's New Users Home GPO setting

2. **The initials UPN stand for _____.**
   a. Universal Private Name
   b. User Principal Network
   c. User Principal Name
   d. Universal Principal Name

3. **A UPN is used for _____.**
   a. identifying the user's home folder
   b. registering the user with their domain GC
   c. registering the user's account with the DDNS service
   d. supporting universal logon anywhere in the domain

4. **For a UPN to work, the users must be able to contact a _____ server in the AD site.**
   a. DDNS
   b. DHCP
   c. GC
   d. ISA

5. **It is now 3:00 p.m. You have just been given a spreadsheet with the account information for 500 new users. You must add these users to your AD domain by 6:00 p.m. What should you do?**
   a. Import the users using the CSVDA tool and file format.
   b. Import the users using the CSVDE tool and file format.
   c. Import the users using a batch file process.
   d. Select some team members and begin adding the new users manually.

6. **Because of a recent business reorganization decision, you must update the Department attribute for 1000 pre-existing users in your AD domain by the close of business tonight. It is now 11:00 a.m. How can you accomplish this?**
   a. Contact your administrative team members and divide the list of 1000 users.
   b. Use the Find function in AD to locate all the users by the current department, and then modify their accounts.
   c. Create a CSVDE script to make the changes for you.
   d. Create an LDIF script to make the changes for you.

7. **A default user attribute in AD for a normal user is _____.**
   a. telex number
   b. mother's maiden name
   c. passport number
   d. NDS context

4.1.2 Troubleshoot groups. Considerations include nesting, scope, and type.

BASIC GROUP MANAGEMENT

UNDERSTANDING THE OBJECTIVE

Groups and their proper use and management form the backbone of any Microsoft domain environment. To provide the maximum level of security for you and the maximum level of functionality for the users, permissions to access resources in Windows 2000 and Windows NT 4.0 should always be controlled and assigned by using either built-in or custom groups.

WHAT YOU REALLY NEED TO KNOW

- ◆ There are several different kinds of groups in a Microsoft domain. Windows NT 4.0 supports only two kinds of groups: Local groups and Global groups. Windows 2000 supports Local groups, Domain Local groups, Global groups, and Universal groups. Each group type has specific use and function constraints.

- ◆ The simplest type of group is the Global group. A Global group is simply a container object that holds user accounts that must be grouped together in a particular fashion for functionality within the domain. Global groups hold users from only their own member domain—and from no other domain. Global groups cannot have permissions assigned to them. However, while they cannot hold users from other domains, Global groups can cross domain boundaries to allow users from one domain access to resources in another domain.

- ◆ Local groups are another type of container object. They are intended to hold Global groups for rights assignments to domain objects. However, they will also hold individual users, although this practice is discouraged. Local groups live on a computer and can never leave that computer. They cannot cross over to other domains. They will, however, hold Global groups from other domains. Permission to access resources in the network is assigned to Local groups. Local groups live on individual computers; Domain Local groups live in the AD domain itself.

- ◆ Universal groups are a supergroup found only when a Windows 2000 domain has switched from Mixed Mode to Native Mode. A Universal group is a container object that cannot directly receive the assignment of permissions. It instead receives permissions through its membership in Local groups. Universal groups exist as Forest-wide objects and may access any domain within a Windows 2000 AD environment.

- ◆ Group nesting is a new concept for groups in Windows 2000. Group nesting means that when a Windows 2000 domain is switched from Mixed mode to Native mode, it is possible to place a group inside another group of the same type.

OBJECTIVES ON THE JOB

Proper administration of the revised and additional group types in Windows 2000 will be an important task for you in a Windows 2000 domain environment.

PRACTICE TEST QUESTIONS

1. **As the administrator of a Windows 2000 AD domain, you want to use Universal groups to simplify assigning permissions for domain resources. However, you have been unable to implement this plan because you can see the Universal group assignment button, but it is dimmed. What is wrong?**
   a. You don't have the permissions necessary to use Universal groups.
   b. You are unable to contact a GC.
   c. Your domain is in Mixed Mode, not Native Mode.
   d. Your domain is in Native mode, but Universal groups have been turned off through the Registry to optimize replication.

2. **You want to add a user to a new group, but every time you add the user to the group, their account is automatically disabled. After you remove the group, their account is active again. What should you suspect?**
   a. Their account is corrupt and must be re-created or restored.
   b. They belong to too many groups.
   c. Their account is the victim of conflicting GPOs in the AD.
   d. Their X.509 certificate has expired.

3. **Individual users should not be placed into Universal groups because of _____ issues.**
   a. security
   b. management
   c. access
   d. replication

4. **An irate user has called you to complain about not being able to log on to the AD after a member of your staff reset the account and added the user to another group. As you troubleshoot the account you notice that the account was reset and that this user belongs to 1024 groups. What is the problem?**
   a. The account was reset and this disconnected the user from their AD GUID.
   b. The account was reset and the password has not synchronized yet.
   c. Because the user belongs to 1024 groups, their account automatically disabled itself.
   d. The user needed to be given their new UPN for the logon to complete.

5. **You want to nest Global groups in your Windows NT 4.0 domain. How can you accomplish this?**
   a. Use the Active Directory Domains and Trusts snap-in to connect to the NT 4.0 domain, and implement your change there.
   b. Upgrade the NT 4.0 domain to Windows 2000.
   c. Apply the ADTools Hot Fix from Microsoft.
   d. Add the GroupNestingOn entry to the NT 4.0 Registry as a type DWORD with a value of 1.

4.1.3 Configure a user account by using Active Directory Users and Computers. Settings include passwords and assigning groups.

USER ACCOUNT IMPLEMENTATION

UNDERSTANDING THE OBJECTIVE

Windows 2000 User accounts are configured using Active Directory Users and Computers, which is an MMC snap-in. All user account properties can be configured from a single interface, and connections are allowed to other domains in the AD forest.

WHAT YOU REALLY NEED TO KNOW

◆ When a user account is configured in Windows 2000, the account is initially created using the New User screen in AD Users and Computers. This allows the administrator to enter basic user information, such as the user's name, the Windows 2000 logon name, and a down-level logon name. After the name information has been entered, the next screen allows the assignment of a domain password and password settings such as expiration date. At the final screen, the administrator commits the addition to the AD schema, and then the user may begin using the account. The account has not been completely configured, however.

◆ Unlike previous versions of Windows, AD User accounts can be created in any OU within the AD environment. An administrator must know the intended location for the new user when the account is created. If this information is not known or changes, the newly created user account can be moved to another part of the AD environment as necessary.

◆ Right-clicking the newly created user reveals several options. These options have been designed so that the administrator does not have to open many different GUI screens. Choosing the Properties option will open the account for complete editing by the administrator or delegated support personnel.

◆ After the tool is opened, you will see approximately 15 separate tabs, depending on how many AD-enabled applications and services are running in the domain. Each tab supports the configuration of a different part of the individual user account setting. The individual settings include the ability to assign group memberships and passwords; other settings include multiple telephone numbers and direct reports.

OBJECTIVES ON THE JOB

The Active Directory Users and Computers snap-in allows an administrator to configure all user account settings from a single GUI interface. This tool simplifies your creation of user accounts because you no longer must access many different tools to effectively configure these individual accounts. As additional AD-enabled applications and services, such as Exchange 2000, are installed into the AD forest, the user configuration information is added to this centralized view for your convenience as an administrator.

PRACTICE TEST QUESTIONS

1. The initial account setup screens for new user accounts in AD include the _____ screens. (Choose all that apply.)
   a. User logon name
   b. Confirm password
   c. User logon name (pre-Windows 2000)
   d. E-mail address

2. By default, a newly created user belongs to the _____ group.
   a. Everyone
   b. Authenticated Users
   c. Domain Users
   d. AD Users

3. While searching your list of Global groups in AD, you noticed that the icon associated with several Global groups looked different than the icon for other Global groups. The hair color of the icon looked gray, not black. The groups seem to function without difficulty. What might cause this difference?
   a. These groups are corrupt and must be re-created.
   b. Your AD NTDS.DIT file is fragmented and must be defragged as soon as possible.
   c. These groups contain users from another domain.
   d. These groups contain more than 500 members.

4. You are the administrator of a Windows 2000 AD domain. You have been given the job of compiling a database that shows the groups to which every user in the corporation belongs. How can you accomplish this?
   a. Create a script to run in the ADSI tool.
   b. Use the showgrps.exe tool from the Server Resource Kit.
   c. Use the Countgroups.vbs script that installs with Dcpromo.
   d. Use Active Directory Users and Groups to count the groups.

5. Your corporate HR team wants to automate the process of adding user accounts to AD. What steps should you take to enable this functionality for them? (Choose all that apply.)
   a. Test your script.
   b. Give the HR Team full access to your AD structure.
   c. Create an LDIF script to add the users.
   d. Use the Delegation of Control Wizard to assign appropriate permissions to the HR team.

6. One difference between CSVDE and LDIF is that _____.
   a. CSVDE works only with Microsoft applications
   b. LDFE works only with Microsoft applications
   c. CSVDE can create passwords
   d. LDIF can be used to modify data in AD

4.1.4 Perform a search for objects in Active Directory.

SEARCHING ACTIVE DIRECTORY

UNDERSTANDING THE OBJECTIVE

An important new feature for supported users in Windows 2000 AD is the ability of users and administrators to search the entire AD for objects. The AD version in Windows 2000, Version 1 of the AD, has a published capacity of 100,000,000 objects. An object could include a single user's home phone number or a group of 3,000 users in a remote office. It could also include print devices published in the AD or a published folder.

WHAT YOU REALLY NEED TO KNOW

◆ Locating objects in a database that can contain 100,000,000 objects can be a daunting task. Fortunately, AD has two comprehensive search tools for the AD. The first tool for administrators is located in the Active Directory Users and Computers MMC snap-in and is labeled Find.

◆ To access the Find tool as the administrator you must first open Active Directory Users and Computers, and then either use the Find icon on the menu bar or right-click an object in the AD tree. You can also search the entire AD forest by selecting the top of the AD tree as your search origin.

◆ After the point-of-origin for the search has been selected, you must choose the criteria by which to search or the objects for which to search. Search criteria could include "users, contacts, and groups", "OUs," or "Printers." Examples of search objects might be the name of a user's manager, a telephone number, or a home address. The Find tool also allows the administrator to enter constraints for data fields. The constraints could be, for example, "Starts With" or "Contains." Such constraints allow you to further refine and define your search parameters.

◆ The first tool used for searching the AD environment is a GUI-based tool. The second tool, also GUI-based, is ADSI Edit. ADSI Edit is more powerful than the Find tool in AD Users and Computers and allows you to work with and directly access the AD schema. This tool also allows you to search for specific data types or objects and supports the use of scripted searches of the AD itself.

◆ The ADSI Edit tool also allows the administrator to search for the individual attributes that AD objects comprise. Because each AD object can contain more than 800 separate attributes, there is an enormous amount of data to which you will have access for conducting searches.

OBJECTIVES ON THE JOB

Searching AD may involve using different tools, depending on the level of detail desired and the kind of search being conducted. To conduct a normal search for user information or the location of a print device, you would probably use the Find tool in AD Users and Computers. For detailed, in-depth searches, you may want to use ADSI Edit.

PRACTICE TEST QUESTIONS

1. **As an administrator, you need to search AD from time to time. Which tool will let you search the AD? (Choose all that apply.)**
   a. Start/Search
   b. Active Directory Users and Computers/Find
   c. Start/Programs/Administrative Tools/Find
   d. LDP

2. **Using the Find tool in Active Directory Users and Computers, you could locate print devices that support _____.**
   a. input trays
   b. printing photographs
   c. Apple print servers
   d. SCSI ports

3. **Which AD administration tool installs by default and supports the Find command?**
   a. Active Directory Sites and Services
   b. Active Directory Domains and Trusts
   c. Active Directory User and Groups
   d. Active Directory Replication Monitor

4. **As an administrator, you want to write a script to search the AD for a specific attribute in the 23 domains that are part of your corporate forest. What tool will let you search the AD using a scripted solution?**
   a. ADSI Edit
   b. LDP
   c. Dsquery
   d. Find

5. **How many searchable attributes exist for each user in the AD?**
   a. 20
   b. 55
   c. 80
   d. 40

6. **You have just taken a call from users who complain that they cannot search the AD for the telephone number of a co-worker, but they could do so earlier today. They need a resolution quickly to complete a business project. You know that they are in a small office that connects to the corporate infrastructure using a dial-on-demand router. Because they are working in this small office, what do you suspect may be preventing them from searching the AD?**
   a. an incorrectly configured dial-on-demand router
   b. a failed network connection
   c. faulty telephone lines
   d. a failed GC server

4.1.5 Use templates to create user accounts.

DUPLICATE ACCOUNT CREATION

UNDERSTANDING THE OBJECTIVE

The use of account templates allows you to create default accounts for AD users and then populate these accounts with information that is specific to the individual users. These account templates can speed up your account-creation process and make it easy to reproduce your most frequently used account types.

WHAT YOU REALLY NEED TO KNOW

◆ To create an account template, you begin with either a new empty account or with an account that already exists in the AD environment. The creation of the templates differs, depending on which option you select.

◆ If you want to begin with a new empty account, you must create that account from scratch just as you would to create the account for an actual user. Make certain to configure all settings that you wish to transfer to the accounts created with the template. It is extremely important to remember that even though this is an account template, it is a completely valid, usable AD account. Be sure to assign a strict password to the account and also disable the account so it cannot be used to gain access to your AD environment. When the account is copied for a new user, the copy becomes active—the newly created account will not be disabled. Consider the option of creating a special OU specifically to hold these account templates, and then assigning strict GPOs to this OU.

◆ The other process for creating account templates is much easier. It involves finding the account of a person who currently has the appropriate permissions and settings and then copying that account. All account settings and permissions copy to the new account. Personal settings, such as name, telephone number, and home address, will not. This technique creates a duplicate of the original account; the duplicate functions exactly as the original account functioned. A possible issue may arise from any Access Denied settings that you were unaware of at the time of creation. This issue does not exist when you create a brand new account. An account that was copied does not have to be created as disabled because copying does not take place until a new account is actually needed. This contrasts with having many preconfigured accounts in your AD environment waiting for a new user.

◆ After you have created account templates, you may use them in exactly the same fashion as any other account in the AD.

OBJECTIVES ON THE JOB

Creating account templates is a valuable technique for your daily administration of a Windows 2000 AD environment. If proper security configurations are used, these templates are safe and can greatly speed up the process of adding new AD member accounts.

PRACTICE TEST QUESTIONS

1. **Your corporate HR staff wants to be able to create a variety of user accounts without waiting for the IT staff to create them. What resource could you make available to the HR department for this process?**
   a. Training on how to use LDIF files
   b. Complete access to Active Directory Users and Computers
   c. Visio Enterprise
   d. User account templates

2. **A recently hired administrator in your office created a new user template and stored the template in the Users Container object in the AD. You are now noticing some activity from this account. You disabled the account quickly but this should not have happened in the first place. What did the other administrator do that was incorrect?**
   a. The administrator placed the account template into the Users Container.
   b. The administrator created the template without following corporate guidelines.
   c. The administrator forgot to disable the account template after creation.
   d. The administrator forgot to assign a password.

3. **An account template can be created in several different ways. The easiest method is to _____.**
   a. create an account from scratch
   b. populate an account with values from several different accounts
   c. copy an account that already has the settings you need
   d. use the ADSI Edit tool

4. **You should always start account template names with a nonalphabetic character because this will cause the account to be _____.**
   a. listed first in the account listings
   b. disabled automatically
   c. activated automatically when a user name is added
   d. configured with the AD Disabled Account flag

5. **By default, account templates in the AD are assigned a password length of _____.**
   a. 8 characters
   b. 12 characters
   c. 0 characters because you must assign a password manually
   d. 0 characters because you must create a SmartCard PIN

6. **Account templates can be used _____.**
   a. only in the OU in which they were created
   b. only in the domain in which they were created
   c. only in the forest in which they were created
   d. anywhere in a Windows 2000 AD environment

4.1.6 Reset an existing computer account.

AD COMPUTER ACCOUNT MAINTAINENCE

UNDERSTANDING THE OBJECTIVE

In AD, just as users have accounts, computers also have accounts. All computers that belong to an AD environment have an associated computer account. One key difference between user accounts and computer accounts, however, is that while many users (each with a different account) may share one computer, the computer remains the same no matter which user is currently logged in. This is a one-to-many relationship, which is one computer to many users.

WHAT YOU REALLY NEED TO KNOW

◆ Just as users may need their accounts reset from time to time, computers may also require periodic account maintenance. This is done using AD Users and Computers after the particular computer account has been located. One possible maintenance activity is the resetting of computer accounts. Note that only user workstations and member servers can have their accounts reset.

◆ To reset a computer account in AD for a computer that no longer exists, the administrator must locate the computer account in its parent OU and, once located, right-click the computer object. You will then see the option to Reset Account. Click this setting and then click the Yes button to reset. If you were successful, you will see a message that says the account was successfully reset. If you reset a computer account for a computer that had a functioning AD account and could use AD resources before being reset, you have now completely disconnected that computer from the AD domain and it can no longer authenticate to AD. This may cause significant problems for your users.

◆ When a user account is reset, the user's password is reset. To gain access to AD, the user simply needs to log in and, when prompted, supply the new password. When a computer account is reset, the password used by the computer is reset to a default value. However, computers cannot log in using the new password because the initial value was used only the first time this machine joined the domain. After the initial use, the passwords are changed and maintained by the computer and AD. Resetting the computer account tells the AD that this computer no longer exists and that any computer presenting itself with the old name and a new password is, in fact, a new computer. AD does not allow the computer to use the old account.

◆ The process of resetting a computer account can be used if a computer needs to be rebuilt because it allows the same name to be reused with a new account password. But the original machine must be re-created because its AD GUID is no longer valid.

OBJECTIVES ON THE JOB

As an administrator you must remember to reset a computer only when needed, and only when the computer no longer exists in the AD environment.

PRACTICE TEST QUESTIONS

1. **A technician was working with a user on the telephone clicked the wrong setting, and reset the user's computer account. This user was working on a special project and needs access to the AD to complete the project. How can you help this user?**
   a. Simply have the user restart the computer and resynchronize the account.
   b. Back up the data and format the computer, then restore from the backup tape.
   c. Remove the computer from the domain and join it to another domain.
   d. Rename the computer and join it to the domain again.

2. **Only Windows 2000 member servers and Windows 2000 _____ can have their accounts reset.**
   a. domain controllers
   b. stand-alone servers
   c. Web servers
   d. workstations

3. **You are working in a remote office and need to add a new computer to the AD Computers container. You do not have access to a computer with the Windows 2000 administrative tools, but you do have access to another computer that is connected to the AD forest. This computer account has not been created in advance. How can you join this computer to the domain?**
   a. Call your office and ask someone there to create the computer account.
   b. Create the account yourself using the netdom join command.
   c. Create the account yourself using the netdom create command.
   d. Use the ADSI Edit command of create computer.

4. **A computer account in the AD should only be reset after the computer _____.**
   a. account has been deleted from the DDNS database
   b. has been rebuilt
   c. has been renamed
   d. has been deleted

5. **If you are having trouble joining a computer to a domain or resetting a computer account, you should use the _____ command to troubleshoot.**
   a. netdom
   b. nltest
   c. netdiag
   d. ldp

6. **If you are having trouble with a computer that is unable to join a domain, you can examine the contents of the _____ file to troubleshoot.**
   a. netsetup.log
   b. domainjoin.log
   c. netdiag.log
   d. netdom.log

4.2 Manage object and container permissions.

MANAGING AD OBJECT PERMISSIONS

UNDERSTANDING THE OBJECTIVE

As you add objects to the AD, you must assign the permissions required to control these objects. Because it is unlikely that you will work entirely by yourself to administer the AD environment, you will need to delegate your administrative authority to selected individuals within your organization. Along with the delegation of authority, you must assign permissions to match the administrative control assignments. Once made, you may also have to troubleshoot the assignments. Fortunately, AD provides tools for both of these administrative duties.

WHAT YOU REALLY NEED TO KNOW

◆ After selecting key members of your organization to share your administrative duties, you will need a method to assign permissions and rights to AD objects to these members. Because the AD environment is so granular, assigning permissions and rights can be a formidable task.

◆ The native tool to make these assignments in Windows 2000 AD is the Delegation of Control Wizard. Anyone with the permission to open the tool is allowed to take advantage of its intuitive graphical interface. That person can easily make permission and rights assignments in AD, without having to access AD at the **ACL** level.

◆ The Delegation of Control Wizard uses its GUI interface to simplify the assignment of permissions for objects in the AD by supporting a standard set of permissions and assignments. However, if desired, considerable customization is also supported. This makes the tool ideal for such tasks as assigning permissions to members of a help desk. Such permissions would allow specific, but limited, job-related roles in the AD.

◆ Because assignments of rights or permissions can be problematic, you can troubleshoot the assignment of rights using the Delegation of Control Wizard. As an administrator, you have the ability (unless removed by a higher authority) to access the ACL of objects within the AD and configure individual permissions manually. This technique fully exposes the rights configuration interface in the AD and allows extremely precise control of rights and permissions.

◆ The property tabs associated with this set of tools are context-sensitive and change their lists of assignable permissions as the Apply Onto selection is changed. This enables control over specific functions in AD.

OBJECTIVES ON THE JOB

As the administrator of an AD environment, the ability to delegate control for certain parts of your environment (which is a feature that Windows NT 4.0 never supported), is an important tool. Your use of this tool benefits your supported users and your own support staff, who can now have only the permissions required by their job code.

PRACTICE TEST QUESTIONS

1. **As an administrator, you will need to configure user account permissions to support job functions. The tool of choice for configuring these permissions is the _____. (Choose all that apply.)**
   a. User Rights Configuration tool
   b. Security Tab for the required user account
   c. Delegation of Control Wizard
   d. Active Directory Users and Computers tool

2. **You are the administrator of your Windows 2000 AD forest. You need to configure permissions for a newly hired help desk technician. However, the previous administrator who configured the help desk technician accounts assigned too many rights. Problems arose because these technicians had so many rights. How can you avoid this problem? (Choose all that apply.)**
   a. Redesign the AD environment and create a separate OU for the technicians.
   b. Move the technicians into the same OU as the users, and then create a strict GPO to control these users. Apply a filter to the technicians' accounts to block the GPO.
   c. Test the newly created technician's OU to verify the correct permissions.
   d. Use the Delegation of Control Wizard.

3. **The Delegation of Control Wizard works by adjusting the _____ of the target object.**
   a. SACL
   b. DACL
   c. ACL
   d. ACE

4. **To troubleshoot the permissions assigned by the Delegation of Control Wizard to AD resources, you should use the _____.**
   a. Effective Permissions tab associated with the AD object
   b. Resultant Permissions tab associated with the AD object
   c. Active Directory Users and Computers/Advanced features
   d. Security/Advanced tab associated with the AD object

5. **The _____ contains the access permissions of an individual user in the AD.**
   a. SACL
   b. DACL
   c. ACL
   d. ACE

6. **An ACL consists of entries called _____.**
   a. permission entries
   b. permissions
   c. user access rights
   d. access control entries

4.2.1 Use the Delegation of Control Wizard to configure inherited and explicit permissions.

AUTOMATING PERMISSION ASSIGNMENT

UNDERSTANDING THE OBJECTIVE

As you populate your AD with users, printers, published folders, and other objects, it quickly becomes apparent that you must exercise control and delegate control permissions over the different parts of your AD to effectively manage it. You can use the Delegation of Control Wizard for this process.

WHAT YOU REALLY NEED TO KNOW

- The Windows NT 4.0 domain featured a very simple structure. It contained only users and their accounts. It did not contain a great deal of information about the specifics of the user accounts, nor did it permit the inclusion of other kinds of objects within its structure. This is contrary to the AD environment, which can host a tremendous amount of data about and for your users. Another distinguishing characteristic of the AD is the granularity of functional control that you, as an administrator, can exercise or assign to others to exercise. However, this granularity can lead to problems when trying to control access to AD.

- As an administrator you do not need to be involved in the actual daily administration of the AD environment. You can delegate permission to responsible parties to perform the normal, day-to-day administration of AD. However, as the administrator of a Windows 2000 AD Forest, how can you control the kinds of access and the level of functionality that these designated parties exercise in your AD environment? Your tool of choice is the Delegation of Control Wizard for the AD.

- The Delegation of Control Wizard is a GUI tool that functions at the site, domain, or OU level in AD. An administrator or other person with appropriate permissions to use the tool is guided through the process of assigning rights and permissions to resources contained within the AD. The Delegation of Control Wizard has, at a minimum, four configuration windows that support the assignment of permissions.

- The first window in the Wizard is the Welcome window. Choosing Next leads you to the Users or Groups window, which allows you to select the individual users or groups that will receive the permissions. The next window contains the list of default common tasks that can be delegated, or allows for the creation of custom tasks using additional windows. The final window is the Completing the Delegation window.

OBJECTIVES ON THE JOB

The Delegation of Control Wizard lets an administrator delegate differing levels of administrative control over selected parts of the AD environment to authorized individuals to perform designated tasks. You can use the Wizard to lessen the administrative overhead of AD by distributing the administrative functions among a few select individuals.

PRACTICE TEST QUESTIONS

1. You are the domain administrator for 500 employees. Management wants to distribute some of your authority to selected individuals within the company. How could you train a helper without allowing him or her to use AD Users and Computers?
   - a. Use the Delegation of Control Wizard to delegate permissions.
   - b. Create a Taskpad view of AD Users and Computers.
   - c. Place them into an OU and assign a strict GPO.
   - d. Give them full control permission to the AD Users and Computers snap-in.

2. Some user accounts in a specific OU in your domain have been misconfigured with the Delegation of Control Wizard. How can you correct and reconfigure these accounts?
   - a. Use the Delegation of Control Wizard again to correct the problem.
   - b. Right-click the OU and choose the Properties/Security tab, select the incorrectly configured user accounts, and then correct the settings using the Advanced button.
   - c. Create an LDIF script to correct the account configuration settings.
   - d. Delete the accounts and re-create them.

3. Using the Delegation of Control Wizard, you can click the Delegate the following common tasks option button or you can click the _____ option button.
   - a. Delegate the following special tasks
   - b. Delegate the following specific tasks
   - c. Create a common task to delegate
   - d. Create a custom task to delegate

4. As the domain administrator for your AD domain, you want to easily configure permissions for your local on-site administrators so they can work on computers in any domain in different AD sites. How can you implement this plan?
   - a. Configure permissions separately on each domain for these administrators.
   - b. Filter permissions on these administrators in each domain.
   - c. Use the Delegation of Control Wizard on each AD site to configure permissions for the administrators.
   - d. Create the accounts for the administrators in the forest root, and then filter the GPO application.

5. The Delegation of Control Wizard works by adjusting the _____ permissions.
   - a. SACL
   - b. DACL
   - c. ACL
   - d. ACE

4.2.2 Configure and troubleshoot object permissions by using object access control lists (ACLs).

TROUBLESHOOTING THE DELEGATION OF CONTROL WIZARD

UNDERSTANDING THE OBJECTIVE

The Delegation of Control Wizard is a useful tool to configure administrative permissions for the AD; however, sometimes account permissions and rights are incorrectly configured with this tool. You must know how to resolve those issues and at what AD level to implement resolutions.

WHAT YOU REALLY NEED TO KNOW

◆ To troubleshoot the permissions enabled by the Delegation of Control Wizard, you must remember that the AD was designed to use the principle of inheritance of rights and permissions. Rights and permissions flow down through the AD structure from the parent object to the child object. If problems are encountered when dealing with rights that were assigned, you might want to begin troubleshooting by viewing the rights and permissions that flow down from the parent and grandparent objects.

◆ The correct order of inheritance in AD is sites–domains–OUs. This means that if all users with a specific assigned permission or right are experiencing the same problem, you should begin troubleshooting at a level that could affect all of these users, instead on concentrating your time and attention on just one user.

◆ After determining the appropriate level at which to begin your troubleshooting, you should locate that object in AD and right-click to bring up the task menu associated with the object. Next choose Properties, and then select the Security tab. This brings up a window divided into an upper window and a lower window. The upper window contains the names of the users or groups that received permissions for this object. The lower window shows the type of permission granted to the individual or group.

◆ After you have located the user or group experiencing the problems, select this object and then choose the Advanced button. In the next window, select the object and choose the Edit button. This takes you to another window with two tabs: the front one labeled Object and the back one labeled Properties. You can use the context-sensitive menus on these two windows to reconfigure any settings that may have been incorrectly configured using the Delegation of Control Wizard. You will also find settings to assign these permissions to specific objects with this container.

OBJECTIVES ON THE JOB

If permissions assigned by the Delegation of Control Wizard require adjustment, you can apply these adjustments using the ACLs that are associated with each object in AD. This level of control is even more granular and allows you to correct the most serious configuration problems.

PRACTICE TEST QUESTIONS

1. **The acronym DACL stands for _____.**
   a. Discrete Access Control Listing
   b. Directory Access Control List
   c. Discretionary Audit Control List
   d. Discretionary Access Control LIst

2. **The DACL consists of ACLs that contain information about the user's account privileges. If the user has been configured with a(n) _____, this will appear in the ACL.**
   a. Security Certificate
   b. No Access permission
   c. account disabled flag
   d. account tombstoned flag

3. **An OU that has been incorrectly configured through the use of the Delegation of Control Wizard may be reset by reconfiguring DACL permissions. The DACL permissions are accessed by selecting _____.**
   a. LDP
   b. ADSI Edit
   c. OU Properties/Security/Advanced settings
   d. Delegation of Control Wizard

4. **ACEs are refreshed by the client only when the client _____.**
   a. logs off and then logs on again
   b. uses the ACERefresh utility from the Server Resource Kit
   c. uses the secedit /run:aceRefreshNow command
   d. receives the default GPO refresh at its normally scheduled interval

5. **As the domain administrator, you want to deny access to certain key business folders that must have their contents protected. You want to ensure that only a few select scientists can manipulate this data. Without using the Delegation of Control Wizard, how could you make these assignments?**
   a. Use a script to modify the computer accounts.
   b. Use a script to modify the user accounts.
   c. Choose the Security tab on the folder you want to protect, and then configure the DACLs manually.
   d. Publish the folders in a new OU and assign the scientists to this OU. Then use the Block Inheritance permission to deny access to all superior objects in the hierarchy.

6. **You have published a shared folder to the AD in a newly created OU. Not counting any specific permissions assigned to this OU, how many different layers of permission, by default, are now attached to this published object?**
   a. 4
   b. 3
   c. 2
   d. 1

4.3 Diagnose Active Directory replication problems.

REPLICATION ISSUES INVOLVING THE AD

UNDERSTANDING THE OBJECTIVE

Because you probably will use more than one domain controller in your AD environment, you must become involved with troubleshooting AD replication, slow WAN link connectivity, replication latency, duplicate AD objects, and using the LostandFound container in the AD structure. These are all important aspects of maintenance.

WHAT YOU REALLY NEED TO KNOW

◆ AD replication issues, if they occur, will have a significant impact on your AD environment, particularly if replication involves WAN connectivity. You must remember that, traditionally, a WAN has implied, unreliable, and slow connectivity. You may have only a 28.8-dial-up connection in place between two AD sites. If so, you will need to adjust and configure the underlying replication topology to fully utilize this infrastructure.

◆ Replication across a WAN is the only replication setting that allows the AD administrator to select the replication method—**RPC** versus SMTP—to be used for this important data. Various issues are associated with each technology, however. RPC requires a good-quality, persistent connection and does not support compression of the AD replication data. SMTP was intended for unreliable connectivity and does use compression, but cannot be used to replicate domain topology information. Only the schema partition and the Network partition can be replicated in this fashion.

◆ Another AD component affected directly by your selection of a replication technology is the latency of your AD information. In your environment, how out-of-date can you afford your information to be? The replication latency impacts your network bandwidth utilization along with other factors, such as issues involving account access and the identification and utilization of published resources.

◆ When duplicate objects are created in the AD, both objects will exist; however; the last object created will have a unique name to differentiate it from the first object. This allows you, as the administrator, to determine which object should remain in the AD schema and which object should be deleted.

◆ The AD also supports LostandFound, a special container object. This serves the role of a repository for AD objects that become disconnected from their parent objects. For example, if an administrator deletes the OU that contains a large group of users while those accounts were being accessed, the users have no parent object in AD to return to and will be placed into the LostandFound container until an administrator is able to resolve the problem.

OBJECTIVES ON THE JOB

Your AD replication configuration can present unique opportunities for you to exercise your network troubleshooting skills.

PRACTICE TEST QUESTIONS

1. **Replication latency describes _____.**
   - a. the schema refresh cycle
   - b. the replication cycle
   - c. the time interval between replication cycles
   - d. the time interval between schema refresh cycles

2. **With intersite replication using SMTP, _____.**
   - a. compression is supported when used for intrasite replication
   - b. compression is not supported when used for intersite replication
   - c. domain partition information will be replicated
   - d. domain partition information will not be replicated

3. **The LostandFound _____ is used for AD objects that become disconnected from their parent objects.**
   - a. OU
   - b. folder
   - c. container
   - d. object

4. **WAN-based replication requires the selection of a _____ and a frequency.**
   - a. protocol
   - b. time window
   - c. compression rate
   - d. refresh rate

5. **User accounts with the letters "CNF" in the name indicate that the account is marked _____.**
   - a. for deletion
   - b. with the AD tombstone flag
   - c. with the pending replication flag
   - d. as a duplicated account in this OU

6. **WAN-based replication can be implemented using two different protocols. The first protocol is _____, and the second protocol is SMTP.**
   - a. TFTP
   - b. RPC
   - c. IGMP
   - d. OSPF

7. **The service that manages intersite replication is called the ISTG, or _____.**
   - a. Intersite Topology Generator
   - b. Intersite Technology Generator
   - c. Internet Topology Generator
   - d. Internal Site Topology Generation

4.3.1 Diagnose problems related to WAN link connectivity.

INTERSITE REPLICATION PROBLEMS

UNDERSTANDING THE OBJECTIVE

Remember that in AD, intrasite replication occurs within a site, and intersite replication occurs between two sites. Also recall that a Site in AD is defined as two or more well-connected IP subnets. Knowing these facts, you can approach the issues that arise from faulty or intermittent WAN connectivity between two or more AD site implementations.

WHAT YOU REALLY NEED TO KNOW

◆ Intrasite replication is a nonscheduled, automatic process. Intersite replication, however, requires configuration. Intersite replication was designed with the assumption that this replication process would have to use unreliable connectivity methods to distribute AD-replicated data throughout an AD environment.

◆ One of the first problems to diagnose with intersite replication may be no replication at all. Intersite replication must be configured to operate successfully. If replication is not occurring, you should check the configuration settings at both ends of the connection. Do you have network connectivity from one side of the connection to the next? Can you successfully view resources on the other side of this connection? If not, then why not?

◆ After investigating the ability to connect one network to another, additional areas of investigation include issues when the time windows are configured for replication to occur on both networks. WAN replication is a time-scheduled service; both sides of the connection must have their replication windows open at the same time. If one window closes as the other window opens, no replication can occur.

◆ What protocol was selected for the replication? Specific constraints are attached to the use of RPC and SMTP. RPC is preferred as it affords a more secure connection for the sensitive data in a replication cycle. However, when the network infrastructure does not support the steady, reliable connectivity needed by RPC, your available connectivity may dictate the use of SNTP. Remember that SNTP will compress replication data, while RPC replication does not.

◆ Another issue may arise from the need for site-link bridges. Are you in a fully routed environment? If not, you must configure site-link bridges for the replication paths needed. A site-link bridge is a structure that maps a routed environment and is used to establish paths through your network topology for replication links to follow. It is similar to the concept and configuration of OSPF routing.

OBJECTIVES ON THE JOB

If your AD environment lives in a single site, you will not need to configure intersite replication. If needed, though, intersite replication requires configuration for functionality.

PRACTICE TEST QUESTIONS

1. Your AD forest consists of two sites and one forest. Each site contains one domain. Each domain logically contains three domain controllers, two in its parent site and the third in the other site. Your network topology does not support routing between these two sites. What should you configure to enable communication between these two sites and domain controllers?
   a. ISTG
   b. KCC
   c. OSPF
   d. a site-link bridge

2. When configuring site-link bridges, the default cost on the links is

   _____.
   a. 1
   b. 50
   c. 100
   d. 500

3. The ISTG is the intersite equivalent of the _____ service.
   a. RRAS
   b. KCC
   c. FRS
   d. NetLogon

4. For replication to occur across a WAN connection, the _____ must be configured.
   a. trust password
   b. subnet mask
   c. compression ratio
   d. time window

5. Even though both sides of a connection are using the same time window settings and the RPC protocol, a consistent failure to replicate could indicate

   _____.
   a. incompatible subnet masks
   b. incompatible site-link bridges
   c. faulty bridgehead servers
   d. unreliable network connections

6. In Question 5 above, assuming that the connection between the sites is unreliable, what technology should be used to facilitate the replication cycle?
   a. IPSec
   b. L2TP
   c. SMTP
   d. TFTP

4.3.2 Diagnose problems involving replication latency. Problems include duplicate objects and the LostandFound container.

AD REPLICATION PROBLEMS

UNDERSTANDING THE OBJECTIVE

Replication latency is the measure of how out of date your AD information is. Issues you may need to resolve include refreshing and updating the list of published objects that reside in the AD, or making certain that attributes of a remote print object are current. However, to support this level of functionality for your clients, you must decide if expending the bandwidth to update this data is a valid use of your available network resources.

WHAT YOU REALLY NEED TO KNOW

◆ Replication latency in an intrasite environment should not be an issue because this replication is controlled by the **KCC**, which is running on every domain controller within your domain. The KCC works on a domain-by-domain basis to maintain the Rule of 3, which governs replication of AD data to domain controllers within the same site for the same domain on a 15-minute replication cycle. If replication latency does become an issue in this environment, you may have too many domain controllers for the calculation of the mesh topology needed by the KCC to successfully complete on all domain controllers. Thus, gaps are left in your replication mesh; this causes other domain controllers to work harder to fill these holes in your mesh.

◆ In terms of intersite replication latency, you need to arrive at a reasonable value for the replication of AD objects and events within your forest. If you do not need the existence of published folders replicated to every corner of your AD, you can adjust the replication latency upward to make it less frequent. This reduces the accuracy of the AD information on the domain controllers receiving this information. This also, of course, affects your bandwidth utilization. The less frequent the replication, the less bandwidth used for replication. The inverse, however, is equally true. The less frequent the replication, the larger the size of the replication packets, so more bandwidth is used to complete the cycle.

◆ What happens if a child object in AD becomes an orphaned object? Objects whose parents no longer exist are placed into the LostandFound container until a decision is made regarding their fate in AD.

◆ What about duplicate objects in the AD that may be created by two or more administrators? In the case of duplicates, AD allows both objects to exist, but changes the name of one to a unique value so the administrator can determine which object should be retained and which can be deleted.

OBJECTIVES ON THE JOB

The diagnosis of replication problems and the problem of child objects that have become disconnected from their parents require different tools and techniques for successful troubleshooting.

PRACTICE TEST QUESTIONS

1. **Another administrator was working on an OU that you have just deleted. The OU had 200 hundred user accounts in it. What has happened to those accounts?**
   a. They have been tombstoned for deletion.
   b. They have already been deleted.
   c. They are still in the AD on other domain controllers because replication has not yet occurred.
   d. They have been placed into the LostandFound container.

2. **You are a newly hired administrator of a Windows 2000 AD domain. You are working in the AD Users and Computers snap-in and want to see the contents of the LostandFound container, but you cannot locate this object in the AD. How can you see the LostandFound container?**
   a. Use the Delegation of Control Wizard to assign yourself permission to the container.
   b. Use the Show All Objects setting in AD Users and Computers.
   c. Add the Registry setting HKLM\System\CurrentControlSet\Services\lanmanserver\ViewLostandFound as a DWord with a value of 1.
   d. Select the Advanced Features in AD Users and Computers.

3. **Your users are calling the help desk with some concerns regarding their ability to change account information. Their passwords are being synchronized almost immediately when they change them, but personal information such as telephone numbers takes an unacceptable amount of time to replicate. What setting should you inspect?**
   a. the replication interval
   b. the replication protocol
   c. the replication frequency
   d. the replication method

4. **When two duplicate objects have been created in the AD structure, the object created last is _____.**
   a. sent to the LostandFound container
   b. sent to the Duplicated Objects OU
   c. given a different name
   d. marked for deletion

5. **Your domain administrator calls and asks you how to configure data compression for the schema partition when using RPC as the replication protocol. What should you advise?**
   a. Right-click on the NTDS object in AD Sites and Services, and enable compression there.
   b. Compression must be enabled through the network adapter card properties.
   c. RPC does not support compression.
   d. Copy the schema partition to a shared folder, and send the information using this process.

4.4 Deploy software by using Group Policy. Types of software include user applications, antivirus software, line-of-business applications, and software updates.

GPO-BASED SOFTWARE DEPLOYMENT

UNDERSTANDING THE OBJECTIVE

GPOs can be used to deploy, update, and maintain software of all types, from simple applications to antivirus updates. You can deploy these applications by using the Microsoft Installer technology and the IntelliMirror service. Combine these with the **MSI** files that can be created, and you can deploy applications in your infrastructure that are self-healing, AD-aware, and that support automatic updates. You will also be able to configure your GPOs to uninstall duplicate applications that users have installed to their machines, and replace the applications with copies of the same applications which are covered by your corporate license structure.

WHAT YOU REALLY NEED TO KNOW

- ◆ Any 32-bit software package that supports the MSI format can be deployed by the use of a GPO. Any 16-bit application can be installed after being converted into a format called a ZAP file. Application updates and patches can be deployed using MST and **MSP** files, respectively.

- ◆ You must decide which method of deployment will be used with the GPOs. You can install against the computer, on the desktop, in a catalog, or through extension mapping. Each process has advantages and disadvantages.

- ◆ While only Windows 2000 clients can use GPO-based software deployment, any client operating system with the Windows Installer service installed can use the MSI technology itself in a stand-alone mode.

- ◆ An important benefit of the MSI technology is that applications deployed using an MSI and GPO can be uninstalled cleanly by the GPO. In addition, because during its installation processing the MSI creates a transaction log that records all system changes, including changes to the Registry, the MSI file can reverse the installation process if the install fails to complete successfully. This reversal does not require using a separate uninstall application for functionality.

- ◆ You can use MST files and the Transform structure to apply software updates, as well as other file types such as new virus signatures. The use of MSP files allows the application of patches to your AD clients. On the Windows 2000 installation CD you will find an executable named Swiadmle.msi that allows you to create fully functional MSI packages for use in your AD environment.

OBJECTIVES ON THE JOB

Software deployment using the GPOs that exist in AD can provide you with a great deal of control and flexibility both in your environment and for the support of your users.

PRACTICE TEST QUESTIONS

1. _____ are most commonly deployed using GPOs.
   a. Word-processing applications
   b. Spreadsheet applications
   c. E-mail applications
   d. MSI packages

2. As an AD domain administrator, you want to make certain that the newest version of the corporate e-mail client is deployed to all client computers, regardless of who uses the computer. Therefore, you should deploy the software using software _____.
   a. distribution packages
   b. publishing
   c. deployment
   d. assignment

3. To update antivirus signature files, you should deploy _____ packages.
   a. MSI
   b. MST
   c. MSP
   d. ZAP

4. As the administrator of your corporate infrastructure, you want to deploy a custom application to the corporate desktops using the least-intrusive method possible. Your corporate infrastructure consists of a mixture of new laptop computers and recent and older desktop computers. The complicating factor is that the application is a 32-bit application that was produced only on 45 standard floppy disks. What is the least-disruptive method you can use to deploy this application to your corporate users? (Choose all that apply.)
   a. Purchase a disk duplication machine and many boxes of floppy disks.
   b. Install the application on a model machine, and then create an image of the installed application using a third-party disk-imaging tool.
   c. Install the application on a model machine while using the WinInstallLE tool, and build an MSI package.
   d. Configure a GPO at your Forest root, and deploy the application as a published application.
   e. Configure a GPO at your Forest root, and deploy the application as an assigned application.
   f. Configure a GPO at your Forest root, and deploy the application using a scripted push.

5. The _____ application allows the administrator to create MSI packages.
   a. Windows Installer
   b. GPO Installer
   c. GPO Packager
   d. WinInstallLE

4.4.1 Use Windows Installer to deploy Windows Installer packages.

DEPLOYING APPLICATIONS USING INSTALLER

UNDERSTANDING THE OBJECTIVE

Windows 2000 supports a new technology natively called the Windows Installer service, which is available free at the Microsoft Web site. Windows 9*x* and Windows NT 4.0 can use this technology after the Installer component is installed on these platforms.

WHAT YOU REALLY NEED TO KNOW

◆ The Windows Installer Service is a technology that supports the use of packaged applications for installing software. These installer packages are distinguished by their .msi extension. The Microsoft Installer files are not traditional executables, but are completely self-contained files that support the installation of applications on computers in a preconfigured state.

◆ A characteristic of an MSI file is that it contains all the settings needed to deploy an application in a form that does not require any configuration by the end user. Microsoft natively supports the MSI format with all new applications, such as Word XP and Office 2000. An important benefit of the MSI technology is that it supports the complete removal of MSI applications when they are no longer required. If an application was installed using an MSI, it is removed completely from all parts of the operating system, including the Registry, when the application is uninstalled. Also, if an error during the installation process prevents the successful installation of the application, the MSI reverses the installation process completely using a transaction log created during the process.

◆ If you have access to the installation media for Windows 2000 Advanced Server (which is located in a folder named Support), you will find a copy of an application named Swiadmle.msi, which allows you to create your own MSI files for distribution in your AD environment. These are fully functional MSI packages that work in the same fashion as other MSI packages, allowing you to create MSI files for all clients in your AD environment.

◆ The MSI files can also be configured with additional information. Using the WinInstallLE tool, you can add information such as your help desk support phone number, a product key required for activation, and your company's Web site information. Another advantage of the MSI technology is that it removes the user's ability to modify the application's installation parameters. The MSI is preconfigured with application options, components, and default installation paths.

OBJECTIVES ON THE JOB

The Windows Installer is an important new technology that can be implemented natively for Windows 2000 and for down-level clients after the Installer service is installed. Once installed, you can deploy MSI packages in your environment. The MSI packages allow you administrative control over the applications installed in your environment.

PRACTICE TEST QUESTIONS

1. The extension for the Microsoft Installer Transform file type is

   _____.

   a. .msi

   b. .msp

   c. .zap

   d. .mst

2. Windows 98 computers can support the Windows Installer technology if the
   _____ has been installed on the computer.

   a. Windows Installer Hot Fix

   b. Windows Installer package

   c. Installer.MSI package

   d. most recent service pack

3. The Installer can be used with a GPO to _____ for a Windows 2000
   computer.

   a. publish applications

   b. install applications

   c. list available applications

   d. assign packages

4. If an MSI package does not exist for the application you want to install, you should
   use the tool set located in the path _____ on the Windows 2000
   Server installation CD.

   a. CD_Root\I386\Installer\WinInstallLE.msi

   b. CD_Root\Support\Tools\Installer.msi

   c. CD_Root\Support\Tools\Swiadmle.msi

   d. CD_Root\Installer\Tools\Swiadmle.msi

5. Any _____ application can be installed using the MSI technology.

   a. 16-bit

   b. DOS

   c. Windows 95

   d. 32-bit

6. The WinInstallLE tool allows you to modify the _____ contained in
   the MSI package.

   a. default installation path

   b. help desk contact information

   c. required security settings

   d. application executable

7. An application assigned to a computer will display a(n) _____ on
   the desktop until it is started, at which time the application will install itself.

   a. shortcut to the application

   b. icon for the application

   c. placeholder for the application

   d. datafile for the application

4.4.2 Deploy updates to installed software including antivirus updates.

UPDATING APPLICATIONS AUTOMATICALLY

UNDERSTANDING THE OBJECTIVE

MSI files can be used to install application packages and to create update packages for applications. These are small files that can be deployed throughout your environment when needed, and can support application updates, service packs, and virus signature updates.

WHAT YOU REALLY NEED TO KNOW

◆ Beyond being used for new applications, the MSI technology can apply modifications to applications. These new modification files are called Transforms and are saved with an extension of .mst. The Transform files are used to support application updates such as new versions of virus signature files. Another file type, called an MSP, is used to apply updates, service packs, bug fixes, and application patches without requiring that the applications be reinstalled.

◆ The file type to use depends on the type of file deployed. As with the MSI files, the additional types do not require any configuration by the end users and contain a default installation path in the file. They can also contain unlock codes, help desk information, or other data relevant to your particular situation.

◆ As with the MSI files, an important advantage of these files is that users are unable to participate in the configuration process. If you have access to the installation media for Windows 2000 Advanced Server, you will find a copy of an application named Swiadmle.msi, which allows you to create your own MSI files for distribution in your AD environment. If the computer receiving the package uses a different directory tree structure, the installation may not succeed.

◆ As an administrator of a Windows 2000 AD forest, you benefit from being able to deploy application patches and antivirus signature updates using this method. The client is not required to understand the update process, and must simply log in and receive the updated files.

◆ If you use non-Microsoft applications in your environment, they also can be updated with this technology. A third-party word-processing application could have its software patches placed into an MST file for distribution to your users in the environment. Down-level clients can be configured with the Windows Installer application so they also can benefit from this technology. All your clients can benefit from using the Installer process to refresh virus signatures and antivirus patches to the various operating systems in your network environment.

OBJECTIVES ON THE JOB

When combined with the MSI technology, the addition of MST and MSP file types can simplify your daily administration of client systems. You no longer will need to uninstall applications to apply updates and patches (assuming the applications were installed using the MSI process). You also will be able to seamlessly apply the latest antivirus signature files to your client and server computers, whether they are Windows 2000 clients or down-level systems.

PRACTICE TEST QUESTIONS

1. **As an administrator, you must update the antivirus signatures for computers in your domain. However, after configuring the Transform file and creating the GPO to deploy the package, only half of your supported computers successfully downloaded the Transform file. What should you suspect is causing this problem?**
   a. You downloaded the wrong signature file.
   b. The other computers are using a different antivirus application.
   c. Your GPO was not configured correctly.
   d. Only the computers that received the antivirus application through the GPO process can use the Transform file. The rest of the computers, being hand-built, must be manually updated.

2. **When deploying software updates to your domain users, you can deploy the updates to _____. (Choose all that apply.)**
   a. a specific OU
   b. the entire site
   c. one domain
   d. one computer

3. **When deploying software updates to your OU users, you can provide a _____ update or an optional update.**
   a. working
   b. mandatory
   c. sequenced
   d. provisional

4. **The latest version of a corporate office application suite has just been released with several hot fixes applied. What technique should you use to deploy this new package?**
   a. an upgrade that is accomplished with an MSP package
   b. a replacement using an MST package
   c. an optional replacement using a ZAP file
   d. a redeployment using the new MSI package for the newer version of the application

5. **Suppose a user brings his or her laptop into the office and connects to your AD to install new copies of applications. Your software application GPO can detect other versions of installed applications and _____.**
   a. apply a second installation that will not interfere with the user's original installation
   b. disable the original application in favor of the new installation
   c. remove the user's copy of the application and install the corporate application that is protected with your corporate license
   d. overwrite the original installation with the new copy of the application

4.4.3 Configure Group Policy to assign and publish applications.

ADVANCED APPLICATION-MANAGEMENT TECHNIQUES

UNDERSTANDING THE OBJECTIVE

Now that you understand MSI technologies, you can use them to deploy applications to your AD clients using the Windows 2000 Group Policy Objects. Applications deployed using GPOs have several important advantages: They are self-healing and self-repairing and can be configured for easy, clean removal from the system. This removal process includes deleting application folders and cleaning the application from the Registry. Remember, using GPOs, the application can be installed only to Windows 2000 clients, and not to down-level clients.

WHAT YOU REALLY NEED TO KNOW

◆ The first step in using GPOs to deploy applications is to obtain an MSI for the application you want to deploy. If an MSI does not exist, you can use the WinInstallLE application to create one. The MSI technology was designed to support 32-bit applications; however, should you need to deploy other kinds of applications, even 16-bit application support is provided.

◆ After obtaining the MSI files, the next step is to configure deployment servers to host the MSI packages. The GPO MSI technology and the component that makes the applications self-healing have the additional benefit of their ability to record their own installation source in the Registry. If the application breaks, the application accesses its installation point, connects to this share, and repairs itself. For the deployment server, Microsoft recommends the use of DFS to eliminate any failure points. Be certain to include a DFS server in the sites to which the clients can connect.

◆ After the distribution point has been created, you must decide which type of GPO deployment to use. You have two deployment choices: You may use either application assignment or application publishing. Application assignment means the application is assigned against the computer and will be installed either the next time the computer starts up or it will exist as an icon on the desktop. In the latter case, the application is not installed until the user clicks the icon to start the application.

◆ Software publishing involves creating what is essentially a software catalog that will appear as an option in the Add and Remove Programs applet. This allows the user to select the application he or she wants to install. This method gives you control over application licenses and ensures that only applications purchased by the corporation exist on the client computers. Application publishing also is used to allow users to receive e-mail with an unknown attachment. When the user clicks the attachment to open it, the application will install.

OBJECTIVES ON THE JOB

Using GPOs to install your applications allows you to fully use MSI technology to control software deployment and maintenance in your AD environment for Windows 2000.

PRACTICE TEST QUESTIONS

1. The technique for creating your own MSI package requires two computers, one computer to function as the _____, and the second one to serve as the host machine.
   a. target
   b. installer target
   c. image model
   d. image

2. When creating your own MSI package, it is important that the model computer _____ before you continue with the process.
   a. have the most recent service pack installed
   b. have all relevant hot fixes installed
   c. have its drive defragmented
   d. reboots after the installation

3. The image capture file should always be created from the _____ that is not being used to install the application.
   a. client
   b. software repository
   c. server
   d. computer

4. When software is assigned using a GPO, the package is installed the next time the computer is restarted or a(n) _____.
   a. installation flag is set to trigger the installation when the user logs on
   b. e-mail is received and opened
   c. user clicks the icon placed on the desktop by the GPO process
   d. user selects the application from the Add and Remove Programs applet in Control Panel

5. A user cannot install the corporate office suite on his or her laptop computer. You find out that the user is working remotely through a dial-up connection. What should you tell the user is the reason the software update is not being received?
   a. The user lacks proper account credentials, but you will adjust the account so that the process will proceed correctly.
   b. The GPO-based software installation will not work over a dial-up connection. The user must access the network using some other technology.
   c. The user is probably not a member of the group that was supposed to receive this updated application.
   d. The user's computer may have corrupted Registry settings that make it appear that the MSI package has been already been installed.

4.5 Troubleshoot end-user Group Policy.

RESOLVING GROUP POLICY ISSUES FOR END USERS

UNDERSTANDING THE OBJECTIVE

Group Policy is one of the most important parts of the Windows 2000 AD. It allows you, as the administrator, to control every aspect of your AD environment. However, like any other application or service, difficulties may be encountered

WHAT YOU REALLY NEED TO KNOW

- ◆ Because the AD uses the concept of inheritance to apply access permissions and GPOs to the objects in the Directory, it is important that you use this information in your attempts to troubleshoot the AD.

- ◆ GPOs are controlled not just by the process of inheritance, but also by the use of precedence of application, which is the listing of GPOs for processing in a specific order of application. Listing the GPOs, in order, for processing does not alter the fact that computer GPOs always supercede user GPOs. It simply allows you to influence the end result of the GPO processing as a whole.

- ◆ By using inheritance for the processing of GPOs, AD uses the parent-child relationship for processing order. Child objects can block GPOs that are inherited from the parent object. However, parent objects have the right to deny this blockage and force the child objects to accept the GPOs assigned to them. This combination of settings is the Block Inheritance/No Override combination. These two configuration settings should be used sparingly, if at all, in your AD environment.

- ◆ If you must block the application of GPOs from a specific user or a group of users, you need to configure and apply GPO filtering. For a user or group to be affected by a GPO, they must be able to read and apply the GPO. Denying either of these two rights blocks the assignment of the GPO to these users or groups. This is what GPO filtering does. It denies the ability to read the GPO or denies the ability to apply GPOs to selected user/group objects. Once configured this way, GPO assignment is no longer possible for the configured user/group object in this configured OU. The filtering of GPOs in this OU will not stop GPOs in other OUs from impacting the configured user/group object. Other GPOs, unless specifically filtered, will apply to these user/group objects.

- ◆ When you must manually refresh GPOs in your AD environment or you must use a scripted process to refresh GPOs, you can use the secedit command, which has several optional switches to allow manual control over GPO refreshes.

OBJECTIVES ON THE JOB

From time to time you will need to troubleshoot your GPOs in AD. It is beneficial if you understand several key points concerning the concepts of GPOs and how they interact with each other and with your AD environment. You must use secedit for manual refreshes of GPOs, and to also refresh components such as Certificates and security settings.

PRACTICE TEST QUESTIONS

1. **You are a local administrator and have just finished working on a user's computer. To perform your work, you had to remove all GPOs from the computer. When you stepped out for a moment, the user opened an application on the computer. The application is a database and the user has records open. How can you refresh the GPOs on the computer to the original settings without restarting the computer and disrupting the user's work?**
   a. Use the Hibernate option to hibernate the computer to refresh the GPOs.
   b. Use the resource kit tool Gporefresh with the switch /now.
   c. Use the secedit command and specify the user policy, the computer policy, or both.
   d. Use the runas command with the Gporesult tool from the resource kit.

2. **You received a call from a user who is having trouble accessing a folder that the rest of the team members can access. The user has several GPOs that might be causing the problem, but you forgot the processing order for GPOs. After a phone call of your own, you find out the correct order for processing GPOs is**
   _____.
   a. Child OU; Parent OU; Child Domain; Parent Domain; Site
   b. Site; Parent Domain; Child Domain; Parent OU; Child OU
   c. Site; Domain; OU
   d. Domain; OU

3. **When GPOs are processed, _____ settings always override computer settings.**
   a. system policy
   b. user
   c. loopback
   d. site

4. **Filtering a GPO means _____.**
   a. denying the read permission to a GPO
   b. denying the write permission to a GPO
   c. moving the user to a different OU where the GPO does not exist
   d. setting the global No Access flag

5. **The default refresh interval for user-level GPOs in AD is _____ minutes.**
   a. 5
   b. 30
   c. 60
   d. 90

6. **The default refresh interval for domain controllers in AD is _____ minutes.**
   a. 5
   b. 30
   c. 60
   d. 90

4.5.1 Troubleshoot Group Policy problems involving precedence, inheritance, filtering, and the No Override option.

ADVANCED GROUP POLICY TROUBLESHOOTING

UNDERSTANDING THE OBJECTIVE

Group Policy is used to control your clients, both users and computers, in the AD environment. As powerful as GPOs are, they may require troubleshooting to function correctly in your AD forest. For instance, there are implementation considerations that will need to be resolved.

WHAT YOU REALLY NEED TO KNOW

◆ To correctly troubleshoot GPOs, you must understand several features of GPOs. First, GPOs do not produce permanent changes to the Windows 2000 Registry. The changes caused by the GPOs are in effect only while the computer is logged into the AD domain. Second, GPOs have a hierarchical structure that controls the order in which they are processed. The order is site, domain, OU. As an additional component of this processing order, computer GPOs are always processed before user GPOs. In cases where the same setting was applied to both the computer and the user but with different constraints, the computer setting always supercedes the user setting.

◆ With these factors in mind, you can begin troubleshooting GPOs in AD. You first must determine what GPOs are being applied to the object you need to troubleshoot. The preferred tool for this is Gpresult, which is part of the Windows 2000 Server Resource Kit. This command-line tool shows all of the GPOs being applied to a computer/user. With this information, you can track through the AD to examine the settings for each GPO.

◆ Many problems can be introduced into the AD environment by incorrectly designing the AD forest. Failure to design to support inheritance can lead to situations in which GPOs are applied incorrectly or at the wrong layer. Additional problems can result from the incorrect use of the No Override setting. Filtering, which allows administrators to deny access for GPOs to specific users and or groups, may also have been applied incorrectly.

◆ The No Override setting modifies the default AD GPO inheritance process, which lets child OUs block GPOs applied by the parent object by applying the Block Inheritance setting. The Block Inheritance and No Override settings should not be used in a daily environment. They are intended for occasional use only.

OBJECTIVES ON THE JOB

Group Policy objects provide the maximum amount of control over your Windows 2000 clients in an Active Directory setting. However, they may need to be adjusted to function correctly for maximum flexibility and control. You may also need to apply filtering to deny GPOs to specific users or groups of users. You also might have to adjust specific GPOs to ensure that settings are applied at the correct level in the AD for maximum control.

PRACTICE TEST QUESTIONS

1. **Your help desk received a call from a user with some issues concerning a Windows 2000 Professional computer. The user understands the concept of GPOs slightly—enough to know that when the computer logs off the domain, the group policies should also leave the computer. This user reports, however, that the GPOs remain on the computer. What should you look for when troubleshooting?**
   a. incorrect GPO permissions
   b. System Policies that are being applied
   c. GPO filtering that has been enabled
   d. incorrect domain

2. **The correct order of application for policy objects on the Windows 2000 Professional platform is _____.**
   a. system policies; local policies; site policies; domain policies; OU policies
   b. site policies; domain policies; OU policies
   c. system policies; site policies; domain policies; OU policies
   d. OU policies; domain policies; site policies; local policies; system policies

3. **In the AD, child OUs always have the right to block inheritance from their parent objects, and the parent always has the right to _____.**
   a. filter the block
   b. deny the block
   c. enable the No Override setting
   d. suppress the block

4. **The correct order of application for policy objects on the Windows 2000 Professional platform is _____.**
   a. site policies; domain policies; OU policies
   b. system policies; local policies; site policies; domain policies; OU policies
   c. OU policies; domain policies; site policies; local policies; system policies
   d. system policies; site policies; domain policies; OU policies

5. **GPO inheritance in AD flows from _____. (Choose all that apply.)**
   a. peer to peer
   b. parent to child
   c. grandparent to parent to child
   d. grandparent to peer

6. **To filter GPO from an object in AD, you can either deny the Apply Group Policy setting or deny the _____ setting.**
   a. Enforce Group Policy
   b. Read
   c. Utilize Group Policy
   d. Load Group Policy

4.5.2 Manually refresh Group Policy.

MANUAL UPDATES OF GROUP POLICY

UNDERSTANDING THE OBJECTIVE

The default refresh interval for GPOs in AD depends on the type of computer. For clients and client computers such as one running Windows 2000 Professional, the automatic refresh interval is every 90 minutes. For domain controllers, the interval is every five minutes. You may also manually implement a specific GPO or all GPOs on a specific computer at a different interval.

WHAT YOU REALLY NEED TO KNOW

◆ The tool used to manually refresh GPO settings is the secedit command, which applies the on-demand GPO refresh for AD-enabled computers. You can use the /refreshpolicy switch with it to force the GPO reapplication with the name of the appropriate computer or user GPO. To reapply the default machine policy and force the immediate application of the policy, use this syntax: secedit /refreshpolicy machine_policy /enforce. Likewise, to force the reapplication of the default user policy, replace the string machine_policy with the string user_policy.

◆ Using the /enforce switch causes the secedit command to force the reapplication of the specified GPO. However, the secedit command cannot force the reapplication of a GPO that installs software. If this is the GPO that must be refreshed, you have to use a different technique, such as cycling the power on the system or having the user log off and then log on again. An administrator can use this manual reset capability to reapply a GPO to a user's computer after working on the machine in an administrative capacity.

◆ You can use the secedit command to manually apply or refresh Public Key Policies in a Windows 2000 environment for your clients. These security policies might consist of EFS settings, automatic enrollment for computer certificates, or the addition of trusted root certificates for computer groups. The secedit command can also be used to troubleshoot and reapply the machine policy when configuring client machines for SmartCard usage.

◆ You can also use the secedit command to configure **L2TP** over IPSec connections, which might be found when using secure VPN links. When using such links, the secedit command will be used to create a computer certificate so that machines trying to connect using the VPN will have a secure communications channel.

OBJECTIVES ON THE JOB

You can use the secedit command to resolve many issues where the refreshing or reapplication of Group Policies, user policies, or machine policies is required. The command can also be placed into a script for automated application in specific instances.

PRACTICE TEST QUESTIONS

1. **Group Policies may need to be manually refreshed when** _____.
   - a. work is being done locally on the computer
   - b. new GPO settings have been downloaded from AD
   - c. a new user logs on
   - d. there were issues with password synchronization and the GC

2. **You can use** _____ **to manually refresh GPO settings.**
   - a. netdom
   - b. LDP
   - c. secedit
   - d. repadmin

3. **The command for manually refreshing the machine policy on a Windows 2000 Professional computer is** _____.
   - a. /refreshpolicy *machine_policy* /enforce
   - b. /refresh *machinepolicy* /now
   - c. /update *machine_policy*
   - d. /refresh /now

4. **The secedit command can force an update of every machine policy except for** _____ **policies.**
   - a. security
   - b. folder redirection
   - c. software installation
   - d. software renewal

5. **Among other capabilities, the secedit command can** _____.
   - a. analyze security settings
   - b. list GPO authentication
   - c. monitor GPO installation
   - d. monitor the state of secure network communications

6. **The command for manually refreshing user policy settings is** _____ **refreshpolicy user_policy.**
   - a. netdiag
   - b. netdom
   - c. L2TP
   - d. secedit

7. **An advantage of secedit is that it can** _____.
   - a. be scripted
   - b. have a small memory footprint
   - c. run from a command-line environment
   - d. have a simple syntax

4.6 Implement and manage security policies by using Group Policy.

SECURITY POLICY IMPLEMENTATION

UNDERSTANDING THE OBJECTIVE

As the administrator of Windows 2000 in your corporate environment, it is your responsibility to maintain adequate security settings and levels to protect your corporation against security breaches by outside parties. Microsoft has provided tools and capabilities to assist in this process. You need only add your time to develop and implement these settings for your clients.

WHAT YOU REALLY NEED TO KNOW

◆ As a first step, you need to examine the security templates that Microsoft has provided as part of the normal installation of Windows 2000. Two additional templates are also included in the Windows 2000 Server Resource Kit; these may be imported into the default security template folder. These two extra templates are designed to secure Web servers.

◆ After examining the templates, you should begin to make some preliminary decisions concerning which templates may be of use in your environment, and which templates can be ignored. For the templates that may be applicable in your environment, determine which kinds of computers should receive which kind of template. Do you have any computers that were Windows NT 4.0 computers and have gone through the in-place upgrade process? If so, they need a specific template, such as hisecdc. Any server that should never support the Terminal Server components needs a different template applied, and so on.

◆ Next determine the exact levels of security to be applied for different types of computers. Security templates support different settings for several levels of secure workstations and several levels of servers. You must familiarize yourself with password settings, file and folder security settings, and Registry protection settings. If you support laptop clients, you may find that a certain template is a better fit for those clients. In addition, remember that this discussion applies only to Windows 2000 computers or computers upgraded to Windows 2000.

◆ Will you deploy these templates through GPOs for the computers? Are some computers isolated from your network, and do they require a manual application of the templates? Remember that GPOs can be deployed at the site, domain, or OU level. Also remember that while site-level GPOs affect all domains in the site, domain-level GPOs must be assigned on a domain-by-domain basis because domains do not inherit OUs. On the other hand, domains do support inheritance, and this can be used to your advantage.

OBJECTIVES ON THE JOB

Applying security policies through the use of templates and GPOs will simplify your security configuration in Windows 2000 AD. By using these two components, you can uniformly apply security settings for your Windows 2000 clients in a corporate environment.

PRACTICE TEST QUESTIONS

1. When a Windows NT 4.0 computer is upgraded to Windows 2000, you must apply
   _____ after the update is completed.
   a. the most recent service pack
   b. a security template
   c. an antivirus application
   d. the most recent security hot fix

2. The Security Configuration and Analysis tool can be used with
   _____. (Choose all that apply.)
   a. Windows NT 4.0
   b. Windows 2000 Web Server
   c. Windows 2000 Advanced Server
   d. Windows 2000 Terminal Server

3. As part of the normal installation of Windows 2000, the security templates are
   installed in the _____ folder.
   a. Winnt
   b. Security Templates
   c. WINDOWS/Security/Templates
   d. %Systemroot%\Securtiy\Templates

4. You are a system administrator with the responsibility for maintaining a small
   working group of 150 users and their computers. You want to automate the
   process of applying a custom security template you have created. What tool allows
   you to automate this process?
   a. AD GPO
   b. Security Configuration and Analysis snap-in
   c. secedit running in a script
   d. secedit running in a script placed in a GPO

5. As an administrator for your AD domain, you want to customize the security
   settings for your domain member servers to make certain that Terminal Services
   will not run on those machines. Which security template will block the application
   and use of Terminal Services for Windows 2000?
   a. compatws
   b. securews
   c. notssid
   d. rootsec

6. You have configured a new security template. You want to attach a description to
   the modified template so that future users will know what the template does. How
   can you attach the description to the template?
   a. Use Edit.com and include a REM statement with the description.
   b. Right-click the template in the Security Templates snap-in, and choose the Set
      Description option.
   c. Change the name to reflect the use.
   d. Create a Notepad document, and attach it to the template.

4.6.1 Use security templates to implement security policies.

APPLYING SECURITY SETTINGS

UNDERSTANDING THE OBJECTIVE

Windows 2000 provides a variety of security tools which system administrators can use. Some of the newest tools are the security templates. These are files that contain preconfigured security settings, which can be applied by an administrator to Windows 2000 computers in your environment. They can be used for either Professional or Server computers and can be modified if you want to change specific settings in the template itself.

WHAT YOU REALLY NEED TO KNOW

◆ The security of your computer systems is one of your primary responsibilities as a system administrator. Windows 2000 can be an extremely secure system if you are proactive in implementing and assigning security settings. To fulfill this requirement, you must consider security settings for laptop and desktop computers running both Windows 2000 Professional and Windows 2000 Server.

◆ To assist you in the process of security configuration, Microsoft has included with the Windows 2000 products a number of default security templates. These templates can be used to control and/or implement security configuration settings in a Windows 2000 environment. The templates are usable only on Windows 2000 computers. However, because the status of the settings can be printed, you could apply some of the same settings to your down-level clients when such configuration settings are supported by those operating systems.

◆ There are eight security templates in Windows 2000, covering a range of security configurations from secure workstations and domain controllers to secure Web servers. Each template can be applied in a specific circumstance to a specific type of machine. Each template can also be modified to fit your particular security model. However, it is recommended that the original templates never be modified. Rather, these originals should remain untouched and any changes applied should be saved as a new template with a new name. If you are uncertain what each template does, you can right-click the template and click Set Description to view the purpose of each template. If you have modified a template from its original configuration, you may enter new descriptive text here to document the new functional features.

◆ You can also use the security templates when Windows NT 4.0 computers have been updated to Windows 2000 using the upgrade-in-place model. Even though these computers use the Windows 2000 operating system, they do not have Windows 2000-level security settings applied. Security templates must be used on these computers to apply Windows 2000 security settings.

OBJECTIVES ON THE JOB

Microsoft security templates help you configure security settings for your Windows 2000 computers. You now have consistent, repeatable templates that can ensure your Windows 2000 computers have the same security settings applied, whether they are located in the corporate headquarters or on a remote island office.

PRACTICE TEST QUESTIONS

1. **Security templates can be modified. However, Microsoft recommends that if you do modify them, you _____.**
   a. make certain to change the description attached to the file
   b. store the modified files in a different folder on the system
   c. include REM statements in the files for any comments you may include
   d. copy the original template and modify the copy, leaving the original in place and intact

2. **Windows NT 4.0 computers that are upgraded to Windows 2000 have _____ security configured.**
   a. Windows 2000 default
   b. no
   c. minimal
   d. the same security as native Widows 2000

3. **Windows 2000 security templates exist for clients, servers, and _____.**
   a. DDNS servers
   b. DHCP servers
   c. WINS servers
   d. Web servers

4. **A security template for a Windows 2000 Professional computer can be applied through the AD by using a GPO that will refresh every _____ minutes.**
   a. 10
   b. 30
   c. 60
   d. 90

5. **A security template for a Windows 2000 Server will be applied through the AD by using a GPO that will refresh every _____ minutes.**
   a. 5
   b. 15
   c. 45
   d. 60

6. **The security templates contain _____ settings designed by Microsoft to secure your computers under varying circumstances.**
   a. midrange
   b. preconfigured
   c. basic
   d. advanced

4.6.2 Analyze the security configuration of a computer by using the secedit command and Security Configuration and Analysis.

ANALYZING WINDOWS 2000 SECURITY SETTINGS

UNDERSTANDING THE OBJECTIVE

Besides providing preconfigured security templates for Windows 2000, Microsoft has also designed two tools that are used to analyze and configure security settings in a Windows 2000 environment. Both tools work with the security templates to support either preconfigured or customized security settings for the Windows 2000 computers in your environment.

WHAT YOU REALLY NEED TO KNOW

◆ The first security analysis tool for Windows 2000 is the secedit command. This command can be placed into a script for repeated use and application. This method provides the administrator with repeatability and consistent operation. The tool can also be used from the command line for application and use by the administrator on an as-needed basis.

◆ When the secedit command is used to analyze the security settings of a Windows 2000 computer, several command-line switches must be used in addition to the secedit command. These switches are: /analyze, /db *filename*, /cfg *filename*, /log *filename*, and /quiet. The analyze switch is used to begin analyzing the system for compliance with specific settings; the db switch specifies the name of the database that contains these specific settings. The db switch is required for the analysis function. If you want to use a security template other than the one currently stored in the database, the cfg switch will specify the template file to import into the database. The cfg switch can be used only with the db switch. The log switch creates a log file of the analysis in the location specified by *filename*. If no log file information is specified, the default log and location is used. The quiet switch does not direct information to either the screen or the log file. You still can view the results of the analysis using the Security Configuration and Analysis tool, however.

◆ The Security Configuration and Analysis tool, which is an MMC snap-in, is a GUI version of secedit with the same functionality and features. This tool may be easier for a less-experienced administrator to use because it has a GUI interface. The tool supports analysis of the computer system and will report the results of this analysis to the administrator in a console view. The snap-in version also supports the creation of MMC Taskpad views for building versions of the tool with a more restricted interface.

OBJECTIVES ON THE JOB

By providing the tools and ability to analyze security settings on Windows 2000 computers, Microsoft has provided you with another important tool. You will use this tool daily as you provide your users with a secure computing environment. Both tools will assist you in your task of securing your environment.

PRACTICE TEST QUESTIONS

1. **The Security Configuration and Analysis tool is designed to analyze**
   _____.
   a. workstations only
   b. computers running Windows 2000 Professional only
   c. servers only
   d. any Windows 2000 computer.

2. **Before a snap-in can be used, it must be configured with** _____.
   a. replication technology
   b. a valid user account
   c. a database
   d. a security principle

3. **After performing an analysis of your computer, you may** _____ **and then adjust them as your environment dictates.**
   a. inspect the differences
   b. interpret the results
   c. view the logs
   d. examine the data collection files

4. **The Security templates can be applied by** _____, **or you can assign them through a GPO for more uniform processing.**
   a. installing them locally using a floppy disk
   b. e-mailing them to clients and telling them to double-click the icon
   c. placing them into a batch file
   d. loading them into a script

5. **After the Security Configuration and Analysis tool has finished analyzing your computer, the results of the analysis** _____.
   a. will be stored in the directory labeled Security Templates
   b. will be available for you to examine through the console view
   c. are not available to you but are used by the tool to calculate new settings
   d. are merged into the default security template

6. **Besides the Security Configuration and Analysis tool, another tool exists that can analyze security settings for Windows 2000 computers. The other tool is**
   _____.
   a. Perfmon
   b. Netdom
   c. Netdiag
   d. secedit

7. **The two templates that can configure a Web server in Windows 2000 are available**
   _____.
   a. as part of the default installation of Windows 2000
   b. as part of the Server Resource Kit
   c. as a free download from Microsoft
   d. as part of the installation process for IIS 5.0

4.6.3 Modify domain security policy to comply with corporate standards.

APPLYING ENTERPRISE SECURITY SETTINGS

UNDERSTANDING THE OBJECTIVE

You are now familiar with the preconfigured security templates built into Windows 2000 and aware of the existence of both the secedit command and the Security Configuration and Analysis MMC snap-in. You can now combine these two types of components to support a corporate-wide security policy in your Windows 2000 AD infrastructure.

WHAT YOU REALLY NEED TO KNOW

◆ Your first step should be to define, at a corporate level, what constitutes a secure computing environment standard and who will define this standard. Next you need to collect input from many groups within the corporation on what kinds of security these groups want to see implemented. This may be best handled through the use of a survey directed to leaders and managers of the corporation. After collecting and quantifying the results, you must separate the possible from the impossible and determine which group standards should take precedence when conflicts arise between different implementations proposed by different groups.

◆ After you have determined what constitutes the corporate standard, you will begin the implementation process. The next step should be the preparation and creation of a test lab where each hardware platform that will have Windows 2000 installed can be tested for compatibility with the newly defined standards. This step is necessary because you will apply these security settings to an entire company, possibly over the course of a few hours, and you must prove to yourself and management that the company will continue to function correctly after the deployment.

◆ After you have successfully completed the testing stage, you need to decide on an actual deployment method. Because the centerpiece of your new corporate standards is the Windows 2000 platform, it is reasonable to say that your deployment should be implemented through the use of Windows 2000 GPOs. You will need to know the required number of GPOs and what each GPO will implement. There is an advantage to using several GPOs to implement your security plans, instead of using one larger GPO with all settings contained within it.

◆ After you have determined the types of GPOs to apply, you must assign them through AD. Remember that your domain controllers live in the Domain Controllers OU, while individual computers may live in any OU. In addition, recall that the default refresh rates for GPOs vary according to the type of client being refreshed.

OBJECTIVES ON THE JOB

The application of security policies in accordance with your corporate standards is a necessary part of the Windows 2000 AD implementation. Microsoft has provided the tools to assist you.

PRACTICE TEST QUESTIONS

1. Your corporate security plan should be the result of careful analysis and detailed design by _____.
   - a. the IT staff only
   - b. all involved stakeholders in corporate security
   - c. an external security analyst
   - d. all interested parties

2. Corporate security standards should be applied to your _____ as soon as practicable.
   - a. member workstations
   - b. domain controllers
   - c. OU structure
   - d. Forest Root domain controller

3. You should assess which servers will never need Terminal Server installed. The _____ template should be applied in a GPO after moving these computers into an OU designed for this purpose.
   - a. hisecdc
   - b. rootsec
   - c. notssid
   - d. DC security

4. _____ are also known as biometric security settings.
   - a. SmartCards
   - b. Thumbprint scanners
   - c. Rigorous passwords
   - d. Secret codes

5. The Security Configuration and Analysis tool will provide a comparison between _____ and the security template. It also will provide you an opportunity to modify your settings to more closely match the suggested settings in the template.
   - a. your design goals
   - b. your committee plans
   - c. your actual implementation
   - d. your contractual obligations

6. The _____ command can be used to analyze the security level of your AD environment in a scripted process.
   - a. netdiag
   - b. repadmin
   - c. secedit
   - d. netdom

Section 5

Configuring, Securing, and Troubleshooting Remote Access

5.1 Configure and troubleshoot remote access and virtual private network (VPN) connections.

SUPPORTING VPN CONNECTIVITY

UNDERSTANDING THE OBJECTIVE

The use of **VPNs** is an important function of a Windows 2000 administrator. You will need to understand how to implement, support, and troubleshoot these connections using the Windows 2000 and Windows NT 4.0 operating systems. Because many users telecommute or work from home, the need to implement VPNs will continue to grow.

WHAT YOU REALLY NEED TO KNOW

◆ A VPN is the creation or extension of a portion of your corporate intranet across the pubic Internet. A VPN also must be hidden from your users so that they are unaware of how the connection is made. A secure VPN is designed, implemented, and then supported using the available tools and technology.

◆ Designing a secure VPN requires some hard choices regarding supported client operating systems. For instance, you might need to issue a company directive that Windows 98 will no longer be supported as an operating system, or you might issue a statement that all remote users can use only computer equipment that is supplied by the owner of the corporate VPN.

◆ You also must examine the protocols available for VPN support. L2TP is preferred. However, down-level clients cannot implement this particular protocol and must instead use PPTP. You must examine your security options for each protocol. Before beginning the implementation, you must decide issues such as levels of encryption, and kinds and strengths of passwords.

◆ After your design is fully mapped out, you next need to implement the design. Will you use Windows NT 4.0 RAS servers or Windows 2000 RRAS servers? Your selection will dictate the level of functionality your RAS clients will receive when they connect to the intranet.

◆ After you have implemented your VPN, you must maintain it. From time to time clients will experience connection problems. Portions of the network that should be accessible will not be, and other portions that should not be accessible will be. You must keep current with connection technologies, such as Wireless networks, and do so while still maintaining basic connectivity for your users.

OBJECTIVES ON THE JOB

Configuring RAS and VPN connections will be part of your normal duties in a corporate network environment. It is important that you understand the technologies and that you know the differences between them.

PRACTICE TEST QUESTIONS

1. **The acronym RAS stands for _____.**
   - a. Routed Remote Access Server
   - b. Routing and Remote Access Server
   - c. Remote Routing Access Server
   - d. Routing and Remote Access Service

2. **The implementation of RAS in Windows 2000 is _____ the implementation in Windows NT 4.0.**
   - a. different from
   - b. the same as
   - c. based on
   - d. more advanced than

3. **A Windows 98 client attempting to connect to a Windows 2000 RRAS server can use _____ as a secure dial-up protocol.**
   - a. MS-CHAP v2
   - b. PPP
   - c. EAP
   - d. PPTP

4. **A Windows 2000 client attempting to authenticate to a Windows 2000 RRAS server can use _____ as an authentication protocol.**
   - a. MS-CHAP v2
   - b. PPP
   - c. EAP
   - d. PPTP

5. **When using L2TP, _____ is enabled by default.**
   - a. MS-CHAP v1
   - b. MS-CHAP v2
   - c. EAP-TLS
   - d. IPSec

6. **For a Windows NT 4.0 VPN connection, you should always use _____ as a protocol.**
   - a. PPP
   - b. PPTP
   - c. SLIP
   - d. SPAP

7. **When configuring PPTP, you might want to apply packet filtering. When packet filtering is configured, it can be applied to the intermediate firewall or on the _____.**
   - a. LAN interface
   - b. VPN connection
   - c. VPN server
   - d. dial-up connection

5.1.1 Configure and troubleshoot client-to-server PPTP and L2TP connections.

INITIAL VPN CONFIGURATION

UNDERSTANDING THE OBJECTIVE

Your first step in configuring VPN connectivity for your client is the initial configuration of protocols for the connectivity. Two protocols are supported for VPN connectivity: PPTP and L2TP. Your decision about which one to use will be governed entirely by what operating system you are supporting for the VPN client. Likewise, your troubleshooting approaches will differ somewhat based on these supported clients.

WHAT YOU REALLY NEED TO KNOW

- ◆ Windows NT 4.0 systems use PPTP as their connectivity protocol. Windows 2000 systems implement L2TP, although PPTP is an option. Windows NT 4.0 does not support L2TP as a protocol.

- ◆ To install PPTP for Windows, the RAS server must have the PPTP driver installed. This is a simple process on a Windows NT 4.0 RAS server. From Control Panel, select the Network applet. Click the Protocols tab, select the Microsoft PPTP driver, and then click the Add button. Supply the installation media or point to the installation location and click OK. Select the port for installation, and then allow the computer to reboot. Before you use the newly installed PPTP connection, you must reinstall Windows NT 4.0 Service Pack 6a. This completes the RAS server installation for Windows NT 4.0.

- ◆ When creating a dial-up connection in Windows 2000, select the Properties page for the VPN connection, select the Networking tab, and then manually select either PPTP or L2TP as the desired protocol. You should note, however, that the default setting in Windows 2000 is to automatically detect the protocol in use and then auto-configure either PPTP or L2TP. Manual selection is not really necessary.

- ◆ Troubleshooting VPN connectivity usually falls into four categories: connection attempts are rejected; connection attempts are accepted; there is no pass-through connectivity from the VPN server; and the VPN tunnel cannot be established. For a general troubleshooting approach, you should verify connectivity to the VPN server, verify the state of the RAS service on the RAS server, and, for Windows 2000, verify the status of the remote access policies. For other troubleshooting tips, refer to the Windows 2000 Server Resource Kit.

OBJECTIVES ON THE JOB

A VPN connection allows your remote clients to connect and work with some sense of security. VPN protocols are PPTP and L2TP. Both are easily installed and configured. The Windows 2000 implementation also requires a properly configured RAS policy for connectivity. This policy is configured differently for Windows 2000, depending on whether you are in Mixed mode or Native mode.

PRACTICE TEST QUESTIONS

1. **Which Microsoft operating system supports L2TP? (Choose all that apply.)**
   a. Windows 95
   b. Windows 98
   c. Windows ME
   d. Windows NT 4.0
   e. Windows 2000

2. **If a client calls the help desk with VPN connectivity problems and he or she is using Windows 2000 with IPSec enabled, _____ is the tunneling protocol.**
   a. PPTP
   b. L2TP v1
   c. L2TP v2
   d. PPTP Service Pack v6a

3. **Which Microsoft operating system supports PPTP? (Choose all that apply.)**
   a. Windows 95
   b. Windows 98
   c. Windows ME
   d. Windows NT 4.0
   e. Windows 2000

4. **A Windows 2000 VPN connection using L2TP requires installation of the _____ service on the RAS server.**
   a. VPN
   b. RAS
   c. Restricted Profile
   d. L2TP

5. **PPTP works by tunneling through the _____ to provide connectivity.**
   a. corporate extranet
   b. public Internet
   c. corporate intranet
   d. public extranet

6. **Your help desk received a call from the user of a Windows NT 4.0 workstation who is trying to connect to a Windows NT 4.0 RAS server to use the VPN connection. However, every time the user tries to connect, a message says that no more ports are available on the RAS server. How could you resolve this connectivity issue?**
   a. Add more serial ports to the RAS server.
   b. Add more PPTP ports to the RAS server.
   c. Add more L2TP ports to the RAS server.
   d. Remove and reinstall the RAS service, and then reinstall Service Pack 6a.

5.1.2 Manage existing server-to-server PPTP and L2TP connections.

VPN ROUTER-TO-ROUTER CONNECTIVITY

UNDERSTANDING THE OBJECTIVE

VPNs can be used to provide connectivity between two segments of a private network. This method can avoid the costs of maintaining a dedicated connection using traditional WAN connectivity technologies. The connection can be implemented using either the PPTP or L2TP protocols. If the connection being created is between two Windows 2000 routers, L2TP is preferred.

WHAT YOU REALLY NEED TO KNOW

◆ If your corporate network infrastructure is subnetted, you will need a connectivity method to join the separate subnets. One common method of connectivity is to use demand-dial routers. This method, while reliable, may require the use of dedicated or toll-free phone lines for data transmission. Other issues, such as authentication or encryption of data, may factor in as well.

◆ A VPN connection provides better service than a dial-up connection, and at a substantially reduced cost with greater security. Implementing a VPN connection using PPTP or L2TP allows the remote routers to dial a local ISP and tunnel through the Internet for connectivity.

◆ To configure a Windows 2000 router to use router-to-router VPN connectivity, you must configure the demand-dial interface on both routers with the following parameters: the IP address or host name of the opposing VPN server; automatic or manually configured encryption settings; Automatic, L2TP, or PPTP protocol with the Automatic setting attempting L2TP first, and then PPTP; and a user name, password, and domain, which will be used for verification of the calling router. The demand-dial interface is created using the Demand-Dial Interface Wizard.

◆ You also must choose a temporary VPN router connection or a persistent VPN router connection. Temporary router connections are intended for small environments that use ISPs for connectivity. Persistent connections are intended for environments that have permanent Internet connectivity.

◆ You also must determine a method for updating the routing tables. If using temporary connections, you can use static routing tables with manual updates or auto-static updates to the routing tables. If you have configured persistent connections, you may enable **RIP v1**, **RIP v2**, or OSPF as your routing protocol.

OBJECTIVES ON THE JOB

The ability to configure a VPN connection between routers can have an important impact on your network functionality. Not only does it provide the opportunity to lower costs, but it also provides the opportunity to implement a more efficient methodology for your routing implementation.

PRACTICE TEST QUESTIONS

1. One benefit of using a router-to-router VPN is _____.
   a. improved support from the DHCP servers
   b. simpler implementation because of the subnetting of the network
   c. lowered administrative costs
   d. the ability to implement IEEE 802.11A as a routing standard

2. As the network architect for your corporation, you want to implement OSPF in your network infrastructure. You also want to minimize administrative costs, yet maximize routing efficiency. If you need to connect a router in a remote office with a router in the corporate headquarters, what connection type should you use to satisfy these constraints?
   a. persistent connection with a demand-dial connection
   b. temporary connection with a demand-dial connection
   c. persistent connection with DSL service
   d. temporary connection with DSL service

3. If you are implementing a router-to-router solution with RIP v2 and a temporary connection utilizing L2TP, you should also implement _____ on the routers.
   a. IPSec
   b. PPTP
   c. manual updates
   d. auto-static updates

4. When configuring router-to-router connectivity on a Windows 2000 server, you will configure the demand-dial interface with credentials for the secure connection. How do you create the actual demand-dial interface?
   a. by using the Routing Interface Wizard
   b. by using the Demand-Dial Interface Wizard
   c. by using the Router Connectivity Wizard
   d. by using the Demand-Dial Configuration Wizard

5. When using PPTP as a protocol to support a demand-dial router in a branch office, you will implement two separate interfaces. The first interface uses demand-dial to connect the router to the local ISP. The second interface uses demand-dial to connect the router to the _____.
   a. branch office infrastructure
   b. opposing router in the corporate office
   c. extranet ISP
   d. router-to-router VPN connection

6. When using IPSec to configure router-to-router VPN connections, you must supply _____ on both ends of the VPN connection.
   a. DHCP
   b. host files
   c. computer certificates
   d. PKA certificates

5.1.3 Configure and verify the security of a VPN connection.

VPN SECURITY CONFIGURATION

UNDERSTANDING THE OBJECTIVE

If you are using PPTP or L2TP for your VPN connection, you must configure and verify security configuration settings to enable and maintain functionality. PPTP has a relatively simple security configuration, while L2TP has a more complex security implementation. Either protocol, if configured correctly, will provide a secure VPN connection for your network.

WHAT YOU REALLY NEED TO KNOW

◆ PPTP connections provide two different security settings: user authentication and data encryption. Both settings require configuration for use. These settings allow you to supply your down-level clients with a secure VPN connection.

◆ There are eight authentication protocols used by PPTP: cleartext (the least desirable), **EAP, CHAP, MS-CHAP, MS-CHAP v2, PAP, SPAP,** and **EAP-TLS**. MS-CHAP v2 and EAP-TLS (which utilizes Smart Cards) are highly recommended because they provide mutual authentication.

◆ PPTP supports encryption of data using **MPPE**, which is available only when using MS-CHAP v1/v2 or EAP-TLS. MPPE uses 40-bit, 56-bit, or 128-bit encryption. The default setting is negotiated by mutual agreement between the VPN client and the VPN server, and always results in the highest level of encryption supported by both ends of the connection being used. The 40-bit settings are down-level compatible with non-Windows 2000 platforms.

◆ L2TP security authentication occurs at two levels. Both the computer and the user, in this order, must be authenticated for connectivity to occur. A key concept of L2TP is the use of computer certificates. After the negotiation is completed, the VPN client and the VPN server begin a communication session using an agreed-upon encryption algorithm, a hash algorithm, and encryption keys. Computer certificates used in the process must be installed on both the VPN client and the VPN server. These certificates can be created using a GPO auto-enrollment process, or they can be created manually using the Certificates snap-in in an MMC console.

◆ L2TP encryption can also be applied when using the L2TP protocol. The two available encryption settings are 56-bit **DES** and **3DES**. This level of encryption provides protection against attempts at hacking transmitted data. An additional feature of L2TP IPSec DES encryption is the regeneration of encryption keys every five minutes or 250 MB of transmitted material (whichever comes first) during the encrypted session. For 3DES, new keys are generated after every hour or after 2 GB of data are transmitted.

OBJECTIVES ON THE JOB

The configuration and verification of security settings, while complex, are an important part of Windows 2000 administration. For more information on troubleshooting security settings using PPTP and L2TP, visit the Windows 2000 Server Resource Kit Web site at *www.reskit.com*.

PRACTICE TEST QUESTIONS

1. The PPTP encryption standard that supports 40-bit encryption is

   _____.
      a. EAP-TLS
      b. EAP
      c. SPAP
      d. MPPE

2. _____ is the security protocol required for Smart Card authentication using PPTP.
      a. IPSec
      b. RSA RC4
      c. EAP-TLS
      d. MS-CHAP v2

3. When using 3DES, the _____ is every hour or 2 GB of transmitted data.
      a. data tombstone
      b. low security refresh interval
      c. data integrity check
      d. default key refresh interval

4. Single DES provides only _____ encryption.
      a. 40-bit
      b. 128-bit
      c. 56-bit
      d. 168-bit

5. When configuring L2TP computer authentication, a(n) _____ must be obtained and stored on both the VPN client and the VPN server.
      a. Lmhosts file
      b. digital signature
      c. computer signature
      d. computer certificate

6. Which protocol will L2TP support? (Choose all that apply.)
      a. EAP
      b. CHAP
      c. MS-CHAP v3
      d. SLIP

7. When two computers enabled with _____ begin their initial negotiation, they go through several different steps, including Phase 1 and Phase 2.
      a. AH negotiation
      b. GPO verification
      c. IPSec protocol
      d. ESP negotiation

OBJECTIVES

5.1.4 Configure client computer remote access properties.

ENABLING REMOTE ACCESS

UNDERSTANDING THE OBJECTIVE

When you enable remote access connectivity for your Windows 2000 clients, those remote clients most commonly will be users who are traveling or in **SOHO** environments. You also might need to configure remote access for a small branch office that uses only the telephone for connectivity to your corporate infrastructure.

WHAT YOU REALLY NEED TO KNOW

◆ The center point of remote access connectivity is a supported, working modem. A modem can use the PSTN or the latest bidirectional satellite transceiver. When configuring your client's remote access, begin with the modem. Most new laptops feature an integral modem, which should simplify your installation process. For external or add-on devices, consult the Windows 2000 HCL or the Web site of the manufacturer for the latest drivers and operating system patches. Verify modem functionality before proceeding.

◆ After the functionality of the modem has been verified, you next must configure the remote access properties. In Windows 2000 Professional, you do this using the Network Connection Wizard, which walks you through creating the new connection. You access this Wizard by right-clicking My Network Places/Properties and selecting Make New Connection.

◆ To start the Wizard, click Next and select the type of connection desired. There are five different selections on this interface. Choose the first button for connecting to your corporate intranet or the second button for connecting to the public Internet. Next you must supply a phone number. If you want to control the connection settings, check the Use dialing rules check box, and then supply the required information. Click Next.

◆ Decide whether this connection will be available to all users of this computer or only to the current user. Click Next and name the connection. If desired, click Add a shortcut to my desktop, and then click Finish.

◆ After the dial-up connection has been created, there are several other settings that must be configured. Select the dial-up connection and open the connection. You will now see five tabs that allow you to customize the connection settings. From these tabs, you may configure the modem, select options, adjust security settings, configure network settings, and configure connection-sharing settings.

OBJECTIVES ON THE JOB

Configuring remote access properties for your users is a common daily task. Remote users depend on having connectivity to the corporate intranet, so you must be prepared to describe the process over a telephone and walk them through creating the connection. Practice beforehand.

PRACTICE TEST QUESTIONS

1. You have received a call from a user who wants you to help resolve a problem. The user is currently traveling and works from a small office without a permanent Internet connection. The user has access to one digital PBX line, one analog voice line, and one line that is used for a FAX machine. The user also has a laptop with an internal modem, an external modem that connects using a serial port, and a PC Card modem. Using these three modems and three phone lines, the user wants to improve connectivity in this office. How many telephone lines could be used to support this user? (Choose all that apply.)
    a. All three lines are available to support the user.
    b. the analog voice line
    c. the digital PBX line
    d. the FAX line

2. Returning to Question 1, which modem(s) would you select to enable the remote access the user needs? (Choose all that apply.)
    a. all three modems
    b. the internal laptop modem
    c. the external serial port modem
    d. the PC Card modem

3. Returning to Question 1, if more than one phone line is available, the feature that must be enabled on the user's laptop is _____.
    a. modem sharing
    b. ICS
    c. multilink support
    d. multimodem support

4. Returning to Question 1, the feature that must be enabled on the RAS dial-in server to support the answer in Question 3 is _____.
    a. modem sharing
    b. ICS
    c. multilink
    d. multimodem support

5. Returning to Question 1, the user does not want to pay for the phone calls used during the dial-up sessions. What can be configured to make certain that the company pays for the phone calls?
    a. a corporate phone card
    b. a VPN tunnel
    c. a toll-free number
    d. the callback setting

5.1.5 Configure remote access name resolution and IP address allocation.

SUPPORTING REMOTE IP CONNECTIVITY

UNDERSTANDING THE OBJECTIVE

After configuring computers for remote connectivity, you must still implement support for network connectivity. You must support name resolution for your remote access clients, and use some method to assign IP addresses.

WHAT YOU REALLY NEED TO KNOW

◆ The assignment of IP addresses is handled differently on a Windows 2000 RRAS server than on a Windows NT 4.0 RAS server. The Windows 2000 RRAS server can implement the assignment of IP addresses through the use of DHCP or through the use of a static address pool.

◆ DHCP RAS IP address assignment requires that the RAS server contact a DHCP server or that the RAS server assign addresses using APIPA. If you elected to implement DHCP for the RAS server, then, by default, the RAS server contacts a DHCP server and obtains a block of 10 DHCP addresses at a time. The first address obtained in the block is assigned to the interface supplied for the RAS clients. The remaining nine addresses are available for clients. As RAS clients disconnect from the RAS server and these addresses are released, they are reassigned to new connections. If no addresses are available for assignment, the RAS server contacts a DHCP server and requests another block of 10 addresses. The size of the DHCP request block is configurable through the Registry. When the RAS service is restarted, a new block of addresses is obtained.

◆ If a Windows 2000 RRAS server cannot contact a DHCP server for address allocation blocks, the server will issue addresses using APIPA. The size of this potential assignment block is still 10 addresses, with the RAS interface on the RAS server using the first assigned APIPA address. With APIPA assignment, the network being connected to must also use APIPA.

◆ Windows 2000 RRAS servers can also use a static address pool for IP address assignment. When configured with a static IP address pool, the RAS server takes the first address for its interface and uses the remaining balance for clients connecting to the server. If a separate subnet has been created for the RAS clients, a routing protocol must be configured for these clients, or the existing routers must be reconfigured to support the new subnet for connectivity.

◆ Name resolution can be implemented by using either DNS or WINS, or both, depending on the needs of the client operating system. Where the RAS server obtains its name resolution services affects the assignment for the clients.

OBJECTIVES ON THE JOB

You must provide IP connectivity and name resolution for your connecting clients. This functionality can be achieved by either DHCP assignment or through static address pools.

PRACTICE TEST QUESTIONS

1. If the DHCP server that the RAS server normally contacts to obtain DHCP address pools is unavailable and the RAS server implements APIPA, which operating systems can connect to the RAS server and utilize the APIPA addresses? (Choose all that apply.)

   a. Windows 98
   b. Windows ME
   c. Windows NT 4.0
   d. Windows 2000

2. On a Windows 2000 RRAS server that uses DHCP for IP connectivity for clients, the addresses for DHCP leases used by the RAS server are _____ the RAS server.

   a. assigned against
   b. reused by
   c. released by
   d. reissued to

3. When configuring static IP addresses for Windows 2000 RRAS clients on a Windows 2000 RRAS server, the RAS server always takes _____ address.

   a. the first
   b. the last
   c. a random
   d. an assigned

4. When you use APIPA for IP address assignment for RAS clients, the RAS clients are limited to only the RAS server and cannot browse the network unless _____ has been configured.

   a. APIPA routing
   b. RIP for APIPA
   c. addressing using APIPA for the entire network
   d. static routing to support APIPA

5. The default setting to download only 10 DHCP addresses at a time from the DHCP server can be modified by altering the _____ Registry entry in the Registry path HKEY_LOCAL_MACHINE\System\CurrentControlSet\Services\RemoteAccess\Parameters\IP.

   a. AddressPoolSize
   b. Initial Address Pool Size
   c. InitialAddressPoolSize
   d. Address Pool Size

6. If a RAS server supports VPN connections and has multiple LAN interfaces, the DNS and WINS information from _____ is used to populate the DNS and WINS information for VPN clients.

   a. the oldest connection
   b. the corporate intranet connection
   c. the connection supporting the largest number of hosts
   d. a LAN interface selected at random during startup

5.2 Troubleshoot a remote access policy.

REMOTE ACCESS POLICIES

UNDERSTANDING THE OBJECTIVE

Remote access policies enable your users to work remotely and also support their business needs when not in the corporate infrastructure. By configuring RAS connectivity for your clients, you can provide RAS support. However, after you enable RAS, you may need to troubleshoot your RAS client's connectivity to your corporate infrastructure.

WHAT YOU REALLY NEED TO KNOW

◆ RAS can be a complex implementation that depends on different components, including RAS policies. The failure of any component can cause connection difficulties for your clients and disrupt their ability to work remotely.

◆ Starting from the client and working back toward your corporate network, the first service used in RAS connectivity is the PSTN. The part of the world or part of the United States from which your clients are attempting to connect may have only poor connections available; those connections might cause problems for your client. There are still sections of the United States where connectivity speeds for a RAS connection may not exceed 2.4 Kbps. Some foreign countries may not achieve half this value. How successfully can you troubleshoot RAS connectivity for a client who wants to retrieve e-mail using Outlook over a dial-up connection of 1.0 Kbps?

◆ Another issue might arise if the client tries to dial in and is rejected. If the client can dial successfully but cannot connect, you may need to look at issues regarding the protocol being implemented for the client. For instance, is the protocol used by the client supported on the RAS server?

◆ If the client can dial in and connect but the password is rejected, you may need to check the status of the account. RAS accounts can be locked out or disabled in the same fashion as a normal domain user account. In addition, check whether there are any authentication protocols being used on the RAS server that may interfere with the client's connectivity.

◆ If your clients can connect and their passwords are accepted, they may still encounter connectivity problems when trying to authenticate against a Windows 2000 RRAS server. Windows NT 4.0 RAS servers simply configured user accounts for access. Windows 2000 RRAS servers require dial-in clients to be checked against conditions, permissions, and profiles for connectivity to the RAS server. You may need to troubleshoot all three layers for connectivity. If your Windows 2000 RRAS server is part of a Windows 2000 AD domain in Native mode, the dial-in settings used by AD are also a factor.

OBJECTIVES ON THE JOB

You may need to troubleshoot your clients' remote access connectivity by examining the RAS policies that have been implemented for them. The policies could vary, depending on the type of Windows RAS server hosting the connections for the clients.

PRACTICE TEST QUESTIONS

1. When troubleshooting RAS connectivity from a Windows 2000 member server in a Windows 2000 domain running in Native mode, there are always _____ levels of policy testing.
   a. 4
   b. 3
   c. 2
   d. 1

2. Configuring a Windows NT 4.0 account for dial-in connectivity involves _____.
   a. adding an account for the user on the RAS server and then adding the user to the RAS Users global group in the NT 4.0 domain
   b. adding the user account to the local group RAS Users on the RAS server
   c. enabling the account for dial-in support
   d. adding the RAS service on the server and rebooting the server (support for the clients is automatic after this)

3. _____ is just one condition for a Windows 2000 RRAS connection.
   a. Group membership
   b. BAP configuration
   c. An authentication protocol
   d. The time of day

4. RAS policies in Windows 2000 can include the _____.
   a. name of a DNS server
   b. address of a DHCP server
   c. encryption protocol to be used
   d. routing protocol to be used

5. If a client is trying to authenticate to a Windows 2000 RRAS server using EAP-TLP, the client is using _____, and you may need to add additional configuration settings. (Choose all that apply.)
   a. IPSec
   b. PPTP
   c. Smart Cards
   d. biometric authentication

6. To use EAP-TLP authentication and Smart Cards, you must enable _____ in your domain.
   a. L2TP
   b. IPSec
   c. certificate authorities
   d. NetBIOS

5.2.1 Diagnose problems with remote access policy priority.

RAS POLICY PRIORITIES

UNDERSTANDING THE OBJECTIVE

When your clients have problems connecting, you might suspect policy problems. You need to understand the difference between RAS policies on Windows 2000 Mixed-mode domains and Windows 2000 Native-mode domains. You also must understand how the application of properties for the user accounts and the remote access policies on RAS servers can combine to allow or deny access.

WHAT YOU REALLY NEED TO KNOW

- ◆ Windows 2000 RRAS policies consist of three groups of settings: conditions, permissions, and rights. Each can allow the client to continue processing and move to the next setting, and ultimately to a successful logon. Each also can block the client from processing any further policies and deny the connection attempt. The success of a client's attempt to utilize dial-up connectivity in Windows 2000 also hinges on the combination of the user object's dial-in properties and the remote access policies as they exist on the RAS server.

- ◆ Beyond controlling whether the client can successfully connect, the RAS policies also control the state of the connection, values such as connection idle limits, maximum session connection times, encryption levels, and user authentication settings.

- ◆ Problems with Windows 2000 dial-in connections arise from the fact that more than one dial-in policy may affect the client. Just as conflicts can arise when configuring and applying GPOs, problems can also arise when configuring and applying RAS policies.

- ◆ Because the dial-in rights in Windows 2000 are very granular, a user could simultaneously belong to two different groups with conflicting dial-in permissions. In this instance, the Deny policy would override any successful connections. Another problem may arise from the lack of **RADIUS**-server support in the Windows 2000 dial-in environment. Without a RADIUS server, each Windows 2000 RRAS server maintains its own set of dial-in permissions. The user may be successful with one attempt and unsuccessful with the next.

- ◆ Authentication and encryption settings may also conflict because of the way that Windows 2000 processes the RAS policies for connectivity. For example, if a Windows 2000 RAS server does not use RADIUS and has no configured dial-in policies, all connection attempts are rejected because the default RAS setting for Windows 2000 is to deny connectivity.

OBJECTIVES ON THE JOB

Diagnosing remote access problems in Windows 2000 can be a challenging task because of the differences between RAS implementations. The user must be authenticated against two sets of settings: those that exist for the user, and those that exist on the RAS server.

PRACTICE TEST QUESTIONS

1. When configuring user accounts for dial-up connectivity to your Windows 2000 Mixed-mode domain which does not use RADIUS, you may need to assign users to a specific _____.
   - a. OU
   - b. RAS server
   - c. domain
   - d. IAS server

2. The default dial-up permission in a Windows 2000 Native-mode domain is _____.
   - a. Everyone/Full Control
   - b. Domain Users/Read
   - c. Authenticated Users/Change
   - d. Everyone/No Access

3. When configuring Windows 2000 dial-up connectivity, you can use a _____ server or an IAS server for RAS accounting information collection.
   - a. DDNS
   - b. RAS accounting
   - c. RADIUS
   - d. GC

4. You have received a call from a remote user who is attempting to connect to your Windows 2000 RRAS server. The user is able to connect to the domain, but the connection lasts only 30 minutes. To troubleshoot this problem where would you start looking? (Choose all that apply.)
   - a. Check the maximum connected session time on the RAS server.
   - b. Check the protocol in use for the connection.
   - c. Check the user's RAS password duration settings.
   - d. Check the length of the DHCP RAS lease.

5. A client is reporting problems with dial-in attempts to your Windows 2000 domain. The problems seem to stem from a specific telephone number used for the dial-in service. One particular number does not allow connectivity; the other numbers do. What should you suspect is the cause of the problem?
   - a. a misconfigured RAS server
   - b. incorrect user settings
   - c. absence of a RADIUS server
   - d. conflicting dial-in permissions

6. RAS policy application in a Windows 2000 mixed mode domain is a three-layer process. In a Windows 2000 native mode domain, it is a _____-layer process.
   - a. one
   - b. two
   - c. three
   - d. four

5.2.2 Diagnose remote access policy problems caused by user account group membership and nested groups.

RAS GROUP TROUBLESHOOTING

UNDERSTANDING THE OBJECTIVE

Windows 2000 supports the use of user accounts for dial-in authentication. You may extend the membership to include user membership in groups. You also have the ability to nest groups for tighter administrative control in a domain environment. These implementations may cause problems for users trying to authenticate to your Windows 2000 domain.

WHAT YOU REALLY NEED TO KNOW

- ◆ Just as Windows 2000 users can belong to a variety of groups for administrative control when connected through the corporate intranet, they can also belong to a variety of groups for administrative control when using dial-in connectivity. You must remember this while troubleshooting Windows 2000 RRAS connectivity issues.

- ◆ The RAS servers in Windows 2000 can block access at different levels, including group memberships of the users. If the user attempting the connection is a member of a disallowed group or if the user does not belong to the correct group, he or she will not be allowed to access the Windows 2000 domain using a dial-in connection.

- ◆ For dial-in access in a Windows 2000 domain, the user accounts that require remote access must be configured to support the permission. You must select these accounts and enable the Allow access permission. As a separate configuration step, you then must change the default dial-in permission for your selected dial-in profile for the domain to "Allow access if dial-in permission is enabled." Failure to complete this step results in your dial-in clients being denied access.

- ◆ Instead of configuring individual user accounts, you can create RAS user groups for connectivity. To implement this technique, create a new Windows 2000 global group, and assign domain users to the group. These users should be able to use remote connectivity. Assign this global group to a domain local group. Then assign the appropriate permissions to the domain local group to support the use of dial-in connections.

- ◆ When supporting RAS clients connecting to Windows NT 4.0 RAS servers with Service Pack 4 or later, remember to add the Everyone group to the Pre-Windows 2000 Compatible Access group. This is required because the processing for RAS connectivity in Windows NT 4.0 is the exact opposite of the processing used in Windows 2000. Failure to implement this change results in nonauthentication for users who are connecting to the Windows NT 4.0 RAS server while trying to authenticate to a Windows 2000 domain. This setting also creates a large and undesirable hole in your Windows 2000 security implementation.

OBJECTIVES ON THE JOB

Effective troubleshooting of group and user RAS connectivity in Windows 2000 will help you support your users with their dial-in connectivity problems.

PRACTICE TEST QUESTIONS

1. When using a Windows NT 4.0 RAS server (with Service Pack 3 or earlier) that is a member server in a Windows 2000 domain, you must remember to configure the _____ group with list contents, read all properties, and read permissions for your Windows 2000 domain root node and all sub-objects of the root node.
   a. Dial-in users
   b. Pre-Windows 2000 users
   c. Everyone
   d. RAS users

2. The default permission for RAS connectivity in Windows NT 4.0 is to _____ the connection.
   a. allow
   b. deny
   c. restrict
   d. support

3. The default permission for RAS connectivity in Windows 2000 is to _____ the connection.
   a. allow
   b. deny
   c. restrict
   d. support

4. A user calls and reports problems dialing in to the corporate intranet using a Windows NT 4.0 workstation. The user has the correct phone number to access the RAS server, and you have verified that the server is online. You have also verified the dial-in settings and confirmed that these are correct. You have checked the user's group memberships and they also seem to be correct. What might be the problem?
   a. The user is trying to connect to a Windows NT 4.0 RAS server.
   b. The user is trying to connect to a Windows 2000 RRAS server.
   c. The user's dial-in account is locked out.
   d. The user is using the wrong encryption protocol.

5. As an implementation technique, you have created a Universal group and placed all your users who need dial-in permissions into this group. You then placed the Universal group into a Domain Local group and assigned the dial-in permission for the Domain Local group. Your users cannot dial in. What did you overlook?
   a. You forgot to assign permissions to the Universal group.
   b. You forgot to configure the RAS server to support the Universal group.
   c. You forgot to place a GC in the same site as the dial-in users.
   d. You forgot to grant the Everyone group dial-in permissions.

5.2.3 Create and configure remote access policies and profiles.

ENABLING REMOTE ACCESS

UNDERSTANDING THE OBJECTIVE

As the administrator of a Windows 2000 domain, you need to configure RAS policies and profiles for your remote users. RAS policies in Windows 2000 are a combination of three specific configuration settings: conditions, permissions, and policies.

WHAT YOU REALLY NEED TO KNOW

- ◆ Windows 2000 RRAS access is more complex than the RAS access provided under Windows NT 4.0. When configuring RAS access for Windows NT 4.0 clients, the only setting to enable allowed the specified user to connect remotely. Windows 2000 RRAS policies allow the administrator to configure specific RAS connection policies based on time of day, day of week, or group membership. Many other settings are supported as well.

- ◆ You need to begin with a planning document that specifies which users will and will not have remote access permissions in your Windows 2000 domain. Issues such as method of connection, dial-in versus VPN connectivity authentication protocols in use, and levels of encryption all must be addressed and defined. You also need to consider issues such as the use of **BAP** and multilink settings. Additional considerations regarding the encryption settings are legal constraints on differing encryption levels imposed by international or national legal restrictions. Canada may support 128-bit encrypted dial-in sessions, but does France? You must consider these points.

- ◆ You also must consider the group memberships of dial-in users and whether these dial-in users will connect to a Windows NT 4.0 member server hosting RAS that belongs to a Windows 2000 domain. In addition, you must consider whether they will connect to a Windows 2000 stand-alone server that does not belong to a Windows 2000 domain. Last, remember that dial-in permission for Windows 2000 RRAS servers functions differently, depending on whether the computer belongs to a Mixed-mode domain or a Native-mode domain.

- ◆ Another aspect of Windows 2000 RRAS policies is that the user attempting to connect must meet at least one of the configured policies. Note that a failure to authenticate against either of the two policies will cause the connection attempt to fail completely. As a troubleshooting technique, remember that these policies are arranged in order of application. You may simply need to reorder the policies to achieve a successful dial-in attempt.

OBJECTIVES ON THE JOB

The configuration of Windows 2000 dial-in policies and profiles requires many different settings and rights for success. It is definitely a task that must be thoroughly planned before being implemented.

PRACTICE TEST QUESTIONS

1. **An example of a RAS condition is _____. (Choose all that apply.)**
   a. the day of the week
   b. the BAP setting
   c. group membership
   d. the dialing location

2. **An example of a RAS permission is _____. (Choose all that apply.)**
   a. group membership
   b. OU membership
   c. an encryption setting
   d. a Smart Card setting

3. **An example of a RAS policy is _____. (Choose all that apply.)**
   a. a BAP setting
   b. the time of day
   c. an encryption setting
   d. an authentication protocol

4. **Windows 2000 RRAS servers by default use a _____ dial-in policy.**
   a. centralized
   b. domain-specific
   c. server-specific
   d. consistent

5. **BAP is used to control the bandwidth used by dial-in connections _____.**
   a. that have QOS enabled
   b. that have VPN connections enabled
   c. that have multilink enabled
   d. that have multicast applications such as NetMeeting enabled

6. **When dial-in policies are being evaluated, the user will be denied a connection if _____ fail(s).**
   a. four polices
   b. three policies
   c. two policies
   d. one policy

7. **The assignment of EAP instead of PPTP is an example of a RAS dial-in _____.**
   a. condition
   b. permission
   c. policy
   d. setting

5.2.4 Select appropriate encryption and authentication protocols.

CLIENT CONNECTION SETTINGS

UNDERSTANDING THE OBJECTIVE

In the modern network environment, security is everything. An administrator's failure to properly secure a network infrastructure can lead to significant compromises by unauthorized individuals. The process of securing your environment must extend to your dial-in users, if any, and the methods that they use to work remotely.

WHAT YOU REALLY NEED TO KNOW

◆ Before your dial-in users can access network resources, they must connect to your network. For the connection to succeed, you must select an authentication protocol and an encryption protocol. Your authentication protocol will, to a degree, be dictated by the client operating system that you are supporting. The authentication protocol will in turn dictate the encryption protocols available to you. The capabilities of the RAS server to which your clients will connect also impact connectivity.

◆ There are three authentication protocols available in Windows 2000: **PPP**, EAP, and EAP-TLS. Each is different and can be used for specific clients.

◆ There are also different encryption protocols. The different levels of encryption are: no encryption at all; PPTP using MPPE with a 40-bit encryption key enabled; L2TP with IPSec using 40-bit DES; PPTP using MPPE with a 56-bit encryption key enabled; L2TP with IPSec using 56-bit DES; PPTP using MPPE with a 128-bit encryption key enabled; and L2TP with IPSec using 3DES.

◆ Each encryption and authentication protocol has its place in your RAS implementation design. If you support Windows 2000 clients, they can use any of the listed protocols without difficulty. You will only need to supply proper configuration settings. However, any down-level clients that you support will have very specific capabilities when you are making design choices. Only Windows 2000 clients can support IPSec as a protocol. This eliminates the most secure and robust security implementations from your Windows NT 4.0 and Windows 9x clients.

◆ As the administrator, you must be familiar with the different options available to you. If you decide to implement IPSec as an encryption protocol, can your computers support the additional 15 to 20 percent added workload on their processors? If not, you may need to invest in some new network adaptor cards that have been designed specifically for IPSec. If you have decided to implement EAP-TLS as an authentication protocol, you need to invest in Smart Cards and readers because this protocol requires both components.

OBJECTIVES ON THE JOB

Encryption and authentication protocols can be an important part of your security implementation for a Windows 2000 domain, as well as a vital tool for your supported users working remotely.

PRACTICE TEST QUESTIONS

1. **Smart Cards require that a user attempting to log in must possess both the Smart Card itself and knowledge of the user's login _____.**
   - a. domain
   - b. name
   - c. PIN
   - d. certificate

2. **The most secure authentication protocol that can be used by a Windows NT 4.0 computer for dial-in connectivity is _____.**
   - a. IPSec
   - b. EAP
   - c. PPP
   - d. PPTP

3. **You have received a call from a user with dial-in problems. The user is trying to connect to a Windows 2000 RRAS server using a Windows NT 4.0 workstation. The user can establish an initial connection, but the connection does not last. To solve this problem, you should check the dial-in _____ setting.**
   - a. password
   - b. encryption
   - c. authentication
   - d. protocol

4. **A user is trying to dial in to a Windows NT 4.0 RAS server. The computer is a Windows 2000 Professional laptop with an integral modem, and the user is using L2TP as the authentication protocol. After authenticating they cannot stay connected. From the list below, what should you check?**
   - a. The LCP settings on their internal modem.
   - b. The LCP setting on the dial-in server.
   - c. The dial-in permissions on the RAS server.
   - d. No troubleshooting is possible because Windows NT 4.0 does not support L2TP.

5. **If you have a single Windows 95 client who needs to authenticate to a UNIX server, you should use the _____ protocol.**
   - a. PPP
   - b. IPSec
   - c. SLIP
   - d. PPTP

6. **A characteristic of SLIP is that it _____.**
   - a. has strong encryption
   - b. has weak encryption
   - c. uses 40-bit encryption
   - d. uses no encryption

5.3 Implement and troubleshoot Terminal Services for remote access.

TERMINAL SERVICES

UNDERSTANDING THE OBJECTIVE

Terminal Services can give the Windows 2000 administrator a great deal of control over his or her environment. As implemented in Windows 2000, Terminal Services allows control of a server. It also makes applications available to users who need to run 32-bit applications, but have only 16-bit workstations.

WHAT YOU REALLY NEED TO KNOW

◆ The version of Terminal Services found in Windows 2000 is licensed directly from the Citrix company, which is the premier Terminal Services company. Citrix has a variety of terminal server clients that can be installed on many different operating systems, including DOS.

◆ Microsoft makes a Pocket PC and Windows CE version of Terminal Server. They are available from the Microsoft Web site and are for administrators who need to manage servers remotely using only a telephone connection.

◆ The Terminal Server implemented in Windows 2000 is robust and stable. Unlike the Windows NT 4.0 Terminal Server, which was a separate product, every copy of Windows 2000 can become a terminal server if the terminal server components are installed. Note that Terminal Server is only available for server products. The server component cannot be installed on a client computer.

◆ Windows 2000 Terminal Server can be installed in two different modes, depending on your needs as an administrator. One mode is the Administrative mode, which allows you complete administrative control of the server that supports this service. The other mode is the Application Server mode, which allows clients to connect using a terminal service client and use applications that are actually running on the application server. This is useful in high-security environments or if you have a group of older computers that cannot run Windows 2000, but still need access to newer applications, such as Office XP.

◆ Terminal Server, when installed, places a folder in the path %SYSTEMROOT%\System32\ Clients. The folder contains all the 16-bit and 32-bit clients for Windows operating systems. If additional clients are needed, they must be obtained from the Citrix Web site. The clients located in this folder can be installed across the network or they can be copied to floppy disks or other installation media, and then used to install the client on the desired platforms. Once installed, this client can be used to connect to terminal servers on your corporate intranet.

OBJECTIVES ON THE JOB

Terminal Server and the Terminal Server client are important new tools in the Windows 2000 operating system. They can provide a great deal of utility. At the same time they provide you a safe and secure computing environment that benefits you and your users.

PRACTICE TEST QUESTIONS

1. The Windows 2000 Terminal Server client can accommodate both 32-bit and
   _____ clients.
   - a. Apple
   - b. UNIX
   - c. LINUX
   - d. 16-bit

2. Terminal Server can be installed on the _____ platform.
   - a. Windows 98
   - b. Windows 2000 Web Server
   - c. Windows 2000 Cluster Server
   - d. Windows 2000 Professional

3. Why is the Windows 2000 Terminal Server a secure implementation of network
   connectivity? (Choose all that apply.)
   - a. All processing occurs on the server, not on the client.
   - b. Only bitmaps are transmitted from the server to the client, and vice versa.
   - c. Terminal Server clients do not require floppy drives or hard drives.
   - d. Smart Card authentication can be enabled.

4. A Terminal Server client is available from _____ for use with
   MS-DOS 6.22.
   - a. Microsoft
   - b. Citrix
   - c. UNIX
   - d. Hewlett/Packard

5. If you attempt to install Terminal Server in its application mode after you have
   finished installing applications, the applications will _____. (Choose
   all that apply.)
   - a. work as before
   - b. stop working
   - c. require reinstallation
   - d. run only on the Terminal Server clients, not the terminal server

6. The protocol used by Windows 2000 Terminal Server is the _____
   protocol.
   - a. ICMP
   - b. RDP
   - c. NetBOIS
   - d. IPSec

5.3.1 Configure Terminal Services for remote administration or application server mode.

TERMINAL SERVICES CONFIGURATION

UNDERSTANDING THE OBJECTIVE

One of the most useful and versatile tools in Windows 2000 is Terminal Server. Unlike the Terminal Server product found in Windows NT 4.0, which was a separate product, Terminal Server in Windows 2000 is part of every Windows 2000 server product; it does not require a special version. Terminal Server can be used in two separate modes; however, they cannot be used at the same time on the same server.

WHAT YOU REALLY NEED TO KNOW

◆ The Windows 2000 administrator can install Terminal Server in two different modes. The service does not install by default. The first mode is Remote Administration mode; it allows the administrator to connect to a Windows 2000 server using a Terminal Server console across the network. You can administer the server as though you were sitting directly in front of the server.

◆ To install Terminal Server, use the Add Windows Components applet in the Control Panel, and choose the Terminal Server Configuration Wizard. You will be prompted to decide between Remote Administration or Application Server modes. Make your decision according to the type of server you need, and allow the Wizard to finish. Remember that a Terminal Server can be installed as only one type of Terminal Server at a time, not both. Also, if you have decided to install Terminal Server in its administrative mode, install it as soon as possible after the server has been built, and before any applications are installed. This allows the applications to function under Administrative mode.

◆ The Remote Administration configuration, by default, supports only two administrative connections at a time. You will have complete control over the servers to which you connect, and Administrative mode requires no further configuration beyond the installation. Microsoft has made a Terminal Server client available for Windows CE and Pocket PC devices as a free download. This allows you to manage these devices using remote connectivity as well as by using a normal network connection.

◆ Application Server mode allows you to deploy and manage applications to your network environment using the benefits of Terminal Server. An important benefit of this technique is the ability to install the Terminal Server client on a host machine that normally could not support Windows 2000. It also enables connectivity to a Windows 2000 Terminal Server in Application mode.

OBJECTIVES ON THE JOB

Windows 2000 Terminal Services gives you complete control over your servers. Microsoft recommends that Terminal Server be installed on all Windows 2000 servers to support remote administration. You can also install Terminal Server in Remote Application mode.

PRACTICE TEST QUESTIONS

1. The Windows 2000 Terminal Server in Administrative mode supports
   _____ licensed connection(s) at a time.
   - a. four
   - b. three
   - c. two
   - d. one

2. A client has called your help desk with a problem. The client is using Microsoft Windows 3.11, Windows for Workgroups and needs to use Office XP applications on this computer while retaining the Windows 3.11 installation. How could you implement this for the client?
   - a. Use a third-party application to create another partition on the computer, install Windows 2000 Professional, and then install Office XP.
   - b. This cannot be implemented; the client needs to obtain a second computer.
   - c. The client needs to install the 32-bit version of the Terminal Server console.
   - d. The client needs to install the 16-bit version of the Terminal Server console.

3. When adding applications to a Windows 2000 Terminal Server in Application mode, you can install applications from the Terminal Server console, or by
   _____.
   - a. using the Terminal Server Remote Installation service
   - b. having a field assistant install the software for you under your direction
   - c. using SMS Version 2 to remotely install the application.
   - d. using remote installation

4. _____ clients that connect to Windows 2000 Terminal Servers already have Terminal Server licenses installed and do not need an additional license for connectivity.
   - a. Windows NT 4.0 Workstation
   - b. Windows 2000 Professional
   - c. Windows ME
   - d. Windows NT 4.0

5. Windows 2000 Terminal Server has an administration client available for
   _____.
   - a. Palm devices
   - b. Apple MacIntosh
   - c. Unix servers
   - d. Windows CE

6. The Microsoft _____ contains the database that Microsoft uses to distribute and activate Terminal Services license packs.
   - a. License Server
   - b. Clearinghouse
   - c. Terminal Server Clearinghouse
   - d. Terminal Server License Server

5.3.2 Configure Terminal Services for local resource mapping.

TERMINAL SERVER OPERATION

UNDERSTANDING THE OBJECTIVE

Your control of a Windows 2000 server through Terminal Server extends beyond controlling the computer administratively. You can also control devices on the computer and transfer specific events from the Terminal Server to the Terminal Server client where you are sitting. In addition, if you need audio responses from the Terminal Server, those can be configured to play through the sound system of the computer at which you are currently sitting.

WHAT YOU REALLY NEED TO KNOW

◆ Local resource mapping means the ability to not only control the desktop interface of Terminal Servers, but also to transfer properties such as sound output from the speakers of the Terminal Server to the speakers of the Terminal Server client. Other functionalities include mapping drives on the Terminal Server to the Terminal Server client.

◆ You also can map and connect to print devices for printer support.

◆ You can extend mapping to local drives on the client computer. This lets you map drives, such as CD drives, in a way that causes the Terminal Server to behave as if the drives were actually on the server, and not on a client machine located across the network.

◆ After hardware devices are mapped, you will treat them in the same fashion as if they were located on a machine sitting in front of you. All the data required for the devices to function is transferred across the Internet in a secure transfer because the Terminal Server is performing the work required by the client. It then transfers images of the processed data to the client.

◆ Because all processing takes place on the Terminal Server, only bit maps are sent across the network to clients. If any attempts are made to capture the transmitted data, the captured data consists of bit maps, which show only a screen shot of the information being processed.

OBJECTIVES ON THE JOB

Mapping local resources into a Terminal Server session for administrative connectivity and application support will provide useful functionality for both you and your clients. With these settings configured and the full-screen option enabled, you will view the terminal server as though you were seated in front of it.

PRACTICE TEST QUESTIONS

1. **If you have configured a session with a Windows 2000 Terminal Server, and you have mapped local resources, you should be able to _____.**
   a. control user logons
   b. use local speaker support
   c. transfer audio information from your computer to a guest operating system
   d. make certain that all servers are using Windows 2000

2. **You need to install some software on a server computer that is a Terminal Server. However, the server is more than 500 miles away and you do not have any on-site personnel to install the newest application. How could you solve this problem?**
   a. Create the shared folder for these resources and publish them in AD.
   b. Use the MSI file process to make a shared mapping from the server's hard drive.
   c. Use the Terminal Server Administrative Console to install the software.
   d. Have the server shipped back to you to install the software.

3. **You are configuring a Terminal Server application for a group of clients. For the application to function, a hardware device using USB must connect to the computer hosting the application. How can you accomplish this using Terminal Server?**
   a. You can't, and have to rethink your deployment of this application.
   b. The device can be installed on the Terminal Server, and users can use one instance of this device across the network.
   c. You can test the device and if it is supported on the client systems, install an instance on each user's terminal client. This provides all users with the device they require.
   d. You can purchase a special adapter module from Microsoft that will allow the device to run in a virtual environment for all users.

4. **Because of bandwidth issues, _____ do not run well using Terminal Server.**
   a. word-processing applications
   b. Web browsers
   c. streaming media applications
   d. communication applications

5. **You have been hired to configure Windows 2000 Terminal Server for a small office. They are currently using a UNIX terminal server application with 25 green screen terminals. Your preliminary report to this client states that you can implement Windows 2000 Terminal Server in this environment _____.**
   a. by using the green screen terminals now in the office
   b. by changing only the monitor component of the current terminals
   c. by adding an additional software component to the Terminal Server
   d. by replacing all current hardware

5.3.3 Configure Terminal Services user properties.

USER ACCOUNTS AND TERMINAL SERVICES

UNDERSTANDING THE OBJECTIVE

When you have decided to enable your users with Terminal Server instead of normal desktop computers, you must configure their accounts in AD for the connection to Terminal Server. The traditional settings will still be used, but you now need to configure additional settings. This configuration is accomplished through AD Users and Computers.

WHAT YOU REALLY NEED TO KNOW

◆ There are four tabs that contain user settings for Terminal Server-enabled user accounts. Each tab has a different set of objects to configure. Be advised that as additional services are added to a Windows 2000 AD environment, the number of tabs in AD Users and Computers for each user may increase. Also remember that all other settings in the AD still apply to and can be used by Terminal Server clients. You are not just configuring their Terminal Server options; you are configuring these in addition to the normal AD settings.

◆ The first tab is titled Environment and contains settings for programs to be started when the Terminal Server starts and has created a Windows desktop. You may select one program to start and specify the location of the program. You may also configure client devices in this screen.

◆ The next screen is labeled Sessions and contains settings that control Terminal Server timeouts and reconnection settings. You may configure when to end a disconnected session and what the session time limits and idle time limits will be. You can also specify reconnection settings here, allowing reconnection only from specific clients, or allowing reconnection from any client system.

◆ The third screen contains settings that allow you to configure remote control settings for a Terminal Server session. You may decide to allow remote control and, if so, how extensive you want your control to be. You can require a user's permission to connect or you can connect without the user's knowledge. You also have settings that allow you to either interact with or view the user's session.

◆ The last tab contains settings that allow you to define a network profile path and home folder location. Remember that because these are Terminal Server clients, they do not have any kind of local storage for files or folders. When they create a document, it must be stored offline because when the Terminal Server client powers down, all data not written to disk is lost. You can also choose the drive to which to map with the Terminal Services home folder, and enable the Terminal Server logon from this interface.

OBJECTIVES ON THE JOB

You must configure accounts for your Terminal Server-enabled clients in almost exactly the same way as you configure Windows 2000 client accounts in AD. You must configure Terminal Server-specific settings for your Terminal Server clients.

PRACTICE TEST QUESTIONS

1. The time limit for ending a disconnected Terminal Server connection for a client in Windows 2000 AD is _____
   - a. two days
   - b. one day
   - c. one hour
   - d. never

2. When configuring Environment settings for a Windows 2000 Terminal Server client, you can enable _____. (Choose all that apply.)
   - a. PCCard devices
   - b. client drives
   - c. client printers
   - d. main client printer

3. Your help desk has received a call from a Terminal Server user who is experiencing problems. He can log into his Terminal Server session without problems and he can work without problems. However, he cannot save any work before the terminal is powered down. What is the problem?
   - a. He does not have his Terminal Services Profile configured to allow him to save data.
   - b. His Terminal Services User Profile may not be correct.
   - c. He is contacting a DFS server that is offline.
   - d. He has an incorrect password assignment.

4. A Terminal Server user account can support an Idle session limit as small as _____.
   - a. one minute
   - b. 30 minutes
   - c. five minutes
   - d. one day

5. Windows 2000 Terminal Server offers some unique capabilities for training and troubleshooting. One of these is the ability to _____ to determine where the user may be making mistakes with the operating system.
   - a. view the user's session
   - b. use the PerfMon tool
   - c. interact with the session
   - d. monitor the desktop

6. As a configuration setting, you can create a single global _____ to contain all your Windows 2000 Terminal Server user accounts.
   - a. resource
   - b. object
   - c. group
   - d. unit

5.4 Configure and troubleshoot Network Address Translation (NAT) and Internet Connection Sharing.

SOHO INTERNET CONNECTIVITY

UNDERSTANDING THE OBJECTIVE

If you must support a SOHO environment, you need to know about **ICS** and **NAT**. Both services support small user environments. ICS was designed for the home user with a small home office. NAT was intended for the SOHO environment, such as might be found in a small company or branch office.

WHAT YOU REALLY NEED TO KNOW

◆ ICS is extremely simple to configure. It requires that you have an Internet connection and that you place a check mark in a box to enable the service. You will receive one warning informing you that the network interface on the computer facing your interior network will have its address changed to 192.168.0.1, and that all computers connecting to this interface will receive an IP address somewhere in this range.

◆ NAT is only slightly more complicated. You must select which interface should become your outboard network connection, and which network will be your interior network connection. You then need to determine whether you should allow NAT to function as a small DHCP server and distribute IP addresses, or whether it should obtain this information from an actual DHCP server. This is the basic configuration of both services. If you need more than one scope of DHCP addresses, you should configure NAT to request all information for address assignment from a normal DHCP server.

◆ The next issue concerns the inability of NAT and ICS to function with certain encryption protocols. Any encryption that performs a checksum on a packet before handing it off cannot function using NAT or ICS because these two services modify the information used to produce the checksum. When the information is modified, the checksum is no longer accurate.

◆ NAT features a DNS proxy to handle name-resolution requests from NAT clients. The service works by intercepting requests for DNS resolution and passing these requests to its own DNS server on behalf of the client. When a response comes back, the result of the query is returned to the client who originally made the request for the service. This functionality is not supported for WINS servers, only for DDNS servers.

OBJECTIVES ON THE JOB

NAT and ICS together can form a complimentary service that allows you to handle a variety of Internet connectivity requests from any client in your corporate environment. ICS is the simplest of the two to install and configure, while NAT is only slightly more complicated. Both services require more than one network interface: one facing the public Internet and one facing the private intranet. After these are in place, you can supply Internet connectivity to your home office and SOHO users in Windows 2000.

PRACTICE TEST QUESTIONS

1. **Your NAT server is not forwarding packets as it should be. What should you do?**
   a. Check DDNS name resolution.
   b. Verify that the network interface connecting to the public Internet was added to the list of interfaces in the RAS snap-in.
   c. Verify that your ISP is not filtering out your NAT packets.
   d. Verify that your network interface supports NAT.

2. **If you suspect problems with ICS, ping the ICS host to determine connectivity. It should respond with an IP address of _____.**
   a. 192.168.0.1
   b. 192.168.1.1
   c. 192.168.1.0
   d. 192.168.2.0

3. **Some of your clients are complaining that their database application is not working. How can you troubleshoot?**
   a. Perform a NetMon trace operation to watch where the traffic is going.
   b. Install the application on the NAT host. If it works, your users are experiencing the issues associated with NAT and host headers.
   c. Check whether your users require elevated permissions to use the application.
   d. Check whether NAT requires elevated permissions to send the packets.

4. **Your NAT clients cannot send and receive packets. The NAT host is experiencing no problems. What should you do?**
   a. Verify the status of the Forward packets setting on the outbound network interface.
   b. Verify the status of the Forward packets setting on the interior network interface.
   c. Verify the status of the Public interface connected to the Internet option in the RAS snap-in for routing.
   d. Restart the RAS service.

5. **The DHCP Allocator service in NAT can manage no more than _____ subnet(s).**
   a. one
   b. two
   c. three
   d. four

6. **The DHCP Allocator service in ICS can manage no more than _____ subnet(s).**
   a. one
   b. two
   c. three
   d. none of the above

5.4.1 Configure Routing and Remote Access to perform NAT.

NAT CONFIGURATION SETTINGS

UNDERSTANDING THE OBJECTIVE

NAT is slightly more complicated to configure than ICS, but easier to configure than RAS. NAT can be an excellent solution for a small- to medium-sized office that wants to optimize a single public IP address. It also works for larger companies that may have several public IP addresses to use.

WHAT YOU REALLY NEED TO KNOW

◆ NAT is a dynamic database that maps IP addresses and port numbers in a dynamic database to the single public IP address that is valid on the public Internet. This allows a company to obtain just one public IP address and implement private IP addressing internally.

◆ NAT maps both **UDP** and **TCP** addresses and ports to its database and tracks packets outbound for and incoming from the public Internet. To achieve this functionality, NAT supports either static or dynamic exterior address mapping. If you have a particular resource that must use the same IP address, you can create a static mapping to that resource to ensure that NAT never attempts to assign the address. You can also implement dynamic mappings if you have no such constraints. These dynamic mappings are created whenever a client attempts to gain access to the public Internet from your corporate intranet. The lifetimes of these dynamic mappings are 24 hours for TCP connections and one minute for UDP connections. Both values are configurable on the NAT server.

◆ For NAT to function correctly, it must modify the internal data contained within packets bound for the Internet. This modification occurs at three different levels: either at TCP, UDP, or IP headers. The headers must be modified by NAT to support NAT's functionality. The information being modified is contained within the packet headers and consists of: the source IP address (outbound); the destination IP address (inbound); the IP checksum; the source port (outbound); the destination port (inbound); the TCP checksum; and the UDP checksum. To enable editing of these fields, NAT comes with several editors designed specifically for this purpose. These editors run automatically and are the NAT components that modify the internal tables for address translation.

◆ With address translation, NAT modifies the internals of IP data packets; thus, these packets may be invalidated by the modification. If IPSec, for instance, encounters a packet designated for a digital signature, it sees a packet handled by NAT as having had its internal structure manipulated/violated. Thus, it discards the packet. All IPSec packets would be handled in the same fashion.

OBJECTIVES ON THE JOB

NAT is a very useful tool; however, it has some limitations of which you need to be aware.

PRACTICE TEST QUESTIONS

1. **You want to configure NAT in your infrastructure. What physical hardware is required to implement NAT? (Choose all that apply.)**
   a. a NAT board
   b. a connection to the external public Internet
   c. two network adapter cards
   d. one network adapter card and a modem

2. **A NAT server can assign IP addresses because it can function as a small _____ server.**
   a. WINS
   b. DHCP
   c. DNS
   d. proxy

3. **NAT can be configured to download _____ from a DHCP server.**
   a. the full scope information
   b. only the IP address and subnet information
   c. DNS information
   d. WINS information

4. **The NAT service can be configured only on a Windows 2000 _____ .**
   a. Professional computer
   b. RAS computer
   c. Server computer running RAS
   d. member server running RAS

5. **The NAT service is installed as another _____ in the RAS snap-in on a Windows 2000 server.**
   a. service
   b. interface
   c. protocol
   d. redirector

6. **After NAT connections are configured, you make _____ assignments either automatic or static.**
   a. interface
   b. network card
   c. IP address
   d. DNS information

7. **Because NAT must modify the internals of IP packets, it cannot be used with any encryption protocols because _____ .**
   a. the encrypted data cannot be modified without breaking encryption rules
   b. NAT does not have any protocol editors
   c. IP packets are never encrypted
   d. the modification of IP packets is not the responsibility of NAT

5.4.2 Troubleshoot Internet Connection Sharing problems by using the ipconfig and ping commands

TROUBLESHOOTING ICS

UNDERSTANDING THE OBJECTIVE

ICS is a much simpler form of NAT. ICS has only one configurable setting, which is to turn on the service. ICS is far less complex than NAT, but is still useful in a SOHO environment. Troubleshooting is much simpler because nothing is configurable.

WHAT YOU REALLY NEED TO KNOW

◆ ICS is a simple form of NAT. Unlike NAT, which allows some simple configuration in the implementation of the IP address, ICS simply defaults to the address of 192.168.0.0/16 for its interior network. All other addresses are assigned at random on this service within the 192.168.0.0 range. No other configurations are possible.

◆ Troubleshooting ICS is straightforward. If your computer is an ICS client, use the ipconfig command to determine the exact IP address you were given by the ICS host. After you have this address, ping the address to see if your computer responds. If so, ping the ICS host to determine connectivity to that machine. If it responds and you cannot connect to the public Internet, you need to begin troubleshooting at the ICS host and work through your corporate intranet until you determine the source of the broken link.

◆ Because the ICS service has no configuration settings for DNS or WINS resolution providers, it supports clients using a simplified proxy service to supply needed DNS and WINS configuration information to connected clients. The host providing ICS services will hand out its DNS and WINS information to clients requesting the address of these two servers for name-resolution services.

◆ ICS is a sharing service that exists on the Windows 98, Windows ME, and Windows 2000 platforms. It is not supported on either Windows 95 or Windows NT 4.0, although these latter two systems can function as ICS clients.

◆ The configuration of ICS from the client side can be as simple as enabling DHCP support. With this configuration, the potential ICS client contacts the ICS host and obtains an IP address and subnet mask. The clients can also be manually configured with an IP address, provided that the address is within the ICS range (192.168.0.0/16), and that the ICS client sees the ICS host as its default gateway (or router, as appropriate, although the terms are somewhat interchangeable).

◆ Once enabled, client connectivity to the Internet is basically automatic with no other configuration required if using the DHCP option.

OBJECTIVES ON THE JOB

ICS is a simple service that provides Internet connectivity settings in a SOHO environment. It uses only one IP address range. It always takes the first address in that range as its own, and hands out all other IP addresses based on its own IP address.

PRACTICE TEST QUESTIONS

1. **The IP address of the ICS host is** _____.
   a. 169.254.0.1
   b. 131.107.0.1
   c. 192.168.0.1
   d. 192.168.1.1

2. **All ICS clients are assigned an address somewhere in the** _____ **range.**
   a. 192.168.0.0/15
   b. 192.168.0.0/16
   c. 192.168.0.0/17
   d. 192.168.0.0/18

3. **When using the ipconfig /all command on a computer configured by ICS, the default gateway returned should be** _____.
   a. 192.168.0.0
   b. Localhost
   c. Remotehost
   d. 192.168.0.1

4. **The** _____ **operating system supports ICS. (Choose all that apply.)**
   a. Windows NT 4.0
   b. Windows 98
   c. Windows ME
   d. Windows 2000

5. **The ICS host will direct its clients to use** _____ **for DNS resolution.**
   a. a host file
   b. an Lmhosts file
   c. its own DNS server
   d. a root name server

6. **ICS is an ideal solution for** _____ **environments.**
   a. lnon-standard
   b. SOHO
   c. medium-sized office
   d. remote office

7. **You have a client who is trying to configure IPSec to work from a home network using ICS. Will this client succeed?**
   a. Yes, ICS was designed for this small office/home office environment.
   b. No, ICS modifies the contents of the file headers, and this is the material that IPSec checks for signs of tampering.
   c. Yes, as long as they apply IPSec only to UDP packets.
   d. Yes, as long as they apply IPSec only to TCP packets.

GLOSSARY OF ACRONYMS AND ABBREVIATIONS

3DES – Triple Data Encryption Standard

A

ACL – Access Control List
ACPI – Advanced Configuration and Power Interface
AD – Active Directory
ADSI – Active Directory Service Interface
APIPA – Automatic Private IP Addressing

B

BAP – Bandwidth Allocation Protocol
B2B – Business to Business
BSOD – Blue Screen of Death

C

CA – Certificate Authority
CDFS – CD file system
CHAP – Challenge Handshake Authentication Protocol

D

DAV – Distributed Authoring and Versioning Protocol
DC – Domain Controller
DDN – Defense Data Network
DDNS – Dynamic Domain Name System
DES – Data Encryption Standard
DFS – Distributed File System
DHCP – Dynamic Host Configuration Protocol
DLL – Dynamic Link Library
DMA – Direct Memory Address channel
DNS – Domain Name System
DORA – DHCPDiscover, DHCPOffer, DHCPRequest, and DHCPAck
DoS – Denial of Service

E

EAP –Extensible Authentication Protocol
EAP-TLS – Extensible Authentication Protocol – Transport Layer Security

EFS – Encrypting File System
ERD – Emergency Repair Disk

F

FAT – File Allocation Table
FQDN – Fully Qualified Domain Name
FTP – File Transfer Protocol

G

GPO – Group Policy object
GUID – Globally Unique Identifier
GUI – Graphical User Interface

H

HCL – Hardware Compatibility List

I

ICMP – Internet Control Message Protocol
ICS – Internet connection sharing
IEAK – Internet Explorer Administration Kit
IIS – Internet Information Services
IP – Internet Protocol
IPSec – IP Security
IRQ – Interrupt Request Line
IXFR – Incremental Zone Transfer

K

KCC – Knowledge Consistency Checker

L

L2TP – Layer 2 Tunneling Protocol

M

MMC – Microsoft Management Console
MPPE – Microsoft Point-to-Point Encryption
MS-CHAP (v2) – Microsoft Challenge Authentication Protocol
MSI – Medium-Scale Integration
MSP – Managed Service Provider

N

NAT – Network Address Translation
NIC – Network Interface Card
NNTP – Network News Transfer Protocol
NTFS – New Technology File System

O

OSPF – Open Shortest Path First
OU – Organizational Unit

P

PAP – Password Authentication Protocol
PKI – Public Key Infrastructure
PNP – Plug and Play
PPP – Point-to-Point Protocol
PPTP – Point-to-Point Tunneling Protocol
PSTN – Public Switched Telephone Network
PTR – Pointer Resource Record
PWS – Peer Web Server

R

RADIUS – Remote Authentication Dial-In User Service
RAS – Remote Access Service
RFC – Request for Comments
RIP (v1 and v2) – Routing Information Protocol
RPC – Remote Procedure Call
RSVP – Resource Reservation Protocol

S

SMTP – Simple Mail Transfer Protocol
SOHO – Small Office, Home Office
SPAP – Shiva Password Authentication Protocol
SRV – Service Resource Record
SSL – Secure Socket Layer

T

TCO – Total Cost of Ownership
TCP – Transport Control Protocol
TCP/IP – Transmission Control Protocol/Internet Protocol
TTL – Time-To-Live

U

UDF – Universal Disk Format
UDP – User Datagram Protocol
UNC – Universal Naming Convention
USB – Universal Serial Bus

V

VPN – Virtual Private Network

W

WEC – Web Extender Client
WINS – Windows Internet Name Service
WSH – Windows Script Host

Section 1.0

Objective 1.1

Practice Questions:

1. d
2. c,f
3. b,c,e
4. a
5. d

Objective 1.1.1

Practice Questions:

1. c
2. d
3. c
4. b
5. c
6. c

Objective 1.1.2

Practice Questions:

1. a
2. a
3. b
4. d
5. c

Objective 1.2

Practice Questions:

1. d
2. a
3. c
4. c
5. c,d
6. b

Objective 1.2.1

Practice Questions:

1. c
2. d
3. d
4. d

Objective 1.2.2
Practice Questions:
1. c
2. b
3. b,d
4. d
5. d

Objective 1.2.3
Practice Questions:
1. a,b,c
2. b
3. d
4. c
5. a,b,d

Objective 1.2.4
Practice Questions:
1. c
2. a,b,c,d
3. b
4. b,d
5. b
6. c

Objective 1.2.5
Practice Questions:
1. d
2. a,b,d
3. c
4. d
5. c
6. b
7. c

Objective 1.2.6
Practice Questions:
1. d
2. b
3. a,b,c,d
4. c
5. a,c
6. c

Objective 1.2.7
Practice Questions:
1. a,b,c,d,e
2. c
3. c
4. c
5. b
6. c

Objective 1.3
Practice Questions:
1. b,c,d
2. b
3. d
4. b
5. a

Objective 1.3.1
Practice Questions:
1. c
2. c,d
3. c
4. b
5. c

Objective 1.3.2
Practice Questions:
1. a,b,c
2. b,c,d,e
3. a,c
4. a
5. c

Objective 1.3.3
Practice Questions:
1. b
2. c
3. d
4. b
5. b,c

Objective 1.3.4
Practice Questions:
1. b,c,d
2. a,b,c
3. c,d
4. b
5. a,b,c,d
6. c

Objective 1.4
Practice Questions:
1. c,d
2. c
3. d
4. b
5. a
6. d

Objective 1.4.1
Practice Questions:
1. d
2. c
3. a,c,d
4. a,b
5. b

Objective 1.4.2
Practice Questions:
1. a,b,c
2. a
3. a,b,c,e
4. b
5. b
6. a

Objective 1.4.3
Practice Questions:
1. a
2. a
3 a,b,d
4. a,b,c
5. b,c

Objective 1.4.4
Practice Questions:
1. a
2. b
3. b
4. b
5. a

Objective 1.4.5
Practice Questions:
1. c
2. c,d
3. b
4. b
5. c
6. a

Objective 1.4.6
Practice Questions:
1. a
2. c
3. c
4. b
5. c

Objective 1.5
Practice Questions:
1. b
2. a,c
3. a
4. a
5. b

Objective 1.5.1
Practice Questions:
1. d
2. b
3. c
4. c
5. c

Objective 1.5.2
Practice Questions:
1. c
2. d
3. b,c
4. b
5. a

Objective 1.5.3
Practice Questions:
1. c
2. b,c,d
3. b,c,e,f
4. b
5. b

Objective 1.5.4
Practice Questions:
1. d
2. a
3. c
4. b
5. b

Objective 1.5.5
Practice Questions:
1. c
2. a
3. d
4. c
5. c

Objective 1.5.6
Practice Questions:
1. d
2. c
3. b
4. a,b
5. d

Section 2.0
Objective 2.1
Practice Questions:
1. c
2. a
3. c
4. a
5. b
6. a,b,c

Objective 2.1.1
Practice Questions:
1. c
2. d
3. a,c
4. b,c,d
5. b
6. a

Objective 2.1.2
Practice Questions:
1. d
2. a,c,d
3. a,b
4. b
5. d
6. c

Objective 2.2
Practice Questions:
1. d
2. b
3. a
4. b
5. c
6. b,d

Objective 2.2.1
Practice Questions:
1. c
2. d
3. c
4. b
5. a
6. a
7. a,d

Objective 2.2.2
Practice Questions:
1. b
2. c
3. d
4. a,b
5. c
6. a

Objective 2.2.3
Practice Questions:
1. a,c,d
2. d
3. d
4. a
5. b
6. d

Objective 2.3
Practice Questions:
1. d
2. d
3. b
4. c
5. d
6. d
7. c

Objective 2.3.1
Practice Questions:
1. a
2. d
3. d
4. d
5. d
6. a,c,d

Objective 2.3.2
Practice Questions:
1. d
2. c
3. d
4. a
5. c
6. a,b,c,d

Objective 2.3.3
Practice Questions:
1. d
2. b,d
3. a
4. c
5. d
6. b

Objective 2.3.4
Practice Questions:
1. c
2. a
3. a
4. a
5. a
6. c

Objective 2.3.5
Practice Questions:
1. a,c
2. c
3. c
4. b
5. c
6. a

Objective 2.4
Practice Questions:
1. b
2. c
3. b
4. a,b,c,d
5. b
6. c
7. c,d

Objective 2.4.1
Practice Questions:
1. a
2. b
3. b
4. d
5. b
6. d
7. b

Objective 2.4.2
Practice Questions:
1. d
2. c
3. b,d
4. c
5. a
6. a,c,d
7. d

Objective 2.4.3
Practice Questions:
1. b
2. b
3. c
4. c
5. a,c,d
6. b

Objective 2.5

Practice Questions:

1. d
2. a,b,c,d
3. a
4. b,d
5. c
6. b

Objective 2.5.1

Practice Questions:

1. c
2. a,b,c,d
3. d
4. d
5. d
6. d
7. c

Objective 2.5.2

Practice Questions:

1. d
2. b
3. c
4. c
5. d
6. c
7. b

Objective 2.5.3

Practice Questions:

1. b
2. b
3. b
4. c
5. b
6. d

Objective 2.5.4

Practice Questions:

1. a
2. b
3. d
4. a,b
5. a,b,c,d
6. d
7. a

Section 3.0

Objective 3.1

Practice Questions:

1. a,b
2. c
3. d
4. a,c
5. b
6. b
7. a,b,d

Objective 3.1.1

Practice Questions:

1. a,c,d
2. d
3. d
4. c,d
5. a
6. a
7. b,d

Objective 3.1.2

Practice Questions:

1. a
2. a,c
3. b
4. c,d
5. a
6. c
7. c,d

Objective 3.1.3

Practice Questions:

1. b
2. b
3. a
4. d
5. b
6. d
7. b

Objective 3.1.4
Practice Questions:
1. a,c,d
2. a,b
3. a
4. c
5. b
6. d
7. b

Objective 3.2
Practice Questions:
1. a
2. c
3. a
4. a
5. c
6. c

Objective 3.2.1
Practice Questions:
1. d
2. a
3. c
4. d
5. c
6. d
7. d

Objective 3.2.2
Practice Questions:
1. a
2. a,b
3. c
4. c
5. b,c,d
6. b
7. b

Objective 3.2.3
Practice Questions:
1. a,c,d
2. c
3. d
4. d
5. a
6. d

Objective 3.2.4
Practice Questions:
1. d
2. c
3. d
4. c
5. c

Objective 3.2.5
Practice Questions:
1. c,d
2. b
3. b,c,d
4. b
5. a,b
6. b
7. c

Objective 3.3
Practice Questions:
1. a,b
2. c,d
3. c
4. d
5. d

Objective 3.3.1
Practice Questions:
1. d
2. a
3. b
4. a,b,d,f
5. c
6. c
7. d

Objective 3.3.2
Practice Questions:
1. b
2. d
3. a,b,c,f
4. a
5. b
6. d
7. d

Objective 3.3.3
Practice Questions:
1. a,b,c
2. b,c,d
3. b,c
4. b
5. b
6. a,b,c
7. a

Objective 3.3.4
Practice Questions:
1. e
2. b
3. c
4. c
5. b

Objective 3.4
Practice Questions:
1. a,b,c
2. c
3. e
4. b
5. b

Objective 3.4.1
Practice Questions:
1. d
2. d
3. d
4. a
5. b

Objective 3.4.2
Practice Questions:
1. d
2. a
3. b
4. c
5. d
6. d
7. c

Objective 3.4.3
Practice Questions:
1. a,b,c
2. a
3. b
4. d
5. b,c
6. d

Objective 3.4.4
Practice Questions:
1. c
2. a,c
3. d
4. c
5. b
6. c

Section 4.0
Objective 4.1
Practice Questions:
1. d
2. b
3. a
4. c
5. b
6. b

Objective 4.1.1
Practice Questions:
1. b
2. c
3. d
4. c
5. b
8. d
9. a

Objective 4.1.2
Practice Questions:
1. c
2. b
3. d
4. c
5. b

Objective 4.1.3
Practice Questions:
1. a,b,c
2. c
3. d
4. a
5. a,c,d
6. d

Objective 4.1.4
Practice Questions:
1. a,b,d
2. a
3. c
4. c
5. b
6. d

Objective 4.1.5
Practice Questions:
1. d
2. c
3. c
4. a
5. c
6. d

Objective 4.1.6
Practice Questions:
1. b
2. d
3. b
4. b
5. c
6. a

Objective 4.2
Practice Questions:
1. c
2. d
3. b
4. d
5. c
6. d

Objective 4.2.1

Practice Questions:

1. a
2. b
3. d
4. c
5. b

Objective 4.2.2

Practice Questions:

1. d
2. b
3. c
4. a
5. c
6. b

Objective 4.3

Practice Questions:

1. c
2. d
3. c
4. b
5. d
6. b
7. a

Objective 4.3.1

Practice Questions:

1. d
2. c
3. b
4. d
5. d
8. c

Objective 4.3.2

Practice Questions:

1. d
2. d
3. c
4. c
5. c

Objective 4.4
Practice Questions:
1. d
2. d
3. c
4. c,e
5. d

Objective 4.4.1
Practice Questions:
1. d
2. b
3. d
4. c
5. d
6. b
7. b

Objective 4.4.2
Practice Questions:
1. d
2. a,b,c,d
3. b
4. d
5. c

Objective 4.4.3
Practice Questions:
1. c
4. d
5. d
4. c
5. b

Objective 4.5
Practice Questions:
1. c
2. c
3. a
4. a
5. d
6. a

Objective 4.5.1

Practice Questions:

1. b
2. a
3. c
4. b
5. b,c
6. b

Objective 4.5.2

Practice Questions:

1. a
2. c
3. a
4. c
5. a
6. d
7. a

Objective 4.6

Practice Questions:

1. b
2. c
3. d
4. c
5. c
6. b

Objective 4.6.1

Practice Questions:

1. d
2. b
3. d
4. d
5. a
6. b

Objective 4.6.2

Practice Questions:

1. d
2. c
3. a
4. a
5. b
6. d
7. b

Objective 4.6.3

Practice Questions:

1. b
2. d
3. c
4. b
5. c
6. c

Section 5.0

Objective 5.1

Practice Questions:

1. b
2. a
3. d
4. c
5. d
6. b
7. c

Objective 5.1.1

Practice Questions:

1. e
2. b
3. a,b,c,d,e
4. b
5. b
6. b

Objective 5.1.2

Practice Questions:

1. c
2. c
3. d
4. b
5. d
6. c

Objective 5.1.3

Practice Questions:

1. d
2. c
3. d
4. c
5. d
6. a,b
7. c

Objective 5.1.4
Practice Questions:
1. b,d
2. b,d
3. c
4. c
5. d

Objective 5.1.5
Practice Questions:
1. a,b,c,d,e
2. c
3. a
4. c
5. c
6. d

Objective 5.2
Practice Questions:
1. a
2. c
3. d
4. c
5. c,d
6. c

Objective 5.2.1
Practice Questions:
1. b
2. d
3. c
4. a
5. c
6. d

Objective 5.2.2
Practice Questions:
1. c
2. a
3. b
4. b
5. c

Objective 5.2.3
Practice Questions:
1. a,d
2. a,b
3. a,c,d
4. c
5. c
6. d
7. c

Objective 5.2.4
Practice Questions:
1. c
2. d
3. c
4. d
5. c
6. d

Objective 5.3
Practice Questions:
1. d
2. c
3. a,b,c,d
4. b
5. b,c
6. b

Objective 5.3.1
Practice Questions:
1. c
2. d
3. d
4. b
5. d
6. b

Objective 5.3.2
Practice Questions:
1. b
2. c
3. c
4. c
5. d

Objective 5.3.3

Practice Questions:

1. b
2. b,c,d
3. b
4. a
5. c
6. c

Objective 5.4

Practice Questions:

1. b
2. a
3. b
4. c
5. a
6. d

Objective 5.4.1

Practice Questions:

1. c
2. b
3. b
4. c
5. c
6. c
7. a

Objective 5.4.2

Practice Questions:

1. c
2. b
3. d
4. b,c,d
5. c
6. b
7. b

INDEX

maximum file size supported by, 8–9
partitions, 8, 10–11, 16–19
permissions, 2, 8, 18–19, 28, 40
quotas and, 12–13
volumes, 42, 48
ntldr, 22, 23

O

object(s). *See also* GPOs (Group Policy objects)
configuration of, 6–7, 168–169, 172–173
permissions, 168–169, 172–173
replication of, 174–175
searching for, 4–5, 32–33, 162–163
Office (Microsoft), 34, 182
OSPF (Open Shortest Path First), 176–177, 208–209
OUs (Organizational Units), 2, 172, 200
creating, 156, 164
GPOs and, 56–57, 188–191
lockout settings and, 50–51
replication and, 179
ownership rights, 12

P

pagefiles, 22
PAP (Password Authentication Protocol), 210
partitions
creating, 8, 16
deleting, 8
extending, 16–17
FAT, 8, 10–11
NTFS, 8, 10–11, 16–19
sharing, 8
size limits on, 8, 9
passwords, 44, 52–53, 160–161, 210
patches, 180–181
pathping command, 64–65, 68–69
permissions, 28–29, 32–33, 46–47, 168–173, 222
assigning, 158, 168–171
managing, 168–169
troubleshooting, 172–173

ping command, 64–65, 68–69, 76–77, 238–239
PKI (Public Key Infrastructure), 14–15
Portal Server (Microsoft), 26
PPP (Point-to-Point Protocol), 224
PPTP (Point-to-Point Tunneling Protocol), 204–211
#PRE command, 106
precedence, 190–191
print device(s), 24–25, 30–32, 35
auditing, 58–59
publishing, 2–3, 6–7
remote access and, 230–233
proxy servers, 40. *See also* servers
PSTN (Public Switched Telephone Network), 212, 216
PTR record type, 90, 94–95
PWS (Personal Web Server), 34–35

Q

quotas, enabling/configuring, 12–13

R

RAS (Remote Access Service), 204–207, 214–217, 220–223. *See also* remote access
Read permission, 28
redundancy, 46
refresh intervals, 192–193
Registry, 64, 180, 186, 190
remote access
configuring, 204–231
enabling, 212–213, 222–223
policies, 216–223
profiles, 222–223
Terminal Services for, 226–233
troubleshooting, 216–217, 220–221, 238–239
replication, 174–179
Reset Account option, 166–167
resource(s)
mapping, 2, 3, 4, 86, 230–231
shared, 2–5, 8, 24–29
reverse lookup zone, 96–97
RFCs (Requests for Comment), 86–87, 90

route command, 64–67
RPC (Remote Procedure Call), 174–177
RRAS (Routing and Remote Access Services), 236
RSVP connections, 68–69

S

scope options, 86
scripts
logon, 54–55
processing, in GPOs, 54–55
shutdown, 54–55
startup, 54–55
searching, for objects, 4–5, 32–33, 162–163
secedit command, 192, 198–199
security, 3, 10–11. *See also* encryption; passwords
ACLs and, 168, 172–173
breaches, detecting, 48–49
configuration, analysis of, 198–201
DoS (Denial of Service) attacks and, 64–65, 68, 76–77
hackers and, 47, 48, 64–65
logs, 58, 60–61
monitoring, 48–49
PKI and, 14–15
plans, 48–49
policy implementation, 194–195
settings, applying, 196–197, 200–201
SSL and, 42–43
VPNs and, 210–211
viruses and, 40, 48, 180–181, 184–185
Security Configuration and Analysis tool (MMC), 198, 200–201
server(s). *See also* Windows 2000 Server (Microsoft)
access permissions for, 46–47
caching-only, 92
DFS and, 20
DHCP and, 78–79, 82–83
FrontPage extensions for, 28–29, 40
hiding the name and location of, 46
installing, 86
intranet browsing and, 40–41